Beyond the Barricades

This series of publications on Africa, Latin America, Southeast Asia, and Global and Comparative Studies is designed to present significant research, translation, and opinion to area specialists and to a wide community of persons interested in world affairs. The editor seeks manuscripts of quality on any subject and can usually make a decision regarding publication within three months of receipt of the original work. Production methods generally permit a work to appear within one year of acceptance. The editor works closely with authors to produce a high-quality book. The series appears in a paperback format and is distributed worldwide. For more information, contact the executive editor at Ohio University Press, Scott Quadrangle, University Terrace, Athens, Ohio 45701.

Executive editor: Gillian Berchowitz
AREA CONSULTANTS
Africa: Diane Ciekawy
Latin America: Thomas Walker
Southeast Asia: William H. Frederick

The Ohio University Research in International Studies series is published for the Center for International Studies by Ohio University Press. The views expressed in individual monographs are those of the authors and should not be considered to represent the policies or beliefs of the Center for International Studies, Ohio University Press, or Ohio University.

Beyond the Barricades

*Nicaragua and the Struggle for the
Sandinista Press, 1979–1998*

Adam Jones

Ohio University Center for International Studies
Research in International Studies
Latin America Series No. 37
Ohio University Press
Athens

© 2002 by the
Center for International Studies
Ohio University
Printed in the United States of America
All rights reserved

10 09 08 07 06 05 04 03 02   5 4 3 2 1

The books in the Ohio University Research in International Studies Series
are printed on acid-free paper ∞ ™

Library of Congress Cataloging-in-Publication Data

Jones, Adam, 1963–
  Beyond the barricades : Nicaragua and the struggle for the Sandinista press,
1979–1998 / Adam Jones.
      p. cm. — (Research in international studies. Latin America series ; no. 37)
  Includes bibliographical references and index.
  ISBN 0-89680-223-X (alk. paper)
  1. Barricada internacional. 2. Nicaragua—Politics and government—1979–1990.
3. Nicaragua—Politics and government—1990– 4. Press and politics—Nicaragua—
History—20th century. I. Title. II. Series.

F1528 .J66 2002
070.4'493209'728509048—dc21
                                                                    2002022609

For Noam Chomsky

Contents

Illustrations

ix

Acknowledgments

Long before I thought to study transformations in the Sandinista Front's official organ (by chance, just as especially dramatic transformations were unfolding), my passionate interest in Nicaragua and its revolution was sparked by the political writings of Noam Chomsky. A decade-long private correspondence, similar to those Chomsky maintains with hundreds of ordinary people worldwide, nourished that interest further. I dedicate this work to him with heartfelt thanks.

My direct involvement with Nicaragua began with a stint as a volunteer with Tools for Peace, a Canadian solidarity organization that dispatched millions of dollars in material aid to Nicaragua throughout the Sandinista revolution and after. Through "T4P" I met a lifelong comrade, Peter Prontzos. I also visited Nicaragua for the first time on a Tools for Peace delegation in 1986 and read *Barricada* to the extent my limited Spanish permitted. But the seed of the present project had yet to germinate.

Rex Brynen at McGill University supervised the master's thesis that took me back to Managua in early 1991, just as the "deofficialized" *Barricada* was taking its first tentative steps. He helped with the construction of a number of the analytical frameworks deployed in this study—notably the idea of mobilizing versus professional strands in press functioning. I was fortunate to be able to arrange for his continued participation in my doctoral research project, "The Press in Transition: A Comparative Study of Nicaragua, South Africa, Jordan, and Russia," which occupied me at the University of British Columbia between 1994 and 1999.

The success of the fieldwork in Managua owed an enormous amount to two central figures in the *Barricada* drama, Carlos Fernando Chamorro and Sofía Montenegro. "Let me ask you frankly," Carlos Fernando mused in our first interview in 1991, "Who do you think will be interested in reading about *Barricada*?" Whatever doubts he may have had on that score, he and Sofía took time from absurdly busy schedules to sit for many hours of interviews over the three months of my stay. Carlos Fernando also granted me the run of the *Barricada* offices and library. The latter proved an essential resource, since virtually every back issue of every Nicaraguan publication was conveniently bound or boxed on its shelves, extending back as far as 1940s editions of the Somocista rag *Novedades*. Daniel Alegría at *Barricada Internacional* welcomed me in his inimitably gregarious way to *BI*'s offices, and allowed me to use the computers there to transcribe interviews. *BI*'s Jane Curschmann translated Spanish-language interviews patiently and superbly. Her coworkers, Toby Mailman and Diane Chomsky, were fine sources of company and insight. Thanks also to the magical Mercedes Mon-cada, who showed me there was more to fieldwork than work.

I returned to Nicaragua in 1996 to study the new version of *Barricada* introduced by the architects of the defenestración. One could hardly imagine a more transformed institution. Of all my contacts from the 1991 fieldwork, only Diane Chomsky and a couple of others at *Barricada Internacional* remained. To my great good fortune, Diane cheerfully helped me find my feet, introducing me personally to *Barricada*'s new editors and senior writers. In so doing, she allowed the considerable credibility she had amassed through years of dedicated work at *BI* to rub off on me. I am quite sure this secured me interviews and archival access I would not otherwise have had, and without which the concluding installment of the *Barricada* story could not have been adequately told.

Among the staff of the post-1994 *Barricada*, William Grigsby, Alfonso Malespín, and Julio López were unreservedly accommodating of my fleeting presence. All took time from their own busy schedules to sit for interviews. My own bias toward the previous, Chamorro-directed incarnation of *Barricada* will probably be evident; but I hope that, with the exception of Julio López, all the post-1994 contingent will find themselves treated fairly in these pages. The anecdote of how I managed to erase my taped interview with López before transcribing it is a personally humiliating one that I will spare the reader; his views are at least available in the written record. A major task in the 1996 fieldwork was to reconstruct the story of the defenestración and its immediate aftermath. Many of my earlier contacts thus remained crucial to the project. Again, Carlos Fernando Chamorro and Sofía Montenegro welcomed my protracted interrogations; again, Carlos Fernando was a crucial source of internal documents. I also greatly enjoyed a long lunchtime interview with Daniel Alegría. Liz Light brought her intelligence and deadpan wit to life away from *Barricada*'s environs. The friendly staff at Guest House Santos put a tin roof over my head for four weeks; sold me cold bottles of Victoria, one of the world's great pilseners; and tolerated my odd gringo ways, including an interest in the ice hockey broadcasts on their satellite TV that must have struck them as pathological.

This project could never have been completed without the generous support of diverse granting agencies. The 1991 fieldwork was funded by a McConnell Fellowship from McGill University; the 1996 travels, by a Social Sciences and Humanities Research Council doctoral fellowship. In the summer of 1998, I was able to return to Nicaragua for a brief visit and final updating, thanks to a research stipend from Langara College. My thanks to Claudia Castillo López at Managua's Biblioteca Nacional, who patiently pulled back issues of Nicaraguan newspapers from the stacks.

My editors at Ohio University Press, Thomas Walker and Gill Berchowitz, displayed heartening enthusiasm for this project from the first and invested a considerable amount of time and effort in

preparing the book for publication. Manuscript editor Nancy Basmajian, production manager Beth Pratt, and copyeditor Bob Furnish all took on the herculean task of sharpening and polishing the manuscript; they have earned my deepest gratitude. Sharon Arnold typified the press's energetic commitment to marketing and publicity, helping to ensure—I hope—that this book will do more than gather dust on a few library shelves. Carlos Fernando Chamorro and Kent Norsworthy each read the draft manuscript from cover to cover and provided many helpful comments and insights. I must be held accountable for any errors that remain. My parents, Jo and David Jones, and my brother, Craig, have all been unfailing sources of support over the years, as have Carla Bergman, Terry and Meghan Evenson, Jay Forster, David Liebe, John Margesson, Hamish Telford, and the indispensable and adorable Miriam Tratt.

On one level, I would like to dedicate *Beyond the Barricades* to all Nicaraguans. Their country has largely dropped from Western radar screens since the Sandinista revolutionaries were stymied in the 1990 elections. But while political orders come and go, some things remain constant. One is the inspiring resilience and good humor that ordinary Nicaraguans display in the face of continuing and staggering adversity. The country may no longer be sufficiently chic for Western commentators of both left and right to make it a centerpiece of their critiques, as in the 1980s, but I hope this book provides evidence that the events of recent years deserve attention and consideration in their own right. My fondest wish is that it will contribute to a new round of engagement between international scholarship and Nicaragua's complex postrevolutionary reality.

Introduction

THE ATMOSPHERE AT the Managua offices of the Nicaraguan newspaper *Barricada* on the afternoon of 25 October 1994 has been described as "tense, but in a way festive."[1] It was in any case expectant. With *Barricada* journalists assembled on the front doorstep, Sandinista commanders Tomás Borge and Lumberto Campbell arrived at the paper's plant in Jeeps with tinted windows. A retinue of bodyguards and local party militants trailed in their wake.

Borge, the only surviving founding member of the Sandinista National Liberation Front (Frente Sandinista de Liberación Nacional, FSLN), had served as minister of the interior and chief censor during the revolution's tumultuous years in power (1979–90). He and Campbell were fresh from a meeting of the Sandinista Assembly that had placed a decisive seal on the campaign, probably dating back to 1990, to unseat Carlos Fernando Chamorro as *Barricada*'s director. Chamorro had directed the paper from June 1980, less than a year after it was founded. He was the son of martyred *La Prensa* editor Pedro Joaquín Chamorro, killed apparently at the behest of the Somoza dictatorship in 1978, and his wife Violeta, who would serve as Nicaragua's president from 1990 to 1996. In his own right, Chamorro had become a leading figure in the broad "renovationist" current that sought a far-reaching transformation and democratization of the FSLN's structures and internal processes. Deposing Chamorro, and (as it transpired) replacing him with Borge, would reharmonize a "wayward" Sandinista institution with the dominant *ortodoxo* (orthodox) current of the FSLN, which had gradually gained the upper hand in the intraparty struggle.

As Borge and Campbell made their appearance at the *Barricada* plant, similar purges were underway across town at the FSLN-owned Radio Sandino and Radio Stereo Ya. Three programs were being abruptly pulled from the airwaves—including one that had been on the air for twenty-one years. Their directors were also fired.[2] But none of these events had the air of ceremony and significance of the scene unfolding at *Barricada*. There, the *defenestración* (lit., "throwing out the window") of Carlos Fernando Chamorro proceeded with the dignity and sense of familiarity befitting longtime revolutionaries, comrades in a movement that had always foresworn violent internal vendettas.

Chamorro—looking "tired, but serene," according to one observer[3]—received the two directorate representatives and led them into his office. After a while he emerged to speak to assembled staff, announcing that he accepted the decision as a fait accompli, but protesting that the directorate in fact did not possess the authority to depose him.[4] Then he retired again to his office to pack his belongings and embrace a succession of *Barricada* employees, clinging "much of the while to a small wooden statue of Augusto C[ésar] Sandino, the peasant insurrection leader who lent his name to the [Sandinista] Front."[5]

By the time Chamorro reemerged, more than a hundred representatives from national and international media had flooded to the *Barricada* offices. The place "was just full, chock-a-block," recalled senior editor Daniel Alegría.[6] One staffer, economics editor Roberto Larios, covered his mouth with masking tape as a sign of protest for the assembled photographers.[7] Chamorro strolled through the throng to his Jeep Cherokee (fig. 0.1) and drove off to his suburban home. Many *Barricada* staffers would join him there later for a bittersweet commemoration of the day's events, and of Chamorro's fifteen-year tenure at the newspaper.

The day before his dismissal, Chamorro had written a "final reflection" as director of *Barricada*. In it, he summarized the impasse that had brought about his defenestración:

> Over these last four years, since it was agreed that *Barricada* would cease to be the official organ of the FSLN, I have waged, with the support of the editorial council, an incessant battle to secure the autonomy conferred on this newspaper and its professional profile. I had to overcome pressure from powerful interests to ensure that *Barricada* became a daily dedicated to truthfully informing the reader,

Figure o.1. With national and international media assembled, *Barricada* director Carlos Fernando Chamorro leaves the newspaper offices on the day of his "defenestración" (firing) by the Sandinista Front, 25 October 1994. *Photo: Oscar Cantarero. Courtesy IHCA, UCA archives.*

independently of our own political interests. . . . Only by moving beyond the narrow framework of party interests was it possible to set the precedent of transforming a party institution into a credible and influential national newspaper. . . . However, now the will of those who were never in agreement with the change in editorial profile, and who continue to see the paper as the extension of the party apparatus, has been imposed. Underlying the practical urgency of bringing the paper into line and converting it into their political instrument is the insistence on a totalizing vision of power [*una visión totalizante del poder*], which recognizes as legitimate only those expressions under their strict control.[8]

Chamorro's comments attested to a perennial source of tension in the relations between *Barricada* and its proprietor and owner, the Sandinista Front. Throughout the revolution's years in power, the FSLN had been the newspaper's primary and (within the constraints of a poor and war-torn country) generous sponsor. Revolutionary solidarity in the face of outside attack, and simple material necessity in a resource-scarce environment, bound *Barricada* and the FSLN leadership in an intimate embrace throughout the 1980s.

That solidarity exacted a professional price, however—one that was acknowledged and problematized at the time, even if it was discussed only internally and in the muted tones deemed appropriate to a nation facing far more severe difficulties. This current of self-critique allows us to speak of a professional imperative existing alongside, and subordinate to, the overarching mobilizing imperative common to any official party organ. In chapter 1, I will argue that the professional imperative was evident in institutional transformations dating from early in *Barricada*'s life. Professional concerns fueled both internal debate and repeated petitions to the FSLN leadership, long before the Sandinistas' catastrophic election defeat in 1990 provided *Barricada* with an opportunity to move in the direction of greater institutional autonomy.

The growth of the autonomy project of 1990–94 can be traced

with some certainty to 1987, when Nicaragua started to emerge from long years of conflict and concomitant restrictions on civil liberties, including media freedoms (which nonetheless remained remarkably broad for a revolutionary society at war). But to assign a date to the birth of the project is in a sense arbitrary. In part, it grew out of a "moral economy of journalism" that influenced *Barricada* staff as it has shaped the craft of reporting and editing the world over. It derived too from Nicaragua's specific political, cultural, and journalistic landscape—for example, the heritage of *La Prensa,* a beacon of antisomocista opposition that sundered in 1980 and reemerged as a staunch opponent of the Sandinistas. And as with conceptions of professionalism prevailing in most media systems (especially Western ones), there was a strong material component. Stripped of its privileged relationship with the ruling authorities, *Barricada* was forced to seek sustenance from readers and advertisers—which meant providing them with a journalism worth reading.

If the broad parameters of the autonomy project are discernible (in retrospect) from 1987 onward, *Barricada* hardly abandoned the mobilizing imperative that had given it birth. It faithfully championed the FSLN during the 1990 elections, in a style scarcely different from the boosterism of the previous campaign, six years earlier. *Barricada* staff were as traumatized as any dedicated revolutionaries by the unexpected Sandinista defeat at the hands of the UNO coalition, with Carlos Fernando Chamorro's mother as its presidential aspirant and figurehead. The paper, though, was forced to come to grips with the unfamiliar new environment more rapidly than most Sandinista institutions. It decided to seize the initiative, and in so doing, it carried the autonomy project a decisive step further. It developed a New Editorial Profile, which proposed the radical de-officializing of the paper and its reorientation "in the national interest" (*por los intereses nacionales*). In December 1990 the autonomy project was approved—fatefully—by every member of the National Directorate save one, Daniel Ortega; and the new version of

Barricada hit Nicaraguan newsstands the following month. The legacy of official status was abandoned right down to the familiar logos—Sandino's Tom Mix hat; a guerrilla crouching behind a barricade of paving stones—that had long graced the masthead.

The autonomy experiment formally launched in 1991 capped an uneven, decade-long process in which *Barricada* had worked to carve out a sphere of semiautonomous operation, founded on a distinction between mobilizing and professional imperatives. Despite important transformations, *Barricada* during the revolutionary decade had remained "a predictable newspaper," in the words of its director, Carlos Fernando Chamorro. "It didn't have much ability to surprise," Chamorro said around the time of his dismissal from the paper in 1994. "Its agenda was predetermined."⁹ Internal and external evaluations of the paper almost unanimously criticized *Barricada*'s stilted political coverage and turgidly "official" tone. Professional initiatives—always originating within *Barricada*— aimed throughout the 1980s at humanizing the paper's content, reducing the dosage of clichés, and increasing the overall "agility" of its journalism. The war correspondence of the period, for example, moved from martial propaganda toward a somewhat more nuanced, human, and exploratory style. At the other end of the spectrum of daily coverage, a "lighter" page—the aptly named *De todo un poco* (A little of everything)—was introduced and quickly became *Barricada*'s most popular feature. In 1989, *Gente* (People) was launched—a daring and stylish weekly supplement directed by the irrepressible feminist Sofía Montenegro. It rapidly became the preferred supplement of an outright majority of *Barricada* readers.

The strongly supportive response from readers, advertisers, and nontraditional constituencies to these harbingers of the autonomy project gave *Barricada* important bargaining power in its postelection negotiations with the National Directorate. The FSLN leadership, weakened and disoriented by the election defeat, declared itself willing to grant *Barricada* a looser rein—again, with one crucial exception. But the directorate demanded (and the paper never questioned) that the party should retain ownership of the paper and control over the strategic heights of its operations. In return, under the terms of the agreement hammered out during 1990, party influence was further diffused through an important new mediating institution: the *Barricada* editorial council, which drew its membership from the Sandinista establishment rather than the party leadership per se.

As long as *Barricada*'s sponsor lacked the desire and cohesion to oppose the newspaper's autonomy project—that is, between 1990 and 1994—*Barricada*'s practical independence was impressive. So too was the way in which it was utilized. *Barricada* established professional linkages with a wide range of newspapers both domestically and internationally. It improved its production quality and general appearance. It launched a Sunday edition, a first for Nicaragua. It devoted greater energy and resources to investigative journalism—resulting, on occasion, in agenda-setting scoops. The most notable of these was the paper's May 1993 unveiling of the so-called Buzón de Santa Rosa, an arms cache in Managua belonging to the Salvadorean FPL guerrillas. *Barricada*'s investigations into the Buzón were a defining moment for the autonomy project. They were, of course, extremely sensitive politically, given the close ties between the FSLN and the FPL during the protracted imperialist siege of the 1980s. The paper's decision to prioritize professional considerations—news value—over political ones offered persuasive evidence that *Barricada* had indeed changed its tune, and was more interested in putting the national interest ahead of narrow sectarianism.

Whatever problems *Barricada* faced during the early 1990s, declining credibility was not among them—at least as far as most readers and outside observers were concerned. There was, though, one vital constituency that remained unconvinced. The autonomy project encountered increasingly vehement opposition from the so-called ortodoxo current of the FSLN, which coalesced after January

1994 as the Izquierda Democrática (Democratic Left) tendency.[10] The transformations at *Barricada* were foundational to the critique mounted by key ortodoxo intellectuals like Mónica Baltodano; her husband, Julio López; and Rosario Murillo (a prominent Sandinista poet and companion of former president Daniel Ortega). Ever since the paper abandoned its official status—indeed, even before—ortodoxo commentary depicted *Barricada* as the cutting edge of co-option, revisionism, and the abandoning of revolutionary values within the front. Along with Sergio Ramírez's FSLN bench in the National Assembly, *Barricada* was seen as one of two key "renovationist" institutions within the FSLN. In ortodoxo eyes, if the parliamentary rebels led by Ramírez were not subdued, their creeping social-democratic tendencies would cripple the front in an arena that had grown in significance since the Sandinistas fell from power. Likewise, if *Barricada*'s autonomy project were allowed to endure, it would jeopardize the FSLN's ability to mobilize its own media for the vital 1996 national elections. The front's campaign risked being derailed before it began, and along with it the revolution's chances of returning to national power.

Daniel Ortega had reason to be sympathetic with this view. He had clashed publicly with *Barricada* as far back as the mid-1980s (see chapter 3). He was the single member of the National Directorate who had been absent—mediating in the Gulf crisis—but glowering from a distance as other members voted to approve the autonomy project in December 1990.[11] Since then, Ortega had launched regular attacks on *Barricada*'s new orientation. Like other ortodoxo leaders and intellectuals, including his companion Murillo, Ortega saw *Barricada*'s self-proclaimed professionalism as a mere mask for a project that, regardless of its intentions, could only assist the resurgent forces of counterrevolution within Nicaragua and internationally. His increasingly vehement opposition was the main reason that the defenestración, when it came in October 1994, was indeed "a coup foretold." His statement immediately after the coup, that *Barricada* "had been turned into a mouthpiece for neoliberal, imperialist, and right-wing politics," aptly summarized his own convictions, and those of the ortodoxos more generally.

Barricada's status as a renovationist institution was hardly a figment of the ortodoxos' imagination. The Democratic Left (DL) tendency—basically the alliance between the ortodoxo current and Ortega—crystallized in a seminal meeting at the Pikín Guerrero schoolhouse, near Managua, in January 1994. The gathering approved a manifesto, the "Propuesta desde la izquierda democrática sandinista" (Proposal of the Sandinista democratic left), which was published (in *Barricada*) in early February. It called for "reject[ion of] the principles and measures of liberalism and neoliberalism," and a renewed commitment to revolutionary struggle. A week later, a loose renovationist coalition responded with its own manifesto, "Por un sandinismo de las mayorías" (For a Sandinismo of the majorities). The group urged an extension of the process of "change and renovation" within the Sandinista Front, to build a party that was "open, participatory, and creative, with flexible structures." Among the signatories were four leading figures at *Barricada*: Carlos Fernando Chamorro and Sofía Montenegro, along with senior editors Darwin Juárez and Onofre Guevara.

The renovationist forces never achieved the organizational coherence or intraparty influence of the Democratic Left current—that would have been anathema to their vision of a more grassroots-oriented, decentralized Sandinista movement. But the involvement of the four *Barricada* staffers—who had apparently decided by this point that they had little to lose by appending their signatures to the "mayorías" document—was the last straw as far as the ortodoxos were concerned. The renovationists had to be confronted and (peacefully) purged. As part of the process, substantial changes would be required at *Barricada*—though it is likely that most ortodoxos imagined a less extensive housecleaning than eventually occurred.

With the coalescing of the currents, the battle lines were drawn for the FSLN Special Congress of May 1994. Here, after months of patient preparations at both base and leadership levels, the Democratic Left won its decisive victory, gaining three-quarters of the seats in the Sandinista Assembly, ostensibly the highest decision-making body in the front. A new National Directorate was elected, confirming key ortodoxos in their posts, but pointedly freezing out Sergio Ramírez and other prominent renovationists. From that moment on, recalled Carlos Fernando Chamorro in 1996, the fate of *Barricada*'s autonomy project was never in doubt: "I knew after the congress that the whole experiment was finished. The only thing we could do was try to gain allies outside the front, and to resist until the last day. That is exactly what we did. But in political terms, we knew that we were lost."[12] Six months later, Tomás Borge and Lumberto Campbell arrived with their retinue at the *Barricada* gates.

The National Directorate apparently did not foresee the defenestración of Carlos Fernando Chamorro as necessitating sweeping changes to every aspect of *Barricada*'s staffing and functioning. The leadership likely felt that economic pressures—together, perhaps, with an institutional esprit de corps—would keep the majority of *Barricada*'s journalists and editors in place after the coup. On the first *Barricada* anniversary to be celebrated since the defenestración (25 July 1995), Tomás Borge acknowledged as much: "The journalists identified with the former director of *Barricada* are good at their profession and, in general, good persons. This is the reason why we intended—in vain—to keep them on."[13]

In vain indeed. Over the three weeks following the defenestración, approximately 80 percent of the *Barricada* journalistic staff resigned, or were forced out by a new directorate that finally realized the scale of internal opposition to its project. Only four lower-level veterans remained (though much greater continuity was maintained among blue-collar staff). The circumstances of this larger institutional transformation are still hotly disputed. At the time of my fieldwork in mid-1996, the wider *defenestración* had spawned the longest-running labor dispute in Nicaraguan history.[14]

It is easy, in retrospect, to overlook the three-week interregnum between old and new orders at *Barricada,* since the final house-cleaning was so extensive. Nonetheless, this brief period must be numbered among the most noteworthy sagas in modern Latin American journalism. Day after day the policies and editorial preferences of *Barricada*'s new directorate—and their allies within the FSLN as a whole—were exposed to withering criticism from *Barricada*'s journalists and remaining editors, *within the pages of the newspaper itself.* This tale has not been told in depth, either in English or Spanish, to my knowledge; it delineates with great clarity the clash between mobilizing and professional imperatives that had, by October 1994, been shaping *Barricada* for a decade and a half. It also provides a fascinating and intimate glimpse into an important revolutionary movement and one of its key component institutions, as both underwent wrenching and far-reaching transformations. Finally, the 1994 coup and its aftermath constitute a powerful human drama, as old allies and *compañeros* (comrades) within the FSLN grew estranged from one another, and as a project in which most participants had invested years of their lives was abruptly terminated by its longtime sponsor.

On 31 November 1994, Tomás Borge set a seal on the changes at *Barricada* with his confirmation as new director of the newspaper and president of its (now vestigial) editorial council. Bayardo Arce, a veteran member of the FSLN National Directorate who had served for years as the leadership's point man at *Barricada,* resigned his position, proclaiming, "In these new conditions, the presidency should be in the hands of the National Directorate."[15] Arce's resignation and Borge's ascension in a way brought the story of *Barricada* full circle. The official organ, transformed in 1991 into a champion of civil society, returned in 1994 to its former orientation as a largely passive mouthpiece for the leadership of the FSLN, notably Borge and Daniel Ortega. However this may have suited those atop the Sandinista power pyramid, it held little appeal for readers, even those who were staunchest in their support of the orto-doxo line. Non-Sandinista members of the political class, along with advertisers, had largely supported *Barricada*'s autonomy project under Chamorro. Predictably, they shunned the new incarnation of *Barricada*. The paper's circulation, which had eroded together with that of the other Nicaraguan dailies amid the material privations of the early 1990s, nose-dived below even marginal sustainability.

The new brains behind *Barricada*, subdirector Julio López, tried to put the best face on the downturn. A circulation even of two thousand, he suggested, would be acceptable, "if it was the right two thousand people."[16] But with the overwhelming majority of Sandinista militants unwilling to subsidize the paper with their meager discretionary income, the project was doomed. In September 1997, *Barricada* workers, including photographers and editors, struck to protest the company's failure to pay them two months of back wages. In January 1998, after further months of fruitless negotiations and equally unsuccessful attempts to muster the funding, Tomás Borge made the decision to close the newspaper. The daily *Barricada* was dead before its twentieth birthday.

CHAPTER 1 OF *Beyond the Barricades* represents a distillation, and to some extent a critical reevaluation, of my earlier research into *Barricada*'s origins and evolution.[17] I focus on structural transformations in the newspaper's relationship with its FSLN sponsor; the varied and often divergent conceptions of the newspaper's role in a revolutionary society; and the growing strength of the professional imperative that underpinned the far-reaching reorientation of January 1991.

Chapter 2 discusses *Barricada*'s autonomy project as it developed from 1987 onward. It considers transformations in the newspaper's institutional structure, editorial content, and sense of professional mission, to the extent that these can be gleaned from interviews, internal documents, and published editorial pronouncments. Chapter 3, "Chronicle of a Coup Foretold," traces the rise of opposition within the Sandinista Front to this new vision of a national (but still pro-revolutionary) journalism. It considers the essential points of conflict between the paper's agenda, both professional and political, and the mobilizing priorities of the increasingly dominant ortodoxo current within the front. The chapter then shifts to a detailed narrative of the coup at *Barricada* in October 1994 and the brief but extraordinary interregnum that followed. The new/old order imposed at *Barricada* after the coup is the subject of chapter 4, which compares and contrasts the *Barricada* of Tomás Borge and Julio López with both earlier incarnations of the paper. The final chapter, "The Death of *Barricada*," carries the story through to its messy, melancholy dénouement in January 1998. In the conclusion to the chapter, I seek to place the *Barricada* events in comparative perspective, utilizing the frameworks developed and data gathered for a broader project on the press in transition worldwide.[18]

Abbreviations

AMNLAE	Asociación de Mujeres Nicaragüenses "Luisa Amanda Espinoza" (Luisa Amanda Espinoza Nicaraguan Women's Association [FSLN])
ANDEN	Asociación Nacional de Educadores de Nicaragua (National Association of Nicaraguan Teachers)
CENIDH	Centro Nicaragüense de Derechos Humanos (Nicaraguan Center for Human Rights)
CINCO	Centro de Investigaciones de la Comunicación (Center for Communications Research)
CIPRES	Centro de Investigación y Promoción para el Desarrollo Rural y Social (Center for Research and Promotion for Rural and Social Development)
COSEP	Consejo Superior de la Empresa Privada (Superior Council of Private Enterprise)
DAP	Departamento de Agitación y Propaganda (Department of Agitation and Propaganda [FSLN])
DL	Democratic Left (Izquierda Democrática [FSLN faction])
DN	Dirección Nacional (National Directorate [FSLN])
EPS	Ejército Popular Sandinista (Sandinista People's Army)
FETSALUD	Federación de Trabajadores de la Salud (Health Workers' Federation)

FPI	Fuerzas Punitivas de Izquierda (Punitive Forces of the Left)
FPL	Fuerzas Populares de Liberación (Popular Forces of Liberation [El Salvador])
FROC	Frente Revolucionaro Obrero y Campesino (Peasant-Worker Revolutionary Front)
FSLN	Frente Sandinista de Liberación Nacional (Sandinista National Liberation Front)
GPP	Guerra Popular Prolongada (Prolonged Popular War [FSLN faction])
INSS	Instituto Nicaragüense de Seguridad Social (Nicaraguan Social Security Institute)
MAP	Movimiento de Acción Popular (Movement of Popular Action)
MITRAB	Ministerio del Trabajo (Ministry of Labor)
MRS	Movimiento de Renovación Sandinista (Movement for Sandinista Renovation)
PRI	Partido Revolucionario Institucional (Institutional Revolutionary Party [Mexico])
SMP	Servicio Militar Patriótico (Patriotic Military Service)
UCA	La Universidad Centroamericana (University of Central America)
UNO	Unión Nacional Opositora (National Opposition Union)
UPN	Unión de Periodistas de Nicaragua (Union of Nicaraguan Journalists)

Beyond the Barricades

Chapter 1

Barricada

The Party and the Paper, 1979–1991

Genesis

THE NICARAGUAN REVOLUTION gave birth to *Barricada* in a blaze of truck headlights. Six days after the ragtag Sandinista armies vanquished the last pockets of Somocista resistance and flooded into the capital city, to the cheers of hundreds of thousands of Managuans, the first four-page *Barricada* broadsheet began to circulate through whatever channels were available in the chaotic transitional environment. The banner headline of the 25 July 1979 edition proclaimed: "We've Triumphed—Now, Forward!"

That day, and for three years afterward, *Barricada* was produced in the offices of the old Somocista newspaper *Novedades*. Leonel Espinoza, who would go on to serve as chief of the Sandinistas' Department of Agitation and Propaganda (DAP), managed to protect offices and valuable equipment from the hordes of demonstrators who sought to vent their fury on the dictatorship's mouthpiece. Still, many production basics had to be improvised. "Sometimes," said Sofía Montenegro, "we had to work with the delivery trucks providing illumination for the journalists to write."

Montenegro, then twenty-five, was one of the first Sandinista militants to affiliate herself with the revolution's new official organ. As was commonly the case in the 1970s—though it had little precedent in Nicaragua's clannish history—political fault lines ran down the middle of her extended family. She had entered the revolution with the Movement of Popular Action (MAP), an extreme-left grouping. Galvanized by the killing of Pedro Joaquín Chamorro, editor of the opposition daily *La Prensa,* and by the first failed insurrection—both in 1978—she "began to revise [her] position . . . [and] realized the real revolutionary option was the Sandinista Front." Montenegro had been working underground with the FSLN ever since.

Meanwhile, her brother, Franklin, had followed in their father's footsteps to become one of the most trusted field commanders of Somoza's National Guard. For Montenegro the revolutionary triumph of 19 July was "bittersweet—because I knew my brother had been caught." Franklin Montenegro had been captured while trying to flee across the Gulf of Fonseca to El Salvador with other members of the National Guard (a story related vividly by Christopher Dickey in *With the Contras*).[1] Montenegro felt "the suspicion of the whole population hanging" over her when her family connection to the Somocista commander was made known. "I didn't know who wanted to kill me. . . . The population was so angry. There were executions in the beginning, not because the front ordered it but because you couldn't stop the mob. . . . All you could do was be careful."

Accompanied by these feelings of ambivalence and by the constant threat of harassment—or worse—Montenegro spent the days following the revolution scouring Managua, looking for material assistance and helping hands for the front's new journalistic project. "The problem was, how were we going to get this thing off the ground?" Montenegro remembered. "Because the Somocista journalists, before they left, took with them whatever they could and destroyed some of the teletypes and typewriters." Fortunately, thanks to her fluent English, the immediate prerevolutionary period had brought Montenegro into close contact with the large community of expatriate journalists, many with open or covert revolutionary sympathies, who flocked to Nicaragua to cover Somoza's downfall:

I became a stringer and translator for *Stern* magazine. That way, I could mingle with all the press—get information from them and pass them information, make contact for them with the Sandinista fighters in the mountains. . . . My first duty [after the revolution] was to seek out members of the foreign press in Managua and ask them for help. I went around asking if they could donate negatives, cameras, typewriters, God knows what. I wrote a little advertisement and put it in the lobby of the Hotel Intercontinental, where the international journalists stayed. Donations began to come in: somebody gave us a camera, someone else a typewriter. So international solidarity was important from the start![2]

Those present at *Barricada's* creation numbered perhaps fifteen people, in Montenegro's recollection. The majority of them were

nearly complete amateurs. We had no idea that things like accounting and administration even existed, until some people from *La Prensa* came over to help us out while their offices were being repaired.[3] We didn't sell the paper initially, we just gave it out. We had no distribution network, nothing. And frankly, we didn't give a shit, you know. To show you how naïve we were, I remember one of the members of the FSLN National Directorate, Luís Carrión, arriving at the office. "You need some money, eh? Well, here's some capital to start with." He gave us four hundred dollars. That was the extent of the front's subsidy at the beginning. . . . We all worked as volunteers; wages weren't introduced until 1980.[4]

The very first edition of the paper was overseen by Danilo Aguirre, *La Prensa's* subdirector, described by Carlos Fernando Chamorro as "the most experienced Nicaraguan journalist at the time." A senior editor from *La Prensa,* Manuel Pinell, also came aboard: he was "the only Nicaraguan working in the country who had an M.A. in journalism"—from the University of Missouri.[5] Ignacio "Nacho" Briones, a longtime presence on the Nicaraguan journalism scene, rounded out the professionally experienced cadre of the newborn publication. Further down the chain of authority, such experience evaporated and staffers learned as they went along.

Inexperience characterized the very summit of authority as well. The earliest *responsables políticos*—the *Barricada* commissars, dispatched by the front's National Directorate—had some experience in underground propaganda efforts, but none in professional journalism.[6] The implications of this will be explored in detail later in the chapter; they certainly attracted the attention of twenty-three-year-old Carlos Fernando Chamorro when he took up the post of *Barricada* director in June 1980.

Chamorro would occupy the director's office for a decade and a half, with an interregnum at the Department of Agitation and Propaganda, where he orchestrated the FSLN's successful 1984 election campaign.[7] Chamorro was a scion of one of the most illustrious families in Nicaragua. One of his relatives, Fruto Chamorro, had served as president between 1853 and 1855; another, his mother Violeta, would occupy the same post between 1990 and 1996. His father was Pedro Joaquín Chamorro Sr., the *La Prensa* editor assassinated in downtown Managua on 10 January 1978. Numerous commentators have cited the murder of Chamorro père as a turning point in the revolutionary struggle. It sparked "an unprecedented wave of riots and mass mobilisations which the Sandinistas' October [1977] offensive alone could never have unleashed, and a flurry of international condemnation."[8] The FSLN leadership, it seems, was seeking to capitalize on Pedro Joaquín's legacy when it appointed his son to direct the new official organ of the front. By doing so, it helped to pave the way for a remarkable anomaly. When, in April 1980, *La Prensa*'s increasingly anti-Sandinista line prompted 80 percent of the staff to leave and found *El Nuevo Diario* as a rival publication, Nicaragua gained the status—probably unique in the twentieth century—of having all its daily newspapers owned or directed (or both) by members of the same family.[9]

But the selection of Carlos Fernando to head *Barricada* was not as intuitive a decision as it might appear. He was born on National Journalists' Day (1 March 1956); but into his twenties, Chamorro fils had displayed little of his father's journalistic passion. Though he had dabbled in writing for *La Prensa* immediately prior to the revolution, Chamorro had rejected the idea of a career in journalism. "Since I was very young, I more or less said to myself, 'Well, I want to do something for myself. I don't want to be in my father's shadow,'" Chamorro explained in a 1991 interview. Instead, he spent time at McGill University in Montreal, graduating in 1977 with a bachelor's degree in economics. His father's death, though, was a transforming event: it was only after the assassination that Carlos Fernando took his first serious steps toward the profession that Pedro Joaquín had made his own. He worked at *La Prensa* from February 1978 to June 1979. Dispatched to *Barricada* as a responsable político when the revolution triumphed, Chamorro worked at the paper for a few formative days, from 21 to 26 July. He put in more sporadic appearances until mid-August, then departed the scene entirely to serve as the vice-minister of culture in the revolutionary government. In late November he returned to *Barricada* as codirector with Luís "El Chiri" Guzmán. By the time he became sole director, in June 1980, therefore, Chamorro could claim more than two years of nearly continuous experience with the pro-revolutionary press. That, as much as his surname, might have given him the edge over the other *responsables* considered for the post.

The institution Chamorro oversaw had barely emerged from chaos. "Everything was very spontaneous," he remembered. "We didn't have time to organize anything. Someone would be named general manager, but he didn't have any experience on a newspaper. We had very young people; we were very rhetorical."[10] It was an inauspicious start, but *Barricada* was on its way to becoming one of the most valuable—and in the end one of the most hotly contested—of the revolution's institutions.

The Vanguard's Vanguard

Rather than mere journalists, we are Sandinistas.

—*Barricada*, 7 September 1979

If the material environment was unstable and unpredictable, *Barricada* could at least count on a role and an identity that was all but predetermined. From the moment it first hit the streets, the paper's raison d'être was the Sandinista National Liberation Front and its revolutionary struggle to transform Nicaragua. *Barricada* would be a party-political project, along the classic lines sketched by those two journalists and revolutionists Karl Marx and V. I. Lenin—although a more Gramscian "organic-intellectual" tinge was occasionally evident.[11] The classic Marxist-Leninist conception of the newspaper as a disseminator of revolutionary propaganda had guided the Sandinista press from the first mimeographed pamphlets issued by the FSLN in the early 1960s.[12] Now, with the revolution victorious, Lenin's "idea of the newspaper as an organizer of production" would guide *Barricada*'s journalism, according to Carlos Fernando Chamorro.[13] "There was a tremendous need," Chamorro explained in 1991, "to put on the street a newspaper which would help represent the voice of authority and organization of the new government and society."[14] Sofía Montenegro also described *Barricada*'s organizing principle as "the Leninist idea of what the press should be." The "common understanding" of this model among *Barricada* staffers, she said, was that

> the press should not only be a medium of information, but also should help to organize a totally disorganized society. The whole Somocista state had fallen to pieces, absolutely destroyed. You had to reconstruct institutions, help people to organize and defend their interests, and all the time *keep moving*, advancing the revolutionary project. That was another characteristic of this view, that the press should serve to make propaganda for revolutionary ideas. Finally, it should be an organ of information, to bring people the news they needed to organize their daily lives.[15]

Some sense of the stylistic essence of the project can be gleaned by surveying the headlines of these early editions of *Barricada*. "Victory of the People with Their Vanguard," "Now: Consolidate the Revolution," "Organization in the Revolution"—the message, and the rhetoric, was typical. Anyone who missed the thrust of the polemic needed only consult the paper's published statements of editorial purpose. On 13 August 1979, barely three weeks after the triumph, an editorial praised the "courageous and outstanding participation" of Nicaraguan journalists in the long battle against the dictatorship:

> But in the same way that the insurrection ended on July 19 1979, to give way to the tasks of the revolution and of the government which today occupy our heroic combatants, so our journalism and our journalists stand ready to turn a new page in the struggle which today is constituted in entirely different terms from those of the past. The journalism which we are committed to developing has as its objective the informing, orientating, and educating of our people in the tasks and responsibilities which each and every Nicaraguan must assume—in the short term, to ensure the success of our national reconstruction, and in the future to forge a country in which the injustices evident in the great social contradictions will disappear forever.

Journalists' work, *Barricada* declared, "should be oriented through discipline, through the full identification with the process being mapped out by our leaders."[16] The edition of 25 August, commemorating the first month of *Barricada*'s publication, made the Marxist-Leninist influence even more plain:

> We are, at this moment, the only newspaper written by the revolutionary vanguard. We know that this implies a complex and diverse agenda: to inform, in the sense of making known that which occurs in our country and around the world; to orient the people and contribute to the task of national reconstruction; to disseminate the political line of the FSLN; to help bring about the organization and

normalization that our liberated country so badly needs as it emerges from the rubble of war; to support the measures taken by the Government of National Reconstruction [dominated by the FSLN]; and to provide information that is both truthful and dedicated to the demands of our people.[17]

This conception of the revolutionary vanguard will be familiar to students of Leninism.[18] Though in crucial respects the Sandinistas departed from the standard state-socialist model that Lenin had propounded, on this point—the need for a driving force to propel Nicaragua into the revolutionary future—they demurred scarcely at all. In his unsurpassed study of the FSLN, *Sandinistas: The Party and the Revolution,* Dennis Gilbert calls this notion of "a self-recruited, ideologically motivated, disciplined, self-abnegating, hierarchical, revolutionary elite . . . without doubt Lenin's most important contribution to the ideology of the FSLN." "Vanguard" became in turn "the most common term in the Sandinista lexicon." Indeed, noted Gilbert, "It is difficult to find a party text where it does not occur."[19]

The vanguardist tendencies within the front would only increase throughout the 1980s, as the revolution confronted the implacable hostility of the Reagan administration and the terrorist force, the so-called contras, that the United States armed and sustained along Nicaragua's borders and in the thinly populated zones of the north and south. The first few years of the revolution also saw a flowering of popular organizations, testimony to the forces of civil society unleashed by the struggle against the dictatorship. These to a significant extent offset the commandist tendencies inherent in the vanguard model, and *Barricada*'s news agenda would reflect their influence, along with the dictates or requests of the FSLN leadership. But as war and economic crisis spawned a mounting national emergency, the carapace of the revolution's institutions hardened. Most were brought under the closer supervision of the National Directorate, the nine-man body at the top of the Sandinista power pyramid. Eventually, they became little more than parastatal mechanisms of administration and distribution. At their gatherings, one of the most commonly heard revolutionary chants was: *Dirección Nacional, Ordene!* (National Directorate, Command Us!). No Sandinista institution would remain untouched by the trend— least of all, perhaps, the party's official organ. When *Barricada*'s *perfil editorial* (editorial profile) was finally formalized in 1985, at the height of the contra war and with the economy spiraling ever downward, Carlos Fernando Chamorro was frank in his acknowledgment that "as an official organ, *Barricada* must comply with the following functions":

a) To be a vehicle of mass information of the FSLN for the divulging of its political line, an instrument of support for the mobilization of the masses around the tasks of the revolution, and to convert itself into an effective medium of communication between the masses and the FSLN.

b) To contribute to the formation of the base committees, members, and activists of the FSLN to wage the ideological struggle, arming them with arguments and revolutionary conceptions, and to be a vehicle of support for the organization of ideological work at the base.[20]

In this vanguardist and parastatal conception,[21] there was naturally little room for "bourgeois" virtues of journalistic professionalism and objectivity. In fact, there was barely room for the kind of stylistic agility that would allow a journalist to move beyond ponderous official pronouncements and engage the reader on a more personal, conversational level. It was not that classical notions of objectivity or of the press's watchdog role were dispensed with altogether. Chamorro, for instance, rejected a strategy built around the provision of "isolated information that might otherwise be called objective truth." But he also argued that "without criticism there can be neither journalism nor revolution." The crux, it appeared, lay in the definition of criticism: "We do not refer here to destructive, counterrevolutionary criticism, but rather to criticism that offers a searching analysis of problems and proposes alternative revolutionary solutions for them."[22]

In such fashion were the bourgeois concepts reinterpreted, the better to marshal them for the revolutionary cause. These efforts often required some nimble intellectual gymnastics. Such was the case in 1980, when Comandante Carlos Núñez—newly appointed to serve as a go-between for *Barricada* in its dealings with the National Directorate—lectured staff celebrating the paper's first anniversary on the distinction between objectivity and impartiality: "As for those who bemoan the lack of objectivity in *Barricada,* [be it noted that] *Barricada* is an objective periodical, but what it is not and will never be—let us say this clearly—is impartial. [This is] because it is at the service of the interests of this revolution, which are none other than the interests of the working people. *Barricada* is not impartial because, like the revolution itself, it is a Sandinista organ; like the revolution it is, therefore, popular and anti-imperialist."

Clearly, the vanguardist conception offered *Barricada* relatively little opportunity to develop its own agenda of news coverage and editorial concerns. In earlier research on *Barricada,* I proposed a periodization of the paper's operations during the revolutionary decade, set alongside the shifting priorities of the newspaper's sponsor, the FSLN. The three main phases I isolated as: the era of reconstruction and state building, from 1979 to 1984; an overlapping and eventually overriding emphasis on national defense, from 1982 to 1987; and, as the war against contra rebels wound down from 1986 to 1989, a shift toward economic damage control and political *concertación* (best rendered in English as "conciliation") with opposition forces, both domestic and regional. Unsurprisingly, a close fit was evident between *Barricada*'s agenda and that of its FSLN sponsor, as encapsulated in the decrees of the National Directorate. At the height of the contra war, for example, *Barricada* was overwhelmed with *corresponsales de guerra* (war correspondence). These would serve as the paper's "main dish" until the late 1980s;[23] *Barricada* became "practically a bulletin of information on the war," in Sofía Montenegro's words.[24] This suited the mood of the times, however, and it had professional spin-offs that would prove important to the future course of the paper.

The paper was integral to the propaganda strategy developed by the FSLN—including by Chamorro himself, during his stint at the DAP—to contest the 1984 elections. When the National Directorate, and hence FSLN policy, switched tack again in 1986, *Barricada* followed suit. The paper was directed "to involve ourselves more" in the field of economics, according to *Barricada*'s managing editor for much of this period, Xavier Reyes.[25] And when the front began mobilizing for the 1990 elections, *Barricada*—which by that time had begun to push its own professional agenda in private meetings with FSLN leaders—put that agenda on hold once again, the better to serve (as it had in 1984) as a cheerleader for the party's candidates. "The campaign," said Carlos Fernando Chamorro, "absorbed everything."[26] Throughout, as staffer Guillermo Cortés aptly summarized *Barricada*'s basic orientation, "What was important was not that all opinions and versions [of a story] came out, but that [*Barricada*'s content] coincided with the political interests" of the FSLN.[27]

How, then, was such a project able to do an about-face—to "de-officialize" and establish itself as a more balanced and professional publication "in the national interest"? The answer may lie, in large part, in a strand of *Barricada*'s functioning that can be seen to accompany and partially offset the "mobilizing imperative" bestowed upon it by the National Directorate. For the purposes of this study, and for the comparative analysis of transitional media around the world,[28] I have dubbed this strand the professional imperative.

For if the mostly young and ill-trained journalists and editors who launched *Barricada* in 1979 were imbued with a desire to serve as the "vanguard's vanguard," they were also participants in the building of an institution that, over time, achieved greater internal coherence, amassed important new resources, and established a firmer sense of professional identity.[29] Often this process went hand in hand with the mobilizing dimension of the paper's operations. It was, after all, the front that was the most important provider of the material inputs and training that were indispensable to a deepening of professional sensibilities. Moreover, the revolutionary commitment that *Barricada* journalists brought to—for example—the corresponsales de guerra had important professional implications. The journalist who risked his or her life on the battlefront, to help speed the defeat of the contras and the triumph of the revolution, was also the journalist who found himself or herself exploring a type of journalism without precedent in Nicaraguan history. Carlos Fernando Chamorro called *Barricada*'s corresponsales de guerra (later published in book form) "the key point in our development": "In 1982 and 1983, that's when the newspaper came out strongly in the streets—not simply fighting against *La Prensa* or against the political parties of the right, but bringing to the front page the real situation of the country. No other newspaper could do it like us.... We sent four reporters to different fronts, and we had very impressive coverage."[30]

At least as regularly as the mobilizing and professional imperatives were able to establish a harmonious balance, however, they brought the paper into conflict with those whose main concern was that *Barricada* be a dependable mouthpiece for the vanguard. As *Barricada* entrenched itself as a revolutionary institution—and even before—staff chafed at party-imposed restrictions and experienced regular difficulties in juggling the political and professional obligations implicit in the idea of revolutionary journalism. In earlier research I argued that the professional imperative—a distinguishable "range of . . . ambitions, priorities, standards, and approaches"—had left an anecdotal and occasionally documentary spoor that allowed the analyst to trace its growth and development through the revolutionary decade of the 1980s. Professional considerations had

- sought expression within the parameters of *Barricada's* mobilizing role;

- regularly generated feelings of dissonance for *Barricada* staffers, testifying to a degree of perceived disharmony in the mobilizing and professional [imperatives];

- led the paper to seek a measure of distance, both bureaucratic and editorial, from the FSLN leadership;

- encouraged *Barricada* staffers to advance perspectives and solicit information that reflected the paper's increasing institutional identity, rather than relying exclusively on information resources generated by the FSLN, the revolutionary state, or sympathetic foreign sources;

- spawned discussion of *Barricada's* formal "de-officialization"—that is, the paper's renunciation of official-organ status and a parastatal role; and

- led, on occasion, to open conflict between *Barricada* staffers and National Directorate members, state functionaries, and foreign diplomatic sources.[31]

The roots of the professional imperative in the context of revolutionary Nicaragua, and their presence even in a propaganda organ such as *Barricada* unashamedly was in the 1980s, require some explanation. Perhaps the most important mitigating factor was the overarching character of the Sandinista revolution—by contrast, say, with Cuba or the Soviet Union. Almost uniquely in the annals of leftist revolution, the Sandinistas never sought or exercised a monopoly over Nicaraguan media. As with their decision to leave 60 percent of the economy in private hands, the relatively wide latitude given to opposition-owned newspapers and radio stations reflected the FSLN's desire to avoid scaring away "patriotic producers" domestically, as well as international sympathizers, by imposing a more hermetic and draconian system of control.[32]

The best-known media controversy of the Sandinista era attested to this basic tolerance, though it is usually cited as an example of

13

Sandinista repression. The events centered on regime relations with *La Prensa*, which under the supervision of Pedro Joaquín Chamorro's widow, Violeta, moved from the leading opposition daily under the Somoza dictatorship and a guarded supporter of the postrevolutionary junta, to the leading opposition voice once the FSLN established unquestioned hegemony. The paper's increasingly anti-Sandinista orientation, as noted, prompted an exodus of journalists and editors, who set up shop almost next door as the independent pro-revolutionary daily *El Nuevo Diario*—an internal transformation that in scope and scale compares to the defenestración at *Barricada* in 1994.[33]

After the schism, and with the increasingly blatant sponsorship of the U.S. Central Intelligence Agency,[34] *La Prensa* was free to advance the virulently anti-Sandinista line that it stuck to throughout the 1980s (and after). It served as the flagship of an opposition media campaign that one observer characterized as "relentlessly ideological, propagandistic, one-sided, sensationalistic, negative, and even dishonest."[35] It continued to publish nonetheless, albeit under increasing regime censorship. The nadir of relations between *La Prensa* and the Sandinista regime was reached in 1986–87, when the newspaper was closed for fifteen months after its directors flew to Washington to lobby for contra aid. But even during this period of chill, other opposition publications continued to circulate, and anti-Sandinista radio stations continued to broadcast.[36]

The fractious relationship with *La Prensa* thus attests to the comparatively tolerant media policy adopted by the Sandinistas. That media policy, in turn, reflected the wider political pluralism that was often remarked upon by visitors to Nicaragua during the 1980s (myself included). The country was one of the rare places in Latin America in the 1980s where one could voice contrary opinions in the street without worrying about a visit from a death squad, or pass a uniformed soldier without flinching inwardly. In fact, as Noam Chomsky argued with ironic force in the context of the 1990

Nicaraguan elections, the degree of pluralism was unusual even by the standards of developed Western countries in wartime:

> Under the totalitarian Sandinistas, foreigners were permitted to forge a political coalition [UNO] based upon the terrorist force [the contras] they created to attack the country; and they were allowed to pour millions of dollars into supporting it in the elections. Foreigners engaged in what the World Court condemned as "the unlawful use of force" against Nicaragua were allowed to fund a major newspaper [*La Prensa*] that called for the overthrow of the government and openly identified with the terrorist forces pursuing these ends, proxies of the foreign power funding the journal. Under these totalitarians, such foreigners as Jeane Kirkpatrick and U.S. Congressmen were permitted to enter the country to present public speeches and news conferences calling for the overthrow of the government by violence and supporting the foreign-run terrorist forces. "Human Rights" investigators accompanied by Contra lobbyists posing as "experts" were permitted free access, as were journalists who were scarcely more than agents of the foreign power attacking the country. Nothing remotely resembling this record can be found in Western democracies; in the United States, Israel, England, and other democracies, such freedoms would be inconceivable, even under far less threat, as the historical record demonstrates with utter clarity.[37]

All this is not to deny that opposition media operated under strictures that included the absurdities common to any censorship bureaucracy. But journalists were not found tortured and trussed in ditches, nor were they jailed, nor (with the one early exception of a radical-*leftist* paper) was the material plant of an opposition publication ever seized.[38] Supplies of Russian newsprint and other scarce goods were distributed equally by Sandinista state authorities to all three daily newspapers throughout the revolutionary era.[39]

The pluralism in the political and mass-media spheres reflected a broader cultural openness that was again striking by the standards of left-revolutionary regimes. The Sandinistas took the unusual view that Western popular culture—which in Nicaragua basically meant U.S. popular culture—was a benign force. According to Rosario Murillo, whose ortodoxo polemics against *Barricada* would help to undermine the paper's autonomy experiment in the 1990s, but who even at her most doctrinaire always seemed likelier to quote Lennon than Lenin: "We were able to see the difference between simple, everyday American people and American *policies; we* were also able to see the difference between rock music and American policy. . . . I think we had the cultural privilege of being able to see the difference between *real* imperialist policies and things that were just part of a culture, a way of life. Things that weren't harmful to anybody, and that in many cases were even enjoyable: films, music, art, even hamburgers and hot dogs. And baseball, of course."[40]

The U.S. influence was, if anything, especially prominent in Nicaraguan journalism. The only school of journalism in Nicaragua before the revolution was a wholly owned subsidiary of the U.S. embassy. (Bayardo Arce, later the National Directorate representative to *Barricada,* taught there before slipping underground as a guerrilla commander.) Though enrollment in the school was never large, the school's diet of "objective," Western-style journalism exerted a powerful influence on generations of Nicaraguan journalists. This meant that however vigorously *Barricada* journalists denounced "bourgeois media" practices during the 1980s, they could hardly help but define themselves against—and to some extent in terms of—that same tradition. This resulted in a certain schizophrenia when it came, for instance, to the watchdog function so central to liberal-democratic conceptions of the press. Even when *Barricada* was most shrill in denouncing the hypocrisy of the model—as when its staff argued that capitalism turned journalists into "eunuchs" capable of writing glowingly about "tyrant assassins"—even then, the critique seemed founded not so much on a conviction that objectivity and the critical function were ignoble per se, but that *Western jour-*

nalism fell short of the standards it proclaimed. Thus *Barricada* could be counted on to deliver denunciations of a journalistic model "that always tells us we have to be objective and impartial, while it itself is neither."[41] But *Barricada*'s writers also paid regular, if ambivalent, lip service to the critical function, as we have seen.

Figure 1.1. Detail of a child newspaper vendor, from Cordelia Dilg's beautiful mural adorning the Asociación de Niños Sandinistas "Luís Alfonso Velásquez" in Managua. *Courtesy Peter Hammer Verlag, Germany, and Father Ernesto Cardenal.*

The cultural heritage of the Nicaraguan revolutionaries, and the macro-pluralistic character of the policies they implemented during the 1980s, had two basic implications for the development of the professional imperative at *Barricada*. First, it determined the essential character of relations between the FSLN (for most purposes, the National Directorate) as the sponsor of the revolution's "official organ," and *Barricada* staffers as the day-to-day custodians of that organ and its journalistic project. It is no exaggeration to say that *Barricada* had greater room for maneuver, and more say in establishing the terms of the relationship with its sponsor, than any comparable organ in the history of leftist revolution. I will discuss the evolution of this "norm," and the specific blend of mobilizing and professional imperatives that it entailed, later in the chapter. But it is worth pausing briefly to contrast *Barricada* in the 1980s with the newspaper that might have been expected to serve as its most obvious role model: *Granma,* the official organ of the Cuban Communist Party. It so happened that *Granma* served as a *negative* example for many of those who wrote and edited *Barricada* during the 1980s. Sofía Montenegro, along with many other *Barricada* staffers, visited *Granma*'s offices in Havana in the early 1980s. She emerged feeling not inspired, but "horrified"—and amused: "I couldn't stop laughing. You know, *Granma* is *here,* and the Central Committee headquarters is over *here.* You write an editorial, you have to take it over to the Central Committee. There's some big shot from the party who checks what you write and gives the OK. Only then can it be printed. This sort of thing never happened at *Barricada.*"

Montenegro was struck above all by "the way that the bureaucracy had overwhelmed the editorial staff, let alone the administration." *Granma*'s staff was far more "padded" than *Barricada*'s own relatively lean operation, Montenegro said. The Cubans expressed disbelief "that this bunch of *kids* [*Barricada* staffers] could, in the first place, be given such a degree of responsibility, and second, that we were let loose without Big Brother watching over us."[42]

Carlos Fernando Chamorro too said he "always mentioned the example of *Granma* as something I did not want *Barricada* to be"; it served for him as a veritable "anticoncept" of revolutionary journalism. Daniel Alegría, speaking in 1991 as editor of *Barricada*'s international edition, called the Cuban press "unsmokable. You can't get through it, whether you're talking layout or content. It's pure propaganda from the first page to the last. . . . I personally think *Granma* is a paper that's been imposed on the Cubans, something that goes totally against their cultural makeup. It's so stiff and formal, and the Cubans themselves are a people who are at their best when they're making jokes about themselves."[43]

Are these comments merely self-serving, retrospective attempts to differentiate *Barricada*'s essential propaganda function from *Granma*'s less apologetic version of the same? Closer analysis suggests that Granma *did* serve *Barricada* as an anticoncept in key areas of the paper's coverage. In the first place, *Barricada*'s directorate took steps to avoid *Granma*'s "extreme subordination of news coverage to official requirements"—what Chamorro referred to as a "pre-elaborated" model of press functioning.[44] The micro-control exercised by party commissars and censorship authorities would be bluntly rejected as a modus operandi for the revolutionary journalists at *Barricada*. Not only would the FSLN's presence in the newsroom be strictly regulated (eventually limited to a single, rather easygoing representative); but *Barricada* would also enjoy freedom from the kind of prior censorship imposed on all the other Nicaraguan dailies in the 1980s, including the pro-revolutionary *El Nuevo Diario*. *Barricada* sought to devote greater attention to the human interest component usually so lacking in *Granma*'s coverage, a feature of its coverage that would later emerge as a core element of the autonomy project of the early 1990s. Finally, the range of opinion-editorial material in *Barricada*'s pages would lean toward individual (though sometimes painfully rhetorical) commentary, rather than prefabricated "official statements" from on high.

It could be argued that *Barricada* during the 1980s was more successful in expanding the professional imperative in institutional, rather
than editorial, terms. It undoubtedly established a considerable, likely
unprecedented degree of day-to-day autonomy from its FSLN sponsor. But as anyone who pores through the archives of back issues from
the 1980s can attest, the paper rarely managed to move beyond a generally clichéd, propagandistic tone—a deficiency that was widely recognized in internal documents of the period. It was, nonetheless, a
vision of a more independent, human, "agile" journalism—founded
above all on a further loosening of the sponsor's reins—that determined the character of the norm worked out between *Barricada* and
the FSLN leadership.

The other key respect in which macro-pluralism shaped *Barricada*'s professional agenda in the 1980s was in the paper's conflictive
but curiously interdependent relationship with the reactionary version
of *La Prensa*. The paper was indeed a powerful opponent. Despite
the frequent harassment visited upon it by the Sandinista authorities, including one period of extended closure, *La Prensa* could
count on a solid foundation of material and moral support in Nicaraguan society. Obviously, of the three Nicaraguan dailies, it was
the preferred publication of the élite—including the many thousands who hightailed it for Florida and other foreign destinations in
protest against the character and policies of the revolutionary regime.
La Prensa could count on receiving the bulk of private-sector
advertising revenue—income supplemented by open and covert
contributions from abroad, notably the CIA and affiliated front
organizations, and by the resources that its wealthy owners and directors possessed. More nebulous, but perhaps even more significant,
was the place *La Prensa* held in the hearts of Nicaraguans—primarily
the result of Pedro Joaquín Chamorro's distinguished record of opposition to the Somoza regime. Although the staff of the newly founded
El Nuevo Diario could claim to be the rightful inheritors of *La
Prensa*'s former progressive tradition, the paper as such remained

firmly "rooted in the traditions of the [Nicaraguan] people," according to Xavier Reyes. "I remember when I was a teenager in my house," said Reyes, "when dinner was served, we began with *gallo pinto* [beans and rice], coffee, tortillas—and *La Prensa*." Carlos Fernando Chamorro likewise referred to the unique "flavor of *La Prensa*" under his father's direction—a journalistic style that was "popular, aggressive, and at the same time well-presented."[45]

All these factors meant that *La Prensa* was a powerful competitor for the project of *periodismo revolucionario* (revolutionary journalism) being developed across town at the *Barricada* complex. That challenge was especially acute in the first year of *Barricada*'s existence, before *La Prensa* underwent its internal crisis and returned to the streets with a mobilizing agenda that was the very antithesis of *Barricada*'s pro-revolutionary stance. In 1979–80, according to Carlos Fernando Chamorro, *La Prensa* had managed to "keep the flavor" of its old progressive orientation. By doing so, it left *Barricada* in the dust. "*La Prensa* was a much better newspaper than us in professional terms," Chamorro lamented. "We were much more rhetorical, we didn't have much experience."[46]

The nature of the challenge was altered when *La Prensa* moved to the forefront of the opposition camp, confronting *Barricada* and the FSLN more generally "for the first time [with] a clear and confrontational opposition paper" (Chamorro). Between 1980 and 1984, *Barricada*'s "main concern" was "the political and ideological struggle with the right," symbolized most vividly by the daily bout of political competition and mudslinging with *La Prensa*. Again, the skein of mobilizing and professional imperatives was a tangled one. Initially, Chamorro said, *Barricada* was "very much on the defensive . . . responding to attacks, responding to questions." It was the paper's manifest weaknesses on the political front that prompted *Barricada* to make something of a leap in professional terms. The paper's writers "learned that you didn't have to answer every attack, and you could take the initiative in the debate," said

Chamorro. With that more strategic perspective in mind, *Barricada* found itself able to glean tips on style and presentation from *La Prensa*, again with both mobilizing and professional implications. *La Prensa*, in Chamorro's words, proved adept at "mak[ing] national and political problems out of individual and particular problems. They would take advantage of *anything*. They'd take the tragedy of a single family and say, 'This family has been abandoned by the revolution.' That was for me a discovery, that we were very much behind in dealing with [problems of] everyday life."[47]

The importance of the "reflex relationship"[48] between *Barricada* and *La Prensa* to the professional self-conception of *Barricada* staffers became plainer still in June 1986, when *La Prensa* was closed indefinitely on the orders of the minister of the interior (and future *Barricada* director), Tomás Borge. (The ban was lifted as part of the Esquipulas peace process in October 1987.) Perhaps surprisingly, *Barricada* staffers strongly opposed the closure. According to Xavier Reyes, the opposition derived from a sense that, while "politically we were rivals . . . *professionally we were colleagues*. . . . We imagined ourselves in the same position, being closed down, and imagined how we'd feel about it."[49] Sofía Montenegro's comments are also revealing: "I always said our greatest pride as revolutionary journalists should be for *La Prensa* to exist [unmolested by the regime], and for nobody to read it."

The disappearance of the daily competition for fifteen months left a void at the heart of *Barricada*'s political *and* professional project. "Our reason to fight every day was *La Prensa*," said Montenegro. "And it was very dull, you know, when it wasn't there. Something was missing."[50] The best the paper could do was to seize the opportunity to expand its professional purview in an attempt to reach devoted readers of *La Prensa*. "We had to fill the information vacuum," said Chamorro.[51] According to Xavier Reyes, "We tried to include other points of view, convert people and institutions into news that were not [traditional] sources for *Barricada*. We were trying to be more objective, more balanced."[52]

Throughout, the professional battle with *La Prensa*—and to a lesser extent with the muckraking, pro-revolutionary *El Nuevo Diario*, which given its origins also enjoyed some of *La Prensa*'s prestige—was vital in moving *Barricada*'s coverage toward a more diverse content and a more versatile journalism. The paper's most popular page, for example—*De todo un poco* ("A little of everything"), introduced in 1985—ran a variety of features and tidbits from the entertainment, cultural, and scientific worlds, as well as material on sexuality and gender relations. After *La Prensa*'s closure the following year, *De todo un poco* was expanded, in an effort to draw less-politicized readers away from the temporarily silenced competition.

In a sense, though, the role of other newspapers—whether *Granma, La Prensa,* or *El Nuevo Diario*—in consolidating *Barricada*'s professional identity was always secondary to the core issue of relations between the paper's staffers and their primary sponsor, the National Directorate of the FSLN. It is time to look more closely at the unusual character of this relationship, and the specific means by which *Barricada* sought to establish a degree of day-to-day autonomy in its dealings with the Sandinista leadership. It was, after all, this move toward a limited independence from an externally generated mobilizing imperative that provided the foundation for the remarkable, if eventually abortive, autonomy experiment of 1990–94.

The FSLN and Barricada: *"Norming" the Material Relationship*

For *Barricada,* the status of official organ brought with it significant material privileges. Of course, these were not as pronounced as with similar publications in more developed revolutionary societies. Nicaragua's crippling underdevelopment, the massive damage caused by fifty years of dictatorship and a ruinous civil war, the rapid onset of a new conflict as the Reagan administration aimed its minions against the soft underbelly of the revolution—all these

factors meant that the regime's generosity toward its affiliated institutions was heavily constrained throughout the revolutionary decade. After helping *Barricada* find its feet in 1979-80, the
Sandinista Front was never again able, or never chose, to provide
Barricada with direct financial subsidies. Indeed, by the end of the
decade, it was *Barricada* that was contributing resources to the
front! We have already seen, moreover, that the related phenomena of
an unusually pluralistic regime and the extraordinary sensitivity of
the outside world to perceived Sandinista "abuses" obliged the
FSLN to distribute key resources equally among the politically
opposed Managua dailies. Thus, several of the most common methods by which authoritarian governments discipline a superficially
"independent" press—by selectively granting or withholding ink and
paper, for example—were unavailable to the Sandinistas, or went
unexploited by them.

But if these arrangements left *Barricada* without subsidies "in the
classical sense,"[53] the paper could nevertheless access a wide range
of inputs and advantages as a result of its privileged relationship with
the party and state (a distinction not always easy to draw in a revolutionary society, whether of the left or right). The first significant
endowment—one that I only properly appreciated after Phil Ryan
cited it in his important book *The Fall and Rise of the Market in
Sandinista Nicaragua*—was the old offices of *Novedades* that housed
Barricada for the first two years of its existence. "The physical assets
of the Somoza-owned newspaper, *Novedades,* ended up directly in
FSLN hands, rather than being transferred to the state," Ryan notes.
"These assets formed the basis of *Barricada,* the official party newspaper."[54]

This was only the beginning of a pattern of support that allowed
Barricada, over time, to establish itself as the largest Nicaraguan
daily in circulation terms. Indeed, at one point in the mid-1980s,
Barricada claimed the highest circulation of any newspaper in the
history of Nicaragua—120,000 copies, in a country of a little over

three million people.[55] This unrealistically wide distribution (in a strictly market sense, at least) was the direct result of FSLN policy measures that boosted the circulation of all three Nicaraguan dailies. Notable among these was the distribution of donated Russian newsprint free of charge; and the subsidies on basic goods that for a time boosted the discretionary income of Nicaraguan consumers, particularly the poorer sectors forming the base of *Barricada*'s (and *El Nuevo Diario*'s) readership.[56] Beyond this, though, *Barricada* received an added boost. Its high circulation reflected bulk purchases of the paper for distribution through state channels—to government ministries, Nicaraguan embassies abroad, and especially to the battlefront, where *Barricada* was considered vital to troop morale in the struggle against the contras.[57]

State-sector advertising was another important source of support. It accounted for around 85 percent of *Barricada*'s advertising prior to the electoral debacle of January 1990. The paper thus enjoyed the rare luxury of being selective in its courting of private-sector ad accounts. "We were not advertiser-oriented," Chamorro conceded in 1991: "We had a small advertising department; we didn't have aggressive people out looking for ads, and also we weren't very good clients. Our philosophy was to favor the reader, not commercial interests. So we decided on a policy of advertising which was completely new: we'd put all the advertisements on nonfacing pages. You can go into the archives and see that *Barricada* would give page 6, page 4, page 8 to advertising. That's not the best [thing] for the advertisers themselves—they want to be on the facing page."[58]

Of still greater importance were the state-sector printing contracts that flowed *Barricada*'s way throughout the revolutionary decade. The trend began with the mass literacy campaigns of the early 1980s and took a quantum leap with the 1984 arrival of a Plamag Rondoset printing press, donated by the East German government. The donation itself, said Carlos Fernando Chamorro, was "the result of a political initiative taken by the FSLN at the highest level," with a commensurate response from "the highest level" of the East German Socialist Unity Party.[59] As such, it stands as perhaps the supreme example of the type of de facto aid, short of direct subsidies, that the front could provide for its official organ. The new press nearly quadrupled *Barricada*'s printing capacity, and gave Editorial El Amanecer (*Barricada*'s FSLN-owned publisher) the only color-capable press in Nicaragua. In 1987 the East Germans contributed a bookbinding machine that further boosted the publishing operation.

With these strategic infusions of aid, *Barricada* was able to become far and away Nicaragua's largest publisher. As of 1987, *Barricada* was the largest supplier of books for Nicaraguan primary and secondary schools—some 2,310,000 volumes between 1980 and 1987—and also produced tens of thousands of copies of higher-educational texts. It prepared millions of pamphlets, magazines, cards, and various educational materials for FSLN activists, mass organizations, and armed forces. It handled the major releases of Editorial Vanguardia, the magazines of the Ministries of Defense and the Interior, and the official periodicals of the major urban and rural trade unions, together with the monthly publications of the National Association of Nicaraguan Teachers (ANDEN) and the Health Workers' Federation (FETSALUD). It printed the publications of Special (Military) Zones I and II and Region V, along with large quantities of "educational" materials for the Department of Agitation and Propaganda (DAP).[60] Carlos Fernando Chamorro acknowledged straightforwardly that these publishing contracts were "one of the most important reasons we were able to grow, to capitalize, to earn money and reinvest it in *Barricada* to make it a strong industry." The publishing operation brought in more than twice the revenue of the sales and advertising generated by *Barricada* itself.[61]

As hinted earlier, though, there was a reciprocal dimension to the material relationship between *Barricada* and its sponsor. When the publishing operation is factored in, *Barricada* by the end of the revolutionary decade was probably the most lucrative enterprise in the front's stable (certain obscure holdings in Mexico, Costa Rica, and Panama notwithstanding).[62] Beginning in 1988, and for five years thereafter, *Barricada* became an important *contributor* to the FSLN's coffers—donating between 0.5 and 2 percent of its monthly income, until the strain imposed on the paper's dwindling resources became insupportable. This subsidy in reverse had become by 1992 "an important source of financing for the front," in the estimation of the National Directorate's representative to *Barricada,* Comandante Bayardo Arce.[63] It was also a defining moment for *Barricada* as an institution, symbolizing a new, if temporary, equality in relations between party and paper.

A final important advantage, both political and material, was the special treatment extended to *Barricada* under the censorship regime imposed by successive states of emergency in the mid-1980s. There is no doubt that *Barricada* was spared the kind of prior censorship that rendered *La Prensa*'s content, and sometimes its publishing schedule, inherently unpredictable—censorship that extended even to the robustly pro-revolutionary *El Nuevo Diario*. Although Chamorro stated on a number of occasions in the 1980s that *Barricada* was forced to submit its daily copy to the Ministry of the Interior, like the other dailies, the chief censor at the ministry for much of the 1980s, Nelba Blandón, acknowledged that in fact special treatment was extended to *Barricada:* "It would be a total lie if I told you [the censorship policy] was applied to [*Barricada*] in the same way it was applied to *La Prensa* or *El Nuevo Diario*." Did this mean the other papers experienced day-to-day censorship, while *Barricada* was liable only to ex post facto punitive measures? "That's correct," Blandón replied.[64] It is unclear whether the other Nicaraguan papers were significantly damaged, materially, by the restrictions on content and the bureaucratic formalities imposed by Tomás Borge's Ministry of the Interior. Whatever material risk obtained, though, it was not one that *Barricada* needed concern itself with.

Norming the Political Relationship

I have argued that *both* a staunch mobilizing imperative *and* a drive for professional autonomy are visible almost from *Barricada*'s birth. Let us now consider some of the evidence for the latter proposition.

In the earliest days of *Barricada*'s operations, the task of ensuring a basic harmony between the front's mobilizing requirements and the editorial content of the official organ was achieved through two major institutions. The first was a network of political cadres that directly oversaw and approved every word that made it into the paper's pages. This was the standard state-socialist model, followed at *Granma, Pravda,* and other prototypical institutions. The successor arrangement saw individual members of the National Directorate delegated to serve as dominant, and direct, mobilizing influences. The transformations that took place in both institutions, and from one to the other, were the direct result of the efforts of *Barricada*'s staff, especially its director, Carlos Fernando Chamorro.[65] Likewise, what tensions arose in the party-paper relationship through the 1980s tended to result from *Barricada*'s bridling, primarily on professional grounds, at the mobilizing demands placed on it by its FSLN sponsor.

The first attempt to assert direct party control over *Barricada*'s operations took the form of a political commissariat that included just one trained journalist—Xavier Reyes. In a 1991 interview, Reyes described the operations of the commissariat as follows: "Journalists handed over their articles to a commissar, and he or she made sure that what was written there was in line with the Sandinista line. If it wasn't, he or she would return it to the journalist. If it was OK, it would be passed on to the chief of writing, who would then begin the strictly journalistic work [on it]." *Barricada* journalists, said Reyes, felt their professional sensibilities piqued by "the fact that people who weren't journalists would touch their material. . . . This was like establishing a certain distance between the journalist and revolutionary work: it was like setting up a barrier, like doubting that the journalist was capable of interpreting correctly the new phenomena in society." In 1981, under Reyes's supervision, the commissariat was overhauled and a "normal writing structure" instituted in the news-room—"that is, without any political intervention by the party." *Barricada* won greater professional "breathing-space," Reyes said—more freedom to interpret and apply the ideological tenets of the front in its own manner.[66]

These first intimations of professional autonomy, though, were quickly undermined by another, more personal kind of mobilizing intervention—one that proved no less exasperating on professional grounds. The culprits this time were the individual members of the FSLN National Directorate. The directorate combined three prerevolutionary "tendencies," each of which contributed three representatives (see chapter 3). In addition to their position on the directorate, and reflecting the intertwining of party and state that is standard in revolutionary societies, most directorate members also received ministerial appointments or other privileged state positions. It is notable that this did not lead to major ideological schisms during the years of revolution and national emergency. An impressive revolutionary cohesion instead prevailed—at *Barricada* as well. But if newspaper staff did not have to walk an especially delicate doctrinal line when mediating among directorate members, they *did* have to reckon with the personal quirks and preferences of the nine most powerful individuals in Nicaragua.

The purviews and personal temperaments of directorate members varied widely. But all FSLN leaders, it seems, had something in common—a conviction that their own activities were most central to the revolution, and thus should command the greatest attention in *Barricada*'s pages. "All the members of the National Directorate demanded a strong presence in the newspaper," recalled Xavier Reyes: "[Minister of Agriculture] Jaime Wheelock felt that what he was doing . . . was so important it should take up all eight columns of the front page. Carlos Núñez felt the National Assembly [which he oversaw] was the most important thing. Daniel Ortega felt the activities of the central government were most important. Tomás Borge felt what he was doing was most important. So you had nine telephone calls every day! . . . Some days were more unbearable than others."

Nor was Carlos Fernando Chamorro, as director, the only victim of this self-interested lobbying. "When they failed" with Chamorro, Reyes said, the directorate members "would go down to the level of the writers."[67] Finally, Chamorro took it upon himself to press *Barricada*'s case in an audience with the directorate—citing "our criterion as journalists," according to Chamorro. His argument on behalf of *Barricada* staff "was that you had to take into consideration the political aspect [i.e., the wishes of individual directorate members], but you couldn't subordinate the journalistic importance or the public interest to the political aspect *all* the time." Chamorro described the foundation of the new norm this way:

> If you had five members of the National Directorate participating in different activities, there might be one thing of the five that was really a priority, decided politically by the FSLN. So I would say, "OK, you tell me what's your priority, and from then on *I* decide what is more important, according to my perception of the public interest." . . . We had to negotiate and accept certain things. [But] we fought in order to introduce new concepts. Basically the new concept was: Journalistic criteria have to be respected, and you can't predetermine everything. We had a lot of complaints about how we administered the norm, but I think over time, everybody [in the directorate] started forgetting about it.[68]

The result was the most significant institutional innovation in *Barricada*'s operations during the revolutionary decade: the designation of a single National Directorate member as liaison between the paper and its FSLN sponsors. Under the new arrangement, any directorate member who had a request for coverage could present it to the representative, who in turn "would speak with Carlos and discuss with him, of all the necessities, which one got space," according to Sofía Montenegro.[69] In turn, the representative would serve as a channel to the directorate for *Barricada*'s concerns and requests— for example, the initiative that led to the donation of the East German printing press. As it happened, both representatives—Carlos Núñez until 1984, and Bayardo Arce thereafter—established strong and empathetic bonds with *Barricada* as an institution with its own interests and identity, and lobbied other directorate members on the paper's behalf. Núñez, in particular, appears to have been genuinely loved by *Barricada* staff; his untimely death from cancer, in 1990, was keenly felt.

How did other members of the directorate take to the new arrangement? Some seem to have found it more tolerable than others. Xavier Reyes recalled one illuminating occasion on which Tomás Borge telephoned Marcio Vargas, a *Barricada* senior editor, "and said he wanted a certain news item on the front page": "Marcio told him he wasn't going to do it, because the decision [regarding front-page coverage] had already been made. Comandante Borge told him it wasn't a suggestion, but an order. Marcio said he wasn't going to do it unless he talked with Carlos Núñez [in his capacity as directorate representative] first. They started arguing on the telephone."

In this case, though, matters were resolved to the satisfaction of *Barricada* staff: "Comandante Núñez complained to Borge, and asked for an explanation of his behavior. They both analyzed the situation, and I think on *Barricada*'s anniversary in 1983 or 1984, Comandante Borge publicly apologized to Marcio for having yelled at him over the telephone that night and for having tried to impose on the newspaper. He said he wanted to apologize publicly, because it wasn't the way you should deal with the paper."[70]

Borge was, of course, interior minister for much of this period; his reputation as an ideological hard-liner followed him through his tenure as *Barricada*'s director from 1994 to 1998. But the greatest pressure on the newspaper did not necessarily come from those directorate members with the most autocratic auras. In fact, it was Daniel Ortega—who belonged to the allegedly moderate Tercerista tendency—who seemed to nurse the deepest grudge against *Barricada*'s semiautonomy. Ortega's ideological background is considered further in chapter 3, which explores his mounting, finally decisive antipathy toward the paper and its staff.

These examples suggest that despite the paper's success in reducing the daily interventions by the FSLN leadership, the comandantes' conceptions of *Barricada*'s role still hampered the professional functioning of the paper. An especially piquant instance of conflict was cited by Guillermo Cortés in 1991, recalling a visit to the *Barricada* offices by Minister of Agriculture Jaime Wheelock. On that occasion, Cortés remembered, Comandante Wheelock took the opportunity to lobby staffers, urging them to support an initiative aimed at boosting agricultural production by encouraging peasants on state farms to increase their working hours. "I said to the comandante that this was all very well, but if they were demanding more work from farmworkers, then they should make a greater effort to control state expenses, especially luxury expenses like fancy vehicles." Wheelock, said Cortés, "became furious. . . . He began to explain that there was no problem with luxury cars in the Ministry of Agriculture—whereas in fact that's where there were the most [problems]. Finally he out and out called me a Somocista! So there were those attitudes," Cortés concluded. "If someone came out with a criticism, then came the pressure. An atmosphere was created, an environment that if you didn't quite agree with what was agreeable to those in power, it would go badly for you."[71]

Despite the important steps toward norming the relationship between party and paper, not the least of *Barricada*'s editorial concerns during the 1980s was the tendency of most Nicaraguan and foreign readers to assume that every word in the paper was rubber-stamped by the FSLN leadership. As a result, political coverage was a perennial minefield, in which outright disaster always seemed a step away. The result was an inordinate amount of self-censorship that effectively canceled out much of the hard-won autonomy the paper gained in the early years of the revolutionary decade. Coverage of foreign relations, for example, could impose crushing pressures, as Sofía Montenegro described:

> You were absolutely conscious of your responsibilities toward the front. You didn't have the possibility of writing anything wrong in *Barricada*. Anything you wrote was [perceived as] official. You had no margin of discretion at all. . . . Out of this there developed a *paralyzed* journalism. You were so intimidated by the possible effects of what you could write about the revolution that you always exercised immense self-restraint. . . . That's how self-censorship came along. . . . Everybody was cornering you. You lived constantly in a state of siege. . . . You had to think very carefully, weigh every word that made it into print. There wasn't much possibility to fool around.[72]

A notable taboo area was criticism of the Eastern Bloc countries. Their ossified systems were only a few years away from collapse; but in the meantime they were indispensable sources of material and moral support for the Sandinista revolutionary regime—and, as we have seen, for its official organ. When Eastern Bloc embassies dropped off a press release, according to Carlos Fernando Chamorro, they naturally expected it to be published verbatim, as it would have been in the official organs of Poland or Czechoslovakia. *Barricada* staffers may have had greater discretion when it came to deciding the appropriate amount of space to devote to the item. Staffers could rewrite the news releases "in our own language," according to Chamorro; the "incredibly impersonal" style of state-socialist journalism could thereby be downplayed, along with the "totally ridiculous" cult-of-personality treatment that Eastern Bloc dignitaries were accustomed to receiving from their own media. Still, Chamorro acknowledged that the exigencies of revolutionary self-defense sharply curtailed *Barricada*'s freedom of movement in this sphere. The newspaper was "not critical at all" of the state socialist societies—even though many staffers considered the systems oppressive, often on the basis of firsthand experience:

> I never thought the model for Nicaragua was the Soviet Union or East Germany, still less Cuba [said Chamorro]. But I found myself faced with the contradiction that *Barricada* was the party paper; the FSLN had a certain policy toward these states and their ruling parties. . . . If somebody wrote something very critical of the type of socialism existing in Poland or the Soviet Union, this would be considered an attack on those societies. That would endanger the relationship between the FSLN and those countries and parties. There was simply no possibility of that. I think it would have been much more important at this point in time [during the 1980s] if we had played at least a modest role in allowing people to analyze those societies more critically: how they were based and how consistent they were in applying their principles. But it wasn't possible.[73]

What flashes of outspokenness there were could have rapid, though never brutal, repercussions. Montenegro, *Barricada*'s international editor in the mid-1980s, said she once directed a string of "aggressive" and "impertinent" questions to a Polish delegate addressing a Sandinista gathering on the political situation in his country. After "nagging" the delegate for a while, with some of her peers "pinch[ing] me to shut up," Montenegro received an official sanction from the party, and an in-house dressing-down from Carlos Fernando Chamorro. "What this shows," in Montenegro's view, "is that you didn't only have to watch what you were saying outside; you also had to be concerned about what others within the FSLN would be saying about you. With all these tensions and pressures, where could you find the middle ground—being loyal to the truth, without hurting the interests of the front? What the hell could you do?"[74]

Events in late January and early February 1987, with Carlos Fernando Chamorro away from *Barricada* serving as the chief of the

DAP, amply demonstrated the front's sensitivities to *Barricada*'s coverage. At the heart of the story was a practical joke—but one that precipitated the most severe internal crisis at the newspaper during the entire revolutionary decade. In Chamorro's absence, Xavier Reyes, the paper's acting director, and his deputy, Marcio Vargas, decided to play a prank on subeditor Juan José Lacayo, whom they had long accused of failing to read stories through before writing the headlines for them. In Sofía Montenegro's account:

> [Vargas] took a story written by one of the best journalists at the paper, and he knew that the headline writer would do as he always did—read the first three paragraphs and forget the rest. So Marcio wrote a false final paragraph that was, politically, absolutely explosive. The article was about a meeting between President Ortega and representatives of the Evangelical Church [Baptists] in Nicaragua. It was a time of some tensions between the church and the government, and this meeting was hugely significant to resolving the disagreements. The article talked about the meeting, about the positions held by the Evangelicals concerning the war, the economy, and all that. At the end Marcio stuck his joke paragraph, which went something like: "But the Evangelical Church leaders said they didn't want Ortega to attend the meeting, because they didn't like him much. . . ."
>
> This way, Marcio figured he'd get proof that the articles weren't being read through to the end. And of course the headline writer did his usual cursory job. But in the heat of the moment, Marcio *forgot to take out the false paragraph*—it passed the proofreader, who thought it was strange, but who saw that the headline writer had OK'd the text. And the next morning news of the supposed animosity between the Evangelicals and Daniel Ortega was on every newsstand in Nicaragua.

Predictably, the article sparked a furor:

> The leader of the Evangelical Church was the first to call the paper. It was a scandal! And Ortega got *so* mad. He couldn't understand why *Barricada* had printed such garbage, when none of the church leaders had said anything of the kind about the FSLN directorate.

35

First they [the FSLN leadership] wanted to strangle the journalist that covered the meeting. Then they found out the responsibility lay with the editorial staff. At that point, the National Directorate's first thought was that this article had been planted to sabotage the meeting with the church: there must be a counterrevolutionary inside *Barricada*!

Of course, the paper immediately printed a correction and an apology. But Carlos [Fernando Chamorro] had to find out from the staff members what the hell had happened. When they told him, he said, "Oh my God, I can't go to the National Directorate and tell them the truth, that it was a *joke*"—and in fact he was right; the directorate would have preferred for it to be something more serious and suspicious. They accused the staff of irresponsibility and they kicked Marcio and Xavier off the paper. In so doing, they were firing many years of experience and labor and sacrifice—people who were very respected at the paper and within the front. The workers at *Barricada* threatened to go on strike; many people appealed to the directorate, saying, "Don't be so drastic. Make apologies to the church, explain what happened." Daniel Ortega replied: "How can we go to the church and tell them we were only fooling around?" So that was it.[75]

Sometimes it appeared as though the only person who could remain irreverent in the face of such constraints was Róger Sánchez, whose brilliant caricatures on political and sexual themes enlivened *Barricada*'s pages until the mid-1980s. Sánchez viscerally rejected abject subservience to any state, even a revolutionary one. He delighted in tweaking Sandinista noses along with bourgeois mores. A March 1983 cartoon (fig. 1.2) lampooned the "new" breed of Nicaraguan journalist, whose lickspittle posture toward the authorities sometimes recalled that of his spineless Somocista predecessor. After a number of vexing run-ins with the new officialdom, Sánchez decided that work for the official organ was too confining. He moved to take over an ailing satirical weekly of some decades' standing, *La Semana Cómica*. Sánchez turned *La Semana* into a "back-talking, iconoclastic, anarchic, messy, subversive" publication that was an instant hit with young Nicaraguans.[76] But his lampooning of sexual mores—which revolutionaries often shared—led to several highly public clashes with Sandinista censors in the late 1980s. On two occasions in 1988, *La Semana Cómica* was briefly closed by Tomás Borge's Ministry of the Interior. Still, there was likely no more avidly worshipped Sandinista media figure in Nicaragua. Sánchez's overwhelming popularity, especially among youth, would likely have been enough to ensure that the punishments he faced would never be more serious than a slap on the wrist. The additional fact that he operated within a comparatively pluralistic media environment,

Figure 1.2. The limitations of partisan journalism. A revolutionary state functionary spoonfeeds press conference material to an eager pro-revolutionary journalist: "Open your mouth and close your eyes . . . ." Róger Sánchez's cartoon appeared in *Barricada* on 1 March 1983 (National Journalists' Day in Nicaragua). *Courtesy Marta Sirias.*

as well as his genial and cheerful disposition, also helped him steer clear of real danger. FSLN leaders up to the level of chief censor Borge, along with hundreds of thousands of other Nicaraguans, mourned Sánchez when—like so many creative Sandinistas—he died young, at the preposterous age of thirty, of stomach cancer.[77]

The occasionally fractious relationship between the *Frente* and its quasi-dissidents, like Sánchez or Sofía Montenegro, helps to define some interesting points of conflict between divergent agendas and imperatives. But the clashes should not be blown out of proportion. The small-scale sanctions meted out to these two figures were typical of Sandinista internal discipline. Amid civil war and economic collapse, all hands were needed on deck. The anathematizing of dedicated fellow revolutionaries was a luxury rarely indulged in—at least during the 1980s. Likewise, those registering occasional or even regular notes of dissent tended to stop short of a far-reaching critique of the revolution they passionately believed in. This basic bond would be dramatically severed between 1990 and 1994. Even in the wake of that sundering, however, a comparative civility prevailed among former Sandinista allies—a further tribute to the pluralism of the FSLN, and perhaps to the clannish character of Nicaraguan politics more generally. A year and a half after orchestrating the abrupt *defenestración* of Carlos Fernando Chamorro, for example, Daniel Ortega appeared as an invited guest on Chamorro's new TV talk show, *Esta Semana*. Here, perhaps, lay the real foundation of the norm that guided relations between the front's leadership and avowedly revolutionary institutions, through the 1980s and into the postrevolutionary era.

Professionalism and the "Moral Economy of Journalism"

I have suggested that "professional" considerations underpinned many of the concerns and initiatives pressed by *Barricada* staffers in the face of the mobilizing constraints that confronted them during the 1980s. The sources of this professional imperative were diverse. A number of them appear directly related to Nicaraguan culture and history: the influence of the U.S.-sponsored school of journalism in Managua; the professional model developed by the prerevolutionary *La Prensa;* the day-to-day competition between *La Prensa* and *Barricada* in the supercharged political environment of the 1980s. But there seems also to have been an important ethical dimension to the professional imperative as it developed at *Barricada* over the course of the revolutionary decade. This is to say that in many instances of conflict between party and paper, between mobilizing and professional imperatives, a normative aspect pertained.

In his classic study of subsistence-agricultural societies, *The Moral Economy of the Peasant,* James C. Scott points to those moments in which essential, time-honored strategies and institutions of subsistence are undermined as the conjunctures in which rebellion and revolution are most likely to occur.[78] *Barricada* staffers had not had much time to develop institutions of their own to guide journalistic practice. Rather, the paper's project, at least during the first half of the 1980s, seemed at least as much a matter of daily improvisation and crisis management as of adherence to established norms. ("We have been masters of improvisation, which is a typical characteristic of the Sandinistas," said Sofía Montenegro.)[79] Nonetheless, comparative study suggests that something like a moral economy of journalism may operate even in media that are highly constrained, and directed along classic mobilizing lines. Only at the totalitarian extremes (Stalin's USSR, North Korea) does this moral economy seem truly suppressed, and even in those cases it may still be nascent, ready to emerge when conditions permit.

At its heart, the moral economy seems founded on an essential epistemological assumption, giving rise in turn to a conception of individual and professional responsibility. The epistemological

39

foundation is the notion of a reality that is external to the observer and not infinitely malleable, regardless of personal preferences and perspectives. The professional imperative derived from this stance is based on the journalist's perceived duty to "write the truth . . . trust what you see, not your implanted notions," as one Russian commentator put it.[80] Intimately bound up with this perspective is a notion of the reporter's social responsibility to readers, and the necessity to consult (and reflect the views of) at least a limited diversity of sources.[81]

To see this moral economy at work in the context of *Barricada*'s project during the 1980s, consider the dilemma of Gabriela Selser, a *Barricada* journalist assigned to report on the wartime relocation of Miskito Indian communities along Nicaragua's Atlantic coast. The *costeños*—Indian and black alike—had long felt estranged from the majority mestizo population of the Pacific coast. When confronted with a succession of ill-judged revolutionary initiatives after July 1979, the costeños became fertile ground for contra recruiters. Their sympathies prompted several outright (though not centrally directed) atrocities by Sandinista forces in the region, and eventually resulted in the decision—which *was* centrally mandated—to move entire villages away from the war's front lines along the Honduran border.[82] Selser, witnessing the scenes of anguish as populations were uprooted, spoke of feeling an intense quandary—one that pitted the mobilizing requirements of revolutionary journalism against the reality that assailed her eyes and ears: "The problem was that the people didn't want to live there [in FSLN-designated resettlement centers]. The women were crying, accusing the army of having forcibly removed them from their houses. They asked us [journalists] to tell the truth: that they weren't doing well there. The houses built for them were very different from the kind of dwellings they were used to. In addition, there was the normal feeling of uprootedness: they missed the river, their trees, their house."

Selser returned to Managua and *Barricada* feeling "really traumatized" by the experience. There, she found herself embroiled in a debate over precisely how *Barricada* should cover the events: "We had very strong discussions about how to focus the story. In the end, we managed to write a story in which [the real situation] was outlined, but sort of between the lines, in a disguised way. For example, we said it was natural [the Miskitos] would feel bad [about being relocated], but they would get used to it. I never agreed with that [approach]."

Similar difficulties were experienced elsewhere on the battlefront, and they resulted over time in an evolution in *Barricada*'s war coverage: from triumphalist, highly idealized coverage around the time general conscription was introduced in 1982 (the Patriotic Military Service, or SMP), to somewhat more nuanced and *human* coverage as the war ground on. Selser traced this progression from "idyllic or romantic" coverage to a journalism better able to cope with the "contradictions [that] came into play within the combatants themselves, and their relationships with society and their families":

> I think that one of the greatest mistakes in Sandinista propaganda [in the early stages] was to try and show the Patriotic Military Service as a great big "fight for love." Without trying to evaluate the way it uprooted families, the fear of the combatants, the fear of dying, the danger—normal, natural things. . . . There were even stories about combatants that would say things like, "He's lost an eye, he's lost a leg, he's an orphan, but still he's going to do his military service." In that respect, I think we lost a lot of credibility.

Selser and other originators of the *corresponsales de guerra* worked—with some success, they felt—to "integrat[e] the political propaganda interest" with a more vivid and professional journalism. Dispatched to a military training camp, for instance, Selser said she wrote a story that contrasted the battle-hardened veterans with the frightened new recruits: "I compared the combatants who had just arrived from the city for training—young boys, very scared, with a lot of [internal] conflicts, who just wanted to leave—and those who had two or three months of training and were already feeling much more secure in their capacity to fight. I think that was the only way in which you could deal with the former phenomenon, the fear. You couldn't just write the negative thing, that the boys were scared and so on, without putting in the other side."[83]

In such circumstances, though, "It was very hard to distinguish between our rights as journalists and our political loyalties to the party and the revolution"—according to another war correspondent, Guillermo Cortés. For the most part, the threshold of the moral economy was set rather high by the demands of revolutionary solidarity. "We all knew that what we were doing was not very professional," said Cortés, referring to the highly partisan fashion in which complex issues and events were portrayed.[84]

The professional deficit that Cortés acknowledged was evident too at the level of ordinary language. Despite important variations in tone and approach from the state-socialist standard, *Barricada*'s content was still afflicted by "a highly depersonalized language," in Sofía Montenegro's evaluation. A journalist, said Montenegro, "should be able to recognize [his or her] own voice. But with the frame of mind we had and the political framework in which we operated, this was a no-no. Because in that way, obviously, you opened the door to dissent. Since this was an official organ, it was felt that this would be contradictory."[85] There can be few more succinct summaries of the difficulties of reconciling professional and mobilizing imperatives at *Barricada* during the revolutionary decade.

The idea of the moral economy implies, as noted, a *critical distance* from reality. This is the foundation of the watchdog role that has long been central to liberal-democratic conceptions of the press, and that spawned the idea of the press as a separate estate, distinguishable from other key societal institutions. At *Barricada* throughout the 1980s, however, there was evidently a critical *lack* of distance. That in itself was hardly surprising, given the overriding mobilizing role the paper was created to play and the added pressures of war and national emergency. "Criticism of the revolution and the state," as one journalist wrote in the soberly pro-revolutionary *Pensamiento Propio* in 1986, had come to constitute a "self-criticism" for the revolution's sympathizers. "Our sentiments toward the revolutionary process act to inhibit us," the author wrote. Criticism, however constructive, was seen as "giving arms to the enemy."[86]

It was a signal feature of *Barricada*'s operations that these deficiencies were noted and decried, if internal documents and related evaluations are given credence. The 1985 editorial profile of *Barricada,* the first major attempt to formalize an identity for the paper, placed considerable emphasis on the newspaper's critical function. *Barricada* pledged itself to unearthing all the "deficiencies that affect the execution of the policies of the revolution." But this was little more than the standard Leninist formulation, more honored in the breach than in the observance. The failure was widely acknowledged. The New Editorial Profile of 1990, looking back on *Barricada*'s performance during the revolutionary decade, would criticize the original incarnation of the paper as "extremely predictable," with only the narrowest critical distance, "in many cases none at all," in relations with government and other official sources. *Barricada* was "fundamentally a daily [that served to] diffuse the FSLN line, with few variations," inhibiting the ability of *Barricada* writers to "formulat[e] alternatives that would nourish revolutionary thought." Only "limited and unsystematic" measures had been taken to counteract the trend.[87]

The 1990 verdict echoed conclusions reached two years earlier, in an impressive study written by *Barricada* staffers Guillermo Cortés and Juan Ramón Huerta as part of a degree course at the School of Journalism, and supervised by Carlos Fernando Chamorro himself. Examining the front pages of forty-two *Barricada* editions from 1985 to 1987—some 256 articles in all—Cortés and Huerta cited an "almost absolute preponderance, in *Barricada*'s coverage, of official discourse and official sources." The paper had failed to "exercise systematically a critical function," as its 1985 charter pledged it to do. Concluded the authors:

> In *Barricada* there is not an integral exercising of the journalist's critical function. . . . Superficiality, lack of rigor, absence of investigation and failure to follow cases through to their conclusion . . . characterize the majority of the articles published by the paper in the period under investigation. . . . The daily appears to be highly concentrated on the divulging of official government activity; it acts, moreover, as a mere reproducer of the interests of the various official institutions, without a line of its own which would allow it to satisfy other, more broad and varied, information necessities of the population.[88]

A final dimension of the professional imperative has been alluded to in passing, but merits further examination under the rubric of the moral economy of journalism. I refer to the human interest component of reporting, which bespeaks a basic faith in the validity of ordinary human experience—a radical concept indeed when first propounded in the later nineteenth century. Many modern conceptions of journalism consider it nearly as much of a sin to be dull as to be dishonest. Of course, the obligation to engage on a human level can also undermine other elements of the professional imperative. In the most yellow, or sensationalistic, mass media, with their lowest-common-denominator obsession with sex and crime, that is actually an understatement. But for institutions with ambitions to quality, such as *Barricada* nursed during the 1980s, the obligation to engage—and the regular failure to do so—was one of the most commonly cited professional deficits in the paper's operations. The quandary lay again in the conflict between mobilizing and professional requirements. How was *Barricada* to engage and entertain, when dissemination of a polemical revolutionary line was the paper's raison d'être? How could the steady diet of political pronouncements, diplomatic news, visiting foreign delegations, and broadsides against U.S. foreign policy be made palatable to readers who, though presumably revolutionary, were also hungry for some diversion from the ultrapoliticized atmosphere of war and economic crisis?

The answer, yet again, is that as long as the Sandinistas were in power, the challenge was rarely met. Jonathan Evan Maslow wrote of *Barricada* in 1981 that it was "as boring as any in-house corporate magazine."[89] Despite important transformations at the structural level, and considerable improvements in production and design, there seemed little reason to alter that assessment as *Barricada* headed into the election campaign of 1990 and another round of uncritical boosterism for its FSLN sponsor.

But even if the professional imperative and the moral economy remained secondary, sometimes nearly invisible considerations during the revolutionary decade, there can be little doubt that they remained at least latent in *Barricada*'s functioning. They could be called upon to counter overly invasive party supervision, as occurred at numerous points in the paper's early life. They appear to have infused the internal evaluations and self-critiques of *Barricada* staff. And over time they coalesced into a very different vision of *Barricada,* and of revolutionary journalism more generally. The project to which the professional imperative eventually gave rise was founded, above all, on a clearer separation of *Barricada*'s daily journalism from the mobilizing requirements of its FSLN sponsor. The project was first hinted at in 1987, as Nicaraguan society "decompressed" and domestic politics were liberalized after half a decade of military crisis. But it was only implemented—and probably *could* only have been implemented—after calamity struck the Sandinista movement in 1990. It is to the evolution of this autonomy project, from the late 1980s on, that we now turn.

Chapter 2

Beyond the Barricades

A New Journalism for Nicaragua, 1987–1994

> If the printed press of the 1980s was fundamentally political or, more exactly, partisan, that of the 1990s has already been marked by the irreversible stamp of professionalization and the strengthened autonomy of journalistic institutions. *Barricada* seeks to continue to play a pioneering role in the process of press modernization.
>
> —Carlos Fernando Chamorro, in *Barricada*'s fifteenth anniversary issue, 1994

SANDINISTA-CONTRA CEASE-FIRE TERMED MAJOR BREAK-THROUGH BY NICARAGUA'S RIVAL FACTIONS. On 25 March 1988 readers of the *New York Times* awoke to a four-column headline announcing the decisive step toward resolving Nicaragua's grinding conflict. For years, the Sandinistas had proclaimed that negotiations with the contras would never be entertained—the Sandinistas would only deal directly with the rebels' paymasters in Washington. Now the world watched as members of the FSLN National Directorate, including President Daniel Ortega and his brother, army chief Humberto Ortega, signed a cease-fire and exchanged mutual recognition with contra leaders—all under the approving eye of the conservative strand of the Catholic Church, represented by Cardinal Miguel Obando y Bravo.

The decision was deeply traumatic for many Sandinista militants—including *Barricada* staffers—who had long supported and disseminated the no-negotiation line.[1] Of more direct relevance to the present study, however, was the range of measures that accompanied the cease-fire agreement—notably article 5, which pledged the Sandinista "Government of Nicaragua . . . [to] guarantee unrestricted freedom of expression," and granted demobilized contras and political self-exiles the opportunity to enter (or return to) civilian politics "with equal conditions and guarantees," and "without any conditions beyond those established by the laws of the republic."[2]

The result was a notable thaw in a country that had been a political pressure cooker for many years. The new buzzword was *cocertación*—a somewhat hazy concept that combined national reconciliation with peaceful political competition. The attention of the regime shifted toward the parlous condition of the hyperinflation-ridden Nicaraguan economy. In this sphere, too, significant policy transformations had become evident by the time the cease-fire with the contras was inked. A "hesitant turn towards the market" had occurred as early as 1985, Phil Ryan writes, and 1988–89 saw the "triumph of the market," as "economic reforms scuttled most key elements of the state-dominant economy project."[3] The leadership imposed a range of austerity measures strikingly similar to those being implemented throughout Latin America, as debtor nations sought to curry favor with the International Monetary Fund and other First World–dominated institutions. There were new attempts to court "patriotic producers"—members of Nicaragua's capitalist class who had established a modus vivendi with the Sandinista authorities and whose economic contribution was more desperately needed than ever. In the crucial area of land reform, the Sandinistas continued to shift away from the original emphasis on cooperatives and state farms. That policy was already in abeyance by 1987, as the leadership realized how badly it had alienated Nicaragua's fiercely individualistic peasants—driving them, in some cases, into the arms of the contras.

The economic measures, though popular with the private sector and conservative business classes, caused profound distress to many

FSLN militants. Ryan cites their "fear . . . that government policy had been hijacked by technocrats." Once again, the ripples were felt within *Barricada,* occasioning what Ryan calls "perhaps [the] most critical editorial ever" published in the newspaper while the Sandinistas held power. Written by Carlos Fernando Chamorro and headlined "A Counterpart to the Economic Logic Is Missing," the editorial pointed to the regime's alleged failure to take into account the "social and ideological repercussions" of the austerity measures. Concepts that had long been "slogans and guides for mass action," Chamorro wrote, had now "lost validity." The reforms might well be necessary, the paper argued; but it nonetheless bemoaned the FSLN's failure to successfully convey their "'socialist orientation'"—putting quotation marks around the phrase, Ryan notes, "perhaps for the first time."[4]

Still, neither now nor in the remaining couple of years of the revolution was *Barricada* free to declare itself opposed to a basic tenet of FSLN policy. The paper's more indicative response to the "triumph of the market" in Sandinista Nicaragua was the predicable one of the official organ. The paper's staff digested the new instructions, wrestled with whatever ideological difficulties they engendered— and restructured the paper's content according to the new breeze blowing. *Barricada* moved to deepen and otherwise improve its economic coverage, the better to explain the new Sandinista policies to the movement's sometimes mystified supporters. Economics, unfortunately, was not one of *Barricada*'s traditional strong suits. There were precious few staffers with the training to come to grips with the new phenomenon, though Carlos Fernando Chamorro, with his economics degree from McGill University, did take the lead in exploring the subject in editorials and op-eds. Other staff played catch-up. "We began to concern ourselves with educating journalists in economics, and in writing about agricultural issues," said Xavier Reyes, claiming that in this respect, as in so many others, *Barricada* was responding to instructions from the National Directorate "to involve ourselves more in that field."[5]

There were, nonetheless, signs of a more autonomous and exploratory agenda emerging at *Barricada,* and their ramifications extended further than the interesting editorial cited by Ryan. As with the more dramatic transformations to come in 1990–91, the changes at *Barricada* from late 1987 onward reflected important transformations in FSLN policy, responding, in turn, to perceived changes in Nicaragua's domestic political sphere. But they also—and increasingly—reflected the desire of *Barricada* staff for greater professional self-expression.

The FSLN's policy reversals of 1987–88 decisively shifted the arena of conflict from the military to the political-ideological arena. The measure with the greatest implications for *Barricada* was the decision to allow *La Prensa* to resume publishing after a fifteen-month forced hiatus. This meant a renewal of *Barricada*'s political and professional confrontation with its main competitor, the absence of which, as discussed in chapter 1, had led to a certain lethargy in the paper's sense of mission. It also presented the paper with an ideal opportunity—and a practical reason—to push for greater professional autonomy, since it could be argued that this was necessary to meet *La Prensa*'s challenge. Carlos Fernando Chamorro described the new thinking this way: "The changes in *Barricada* had to take place when the political negotiation process began to be a reality. Because we assumed—and it was logical—that the military contradictions were going to diminish, and that the struggle in Nicaragua was henceforth going to center on political and ideological aspects. Therefore, the media would become more important."[6]

It became easier to contend that success in the political and ideological sphere would require "a much more fresh, agile, informative [revolutionary] press, and one much more capable of going beyond rhetoric," Chamorro added. His views were bolstered by longtime editor Onofre Guevara: now "there was a feeling that you had to make a paper that was more socially acceptable to everyone, less partisan."[7]

This line of argument found a receptive audience among the Sandinista leadership. "The National Directorate was conscious that we needed a change," said Sofía Montenegro. "They felt themselves that [*Barricada*'s] officializing everything had become a straitjacket." That perception, Montenegro added, happily coincided with the interests and desires of "the ones who *really* thought in terms of the newspaper itself"—*Barricada*'s staff.[8]

The thaw of 1987–88 also witnessed the climax of the process to draft a new Nicaraguan constitution, one that would lay a foundation for concertación and national consensus. The constitution was intended to "institutionalize" the Sandinista revolution. *Barricada,* too, felt itself sufficiently strong and coherent as an institution to play a leading role in the process. In charting the future course of the paper, Carlos Fernando Chamorro said he drew on the example of another "institutionalized" revolution—Mexico's—and the press that it had spawned. He cited specifically *Excélsior,* the leading pro-establishment Mexican daily, as the inspiration for a project that

> would not necessarily be official, would not be too tied to the FSLN, but would seek to be more the paper of *consensus* on the basic foundations of [Nicaraguan] society. A newspaper that would be much more preoccupied with defending the constitution than with the party aspects of the FSLN. *Excélsior* is the institution of the political class in Mexico. In a very subtle way, it's oriented to support, not the [ruling] PRI [Institutional Revolutionary Party] itself, but the system the PRI is supporting. It's seen by the society as an institution that speaks for itself; it has a commitment to the basic foundations of the system—the type of economic and political model you're promoting—and at the same time it's not too tied to the party. It's a very sophisticated arrangement.[9]

It is quite likely that this "establishment" project would have prevailed, in some form, had the Sandinistas won the 1990 elections. As it transpired, though, a more drastic reconfiguring of the political landscape loomed—one that would require a more far-reaching response from the leading Sandinista media organ. Few Sandinistas would have proclaimed the outcome of the 1990 vote a desirable one. It did, though, allow—and require—*Barricada* to undergo a political, material, and professional restructuring that was both more wrenching and more interesting than the strategy first mooted in 1987–88.

The Earthquake, 1990

> Right now [1991], the front is going through a very hard time. It[s leadership] has lost authority, credibility, legitimacy. It's difficult for them to lead even their own organizations. Even if they wanted to have greater control over *Barricada,* the situation itself prevents it. Well, we're taking advantage of that.
>
> —Guillermo Cortés, *Barricada* staffer

Carlos Fernando Chamorro spent election night, 25 February 1990, moving between the *Barricada* offices and FSLN campaign headquarters at the Piñata fairground (an ironic choice of sites, given the "piñata" scandal that would descend upon the FSLN after the elections—see below).[10] Like nearly all Sandinistas, Chamorro was anticipating a Sandinista victory "by a wide margin," possibly a landslide.

Around 9:30 in the evening, the first results came in from rural polling stations. They showed the FSLN trailing Violeta Chamorro's UNO coalition badly. For Chamorro's son, the staunch Sandinista supporter, this early tally meant the dream was over: "It was quite clear for me, at that moment, that we had lost." Other Sandinistas held out hope a little longer, waiting to see whether the results from Managua—the FSLN's power base—would turn the tide. But the FSLN lost Managua too.

By one o'clock in the morning, Chamorro was back at *Barricada,* anxiously wondering how to report the staggering developments to the newspaper's readers: "In that moment, in which everybody felt personally depressed, I was thinking about what to do. I couldn't close the edition until I had official results. Then the official results started arriving, but they weren't definite—only 10 percent or so of the vote counted. So I couldn't run a story in which the defeat was decisively announced."[11]

A decision was made. For the time being, *Barricada* would limit itself to announcing that UNO was in the lead. That was the tone of the front-page reporting on 26 February. By the time *Barricada* made it to the streets, though, Daniel Ortega had formally conceded defeat. In its 27 February edition, *Barricada* accepted the verdict. This pat summary of events can hardly begin to capture the shock and tension of these pivotal hours. Observers noted an unnerving stillness in the streets of the capital: Nicaraguans were holding their breath, waiting to see whether the FSLN really would surrender state power, and wondering—perhaps for the first time—what a new, counterrevolutionary regime would mean for them personally.

Once before, a transformation in FSLN policy—responding to changes in the wider political arena—had provided *Barricada* with an opportunity to contemplate expanding its professional imperative and its appeal to the wider Nicaraguan society. But in 1987–88, staffers had envisaged only a gradual reorientation, undertaken at the newspaper's own pace. The catastrophe of 1990 stripped the paper of this luxury of incremental change. It forced *Barricada* to confront a harsh new environment: one in which it could no longer depend on the sympathy and support of the ruling regime; in which the movement that had given it life and provided it with a ready-made constituency was in disarray; in which new rounds of austerity measures and market-oriented reforms would threaten the very material survival of the newspaper.

But if the unanticipated and unwelcome crisis of 1990 nearly proved *Barricada*'s undoing, it also presented the newspaper with an unparalleled opportunity. Uniquely among Sandinista institutions, the days following the election defeat gave the paper a chance to proclaim its professional identity to the society at large—not only to the revolution's secure constituency. In this respect, *Barricada* staffers were perhaps alone in the cohesion and sense of purpose they were able to preserve in the immediate wake of the defeat—if only because the notion of missing an edition or two was too humiliating to contemplate in professional terms. "The thing was, we had to work here," said Sofía Montenegro. "We at *Barricada* were forced to face reality when the whole country was paralyzed. The only things that functioned in the whole Sandinista Front were this paper and the National Directorate—and the directorate never even appeared in public for the first week after the defeat. We had to keep moving. We couldn't close the paper and go home just because we were crying."[12]

The routine of production, together with the sense of obligation to readers who urgently sought a pilot to guide them through suddenly turbulent waters, seems to have anchored *Barricada* staff at a time when they themselves were trying to come to grips with the devastating sense of loss.[13] For Montenegro and many others at the paper, the days following the election defeat were a defining moment in the professional life of the paper:

> You couldn't ignore what had happened, obviously. But I guess all of us were motivated by a need to provide a sense of solidity and continuity. At the same time, it was a chance for us to prove we were an institution by ourselves. I think it became clear to a lot of people that we had a reliable, responsible staff. While everybody outside was passionate, screaming at the top of their lungs . . . well, we kept more or less a sense of self-control. That gained us a lot of credibility. [It was like saying,] "We are here": it was a point of reference for all Sandinismo. For us it was a trial by fire, and we passed the test.[14]

And so *Barricada* pressed on through the uncertain interregnum between the voting and the formal handover of power to the UNO government (25 April 1990). The paper reported extensively on the negotiations surrounding the transition process; published paeans to concertación and the need for national reconciliation; ran investigative reports on attempts to disarm the remaining contra forces; and pondered the likely fate of the revolution's social reforms under the new regime. Old allegiances, of course, remained in force. Notably absent from the paper's coverage was any critical examination of the "piñata"—the derisive term applied to the FSLN's divvying-up of state property among leaders and supporters, from humble slum dwellings to business enterprises and luxury cars and houses.[15] There was probably no more controversial news story in Nicaragua during this period, but it was beyond *Barricada*'s purview as FSLN's official organ. In fact, the taboo would remain in force throughout the period of the autonomy experiment to follow, a subject that will receive attention later in this chapter.

The period of transition for the newspaper also ended, according to Carlos Fernando Chamorro, with the inauguration of the UNO regime headed by his mother in April 1990.[16] The transition sparked "the first sign of a revival of journalism" at *Barricada*. Chamorro seized upon statements by Francisco Mayorga, the incoming president of Nicaragua's central bank, to the effect that the country's precipitous economic decline would be reversed within a hundred days. That, said Chamorro, was "something that allowed you to say, 'OK, now we start a new period. We're going to check up on and be vigilant about [the promises made by] this government.' . . . We took the initiative very rapidly." The sense of professional and political reinvigoration prompted further innovations. "You start discovering this new function," Chamorro said, one "that obliges you to think: 'What's happening? We've changed, but what more do we have to do?'"[17]

The result was a maturing of the earlier plans for quasi-autonomy and their substantial reformulation in the face of radically transformed circumstances. The essential ramifications, for *Barricada,* of the FSLN's fall from power can be summarized as follows:

- The defeat lifted from *Barricada* the burden of supporting the regime in power, eventually decreasing the salience of the mobilizing imperative and radically reducing the dissonance between it and its professional counterpart.

• The normative agenda of political democratization and concertación decisively influenced the National Directorate's own agenda and provided an important political space, enabling *Barricada*'s professional imperative to assume greater prominence.

• The outlines of the FSLN mobilizing agenda were rendered more flexible (and therefore more open to interpretation by *Barricada* staffers) by the directorate's loss of strength and legitimacy, and by the atmosphere of questioning and self-examination that prevailed among Sandinista ranks.

• In the construction of the FSLN's (and therefore its own) mobilizing agenda, *Barricada* came to play a semiautonomous role, encouraging debate about the FSLN's future and seeking to establish itself as a public-opinion leader. Its performance in this respect encountered strong opposition from some Sandinista sectors, including first one National Directorate member and later others.

• The importance of *Barricada* to the FSLN's financial well-being grew, at the same time as material pressures and constraints on *Barricada* dramatically increased.

The global context also should not be overlooked. The FSLN's fall from power occurred only a few months after the cataclysmic changes in Central and Eastern Europe, which obliterated or sharply transformed most of the regimes that had been the Sandinistas' strongest supporters during the 1980s. Clearly, the winds of change were beginning to blow; and they blew through *Barricada*'s pages even before the National Directorate met in December 1990 to approve the paper's New Editorial Profile. In mid-1990 an important structural transformation took place at *Barricada* that paved the way for the paper's formal relaunching in January 1991. It took the form of an editorial council, something Chamorro had been working to get off the ground since at least 1987. The council is best seen as the culmination of a struggle for greater autonomy from the FSLN leadership that had begun with *Barricada* staffers' early bridling at the introduction of political commissars in the newsroom. We saw in chapter 1 that the introduction of a single directorate representative as go-between was designed to streamline relations between the newspaper and its sponsor, and to reduce the day-to-day involvement of the latter in *Barricada*'s professional functioning. Now, with the creation of the council, the role of the leadership would be further muted and *Barricada*'s professional autonomy correspondingly increased. Bayardo Arce, who remained the directorate's representative, was named president of the council. There, however, he would be only one among seven: in addition to Arce, the council comprised three representatives from *Barricada* (Carlos Fernando Chamorro, Sergio de Castro, and Xavier Reyes), and three representatives of what could be called institutional Sandinismo: Alejandro Martínez, the minister of foreign trade in the Sandinista government; William Ramírez, an FSLN representative in the National Assembly; and Rodrigo Reyes, a member and ex-president of the Nicaraguan supreme court.[18] Sofía Montenegro also participated in most council meetings, enjoying "a strange status of observer and invited," in Chamorro's words, and slightly mitigating the council's obvious gender bias.[19]

In the New Editorial Profile that Chamorro now drafted on the basis of council deliberations, the newly constituted body was portrayed as the very anchor of *Barricada*'s continuing role as "an organic medium of the FSLN." In a sense it was. But the initiative for the council, as with all such initiatives in the life of the paper, had come from within *Barricada*. And the primary motivations were professional. In a 1991 interview, Chamorro was surprisingly frank about the council's role as a firewall between the FSLN leadership and *Barricada*'s editorial functioning: "It's much better to know that we're going to have a meeting [of the council] every two weeks; every two weeks we're going to have a brief evaluation, and at the same time share important information dealing with the law, the economy, politics, and foreign policy. I think there is still vigilance [by the FSLN leadership], but this is totally a posteriori. I mean, we don't get any phone calls from anyone saying, 'What are you going to publish tomorrow? What's your headline for tomorrow?'"[20]

After its "deep de-officialization," Chamorro wrote in the New Editorial Profile, *Barricada* would cease to be an organ of the vanguard. If *Barricada* would remain "an organic medium of the FSLN," it would do so by transforming itself into a more amorphous entity—a "newspaper of the revolution, or a newspaper of Sandinismo."[21] This would allow the paper to emerge "as a journalistic institution with its own identity, that is to say, with some degree of autonomy in relation to the FSLN as a political subject, to strengthen to the maximum its potential credibility and influence." *Barricada* would best serve the front's long-term interests, Chamorro argued cannily, if it did not have to be preoccupied on a daily basis with serving those same interests. By "not having to submit [itself] in a rigid way to the tactical requirements of FSLN policy," *Barricada* would have "a greater margin of freedom of action" to cater to its traditional constituency and increase the newspaper's—and hence the front's—appeal to previously hostile or indifferent sectors. After all, Chamorro wrote, "in the final analysis, it is the people [as a whole] that the revolution seeks to attract."[22]

The editorial council was critical to this balancing act. The "Rules of the Editorial Council of *Barricada*," an unpublished internal document drafted by Chamorro during this same period, offers subtle indications of the trade-offs necessary to secure greater autonomy while preserving a broadly Sandinista orientation—or, as the document put it, "to harmonize the newspaper's actions with the global [i.e., overarching] strategy and the specific interests of the FSLN as an opposition force." Taking no chances, Chamorro sought to ensure that *Barricada*'s writers and editors would not have to deal with untoward meddling—even by the council itself. "The editorial council,"

according to Chamorro's rules, "is not an executive organ that inter-
venes in the ordinary decisions of the paper on questions of news and
editorial policies, which are the purview of the directorate of the newspaper in accordance with generally approved policies." Rather, the
council would "aid in the elaboration of the editorial strategy of the
newspaper," including the "definition of its political objectives." This
editorial strategy would be "forwarded at the end to the director of the
newspaper and his team, who are responsible for its application and
execution."[23]

The council's role would remain fairly constant over the course of
the autonomy experiment, though its membership did evolve, with
William Ramírez departing and Emilio Baltodano and *Barricada* editor Roberto Fonseca being drafted to serve. There are indications of a
degree of dissension on certain aspects of the internal Sandinista
debate; a *Barricada* editorial of February 1994 referred to "a variety of
personal opinions" existing among "members of the editorial council,"
as well as among *Barricada* staff.[24] In a 1996 interview, however,
Chamorro properly pointed to the decision by all council members—
including Bayardo Arce—to resign en masse as the defenestración
loomed in 1994 as evidence that a unified vision of the autonomy project had prevailed among council members. The vestigial role of the
council after October 1994, likewise, was an indication that a powerful
linchpin of *Barricada*'s institutional autonomy and professional identity had been discarded.

A Revolutionary Liberalism?

The professional project that took shape at *Barricada* in 1990 derived
above all from liberal-democratic conceptions of the press and its role
vis-à-vis civil society. To see this more clearly, consider a selection of
headings and subheadings from a popular Western journalism text,
expressing the liberal (especially North American) desiderata of obser-

vation, concision, self-discipline, "objective" news sense, and an emphasis on human interest—what Michael Schudson has called "the importance of everyday life":[25]

> *Vision.* To write well, first see well. Acquiring the camera eye. . . . The difference between writer and reporter. A professional attitude toward temporary art. Skepticism for received opinion—and one's own.

> *Focus.* Abstraction. [Avoiding] the language of Vaguespeak. Seeing the war through the single soldier. Detail. Don't ask the reader's emotion—earn it. Avoiding bias. . . .

> *Form.* Grammar and diction. Season, but don't overspice. Arrangement of detail. Construction and unity. Style. Keeping the "I" out.

> *Ideas.* Awareness and news sense. Inspiration vs. hard work. Getting out of the office. . . . What is not news.[26]

Compare this with the essence of the "journalistic strategy" outlined in the New Editorial Profile, which recommended that *Barricada* reposition itself "as a daily of general information with a national reach," rather than a sectarian publication of minimal interest to the unconverted. At the heart of the professional project outlined in the profile were ten components that Carlos Fernando Chamorro and the editorial council considered essential to the paper's new identity. They are reproduced here at some length, with emphasis added, since there is no clearer articulation of the professional vision that was meant to guide *Barricada* in the postrevolutionary era. The drafters of the profile pledged

> (i) [to move toward] a balanced journalism that breaks with the unilateral nature of information predominant in Nicaragua. That is to say, *the consultation of various sources in covering news, the presentation of alternative opinions, and so forth, in order to gain credibility and professional quality.*

(ii) to construct an individual agenda. *Barricada* must reflect daily reality, but above all it must come up with an investigative agenda of news. *To give facts priority over speech [discurso].*

(iii) to combine agility with profundity. . . . Abundant information in short note form, combined with more in-depth material, should [contribute to] a modern and attractive design for easier reading.

(iv) to leave no informational blank spaces [*No hay que dejar vacíos informativos*], even taking into account the fact that there will always exist questions of political convenience that must be considered in deciding whether to publish [an item] or not.

(v) to establish a solid relationship with the public that is linked to the daily. Their minor and major concerns and demands—whether individual or societal—should always receive privileged attention.

(vi) to undertake self-promotion of *Barricada*'s role, its achievements, and those of its journalists, as an institution. Each small victory of *Barricada* should be claimed as a conquest that serves to increase [*Barricada*'s] own space.

(vii) to combine journalistic genres that will permit [the paper] to offer a diversity of reading material and [present] a distinctive journalistic style. . . . To cultivate news [*la crónica*], reporting, interviews.

(viii) *to grant a special importance to human interest [material] and entertainment.* [These serve as] hooks for readers. A surprise every day. A touch of craftiness, pain, joy, without succumbing to unnecessary stridency.

(ix) to cultivate a plain language . . . to purify the language of rhetoric and hyperadjectivization [*sobreadjetivación*].

(x) *to formally separate opinion from information, and to adopt a necessary distance in treatment of informational subjects.* This does not imply that information should be stripped of all its political significance [*intencionalidad política*].

It is quite clear that there is more going on here than a wholesale adoption of liberal-democratic journalistic principles. The reference to "the unilateral nature of information predominant in Nicaragua" acknowledges the partisan character of Nicaraguan journalism in the nineteenth and twentieth centuries—a tradition of which *Barricada* was itself a part. The special nature of *Barricada*'s institutional ties with its FSLN sponsor, and of the revolutionary process that brought it to national prominence, is also evident: hence the acknowledgment that "there will always exist questions of political convenience that must be considered in deciding whether to publish" certain items. Hardly an admission many Western editors would freely make, this accurately reflects the professional trade-offs that were held to be necessary in order for the autonomy project to find its footing without disrupting the symbiotic relationship with the front.

In addition, some elements of the social-responsibility model of journalism are evident in *Barricada*'s post-1990 professional project. "One important feature was the concept of service, or usefulness of information," recalled Carlos Fernando Chamorro in 1998. "We explicitly tried to move beyond the idea that *Barricada* was only useful for the political class. The idea was to expand our readership by offering them useful information on every subject of social interest."[27] Even social-responsibility models must be seen essentially as offshoots of the liberal tradition, however. And it is quite clear that the tenets of classical liberalism *most* influenced the language of *Barricada*'s New Editorial Profile—its determination to "reflect daily reality" with "a balanced journalism," emphasizing "plain language" and "consultation of various sources." The broadly liberal component of the new model received further expression in another seminal document of the new era, "Ethical Principles and Norms of *Barricada*," which circulated internally from April 1991, several months after the formal relaunching of the newspaper. The document included the following passage:

> The primary responsibility that *Barricada* assumes is to truthfully inform its readers. To achieve this purpose, news should comply

with the following requirements: *precision* (taking into account all the important and secondary details of a news item, with exactitude and fidelity); *comprehensiveness* (the panoramic inclusion of [all aspects of] the news story); [and] *penetration* (delving deeply into the significance of the item to discover its importance). The exercise of these three faculties will result in coverage that is faithful to the news story and will determine the primary characteristic of its style: objectivity, the absence of bias [*juicios*], of opinion, [and] of personal evaluation of the item.[28]

It is important to recall briefly, before leaving this subject, a contention made in the previous chapter: that material as well as philosophical factors have shaped the tradition of liberal-democratic journalism. A moral economy of journalism is evident, but so too is a material economy. Ideas of impartiality, critical distance, and human interest were outgrowths of the rise of a truly mass media, in which readers and the advertisers they attracted assumed primary commercial importance. Reduced partisanship, for example, allowed newspapers to cultivate the broadest possible constituency: readers who might have been alienated by a politically partisan journalism could be more easily lured by a reportorial style that abandoned the sectarianism of old. Human interest, meanwhile, though an element of news as old as human communication, was quite consciously adapted for a mass-media era as a lowest common denominator that would again maximize a newspaper's appeal to readers—and hence to advertisers. We will see shortly that such material and commercial considerations were, if not uppermost, at least powerfully present in the minds of those who developed and implemented *Barricada*'s autonomy project between 1990 and 1994.

"In the National Interest"

On 30 January 1991, less than a year after the historic elections that lent a decisive impetus to its drive for autonomy, *Barricada* formally unveiled a new and in some ways radically revamped version of itself. Gone was the insurrectionary logo alongside the masthead: a guerrilla crouched behind a barricade of paving stones, taking aim with a rifle. Gone too were the broad swaths of red and black—the banner of Sandino (though a more subtle version of the color scheme remained). Most striking of all was the change in the paper's slogan, altered to read: "In the National Interest" (*por los intereses nacionales*). As if to emphasize the move away from *Barricada*'s official-organ status, a new logo also appeared: Sandino's trademark Stetson, emblazoned over a Nicaraguan flag. Even this, though, was soon deemed too partisan. A few days after the first edition of the new *Barricada* hit the stands, the Stetson and the flag were separated. There was perhaps no better symbol of the balance—and distance—between mobilizing and professional imperatives that the paper's staff now sought to entrench.

The specifics of *Barricada*'s postrevolutionary editorial agenda received close attention in the New Editorial Profile. As political and programmatic bulwarks for the new orientation, the paper proposed:

(i) the defense of the rule of law, the Constitution, and democratic rights, among which the most important is freedom of expression;

(ii) the widening of space for popular participation, and the democratization of the popular organizations and social movements;

(iii) the unity, democratization, and programmatic relaunching of the FSLN and its projection in society as forger of an authentically democratic, participatory, and representative political culture;

(iv) the struggle for the political depolarization of society, and the channeling of conflicts into democratic forms of expression;

(v) the defense of socioeconomic alternatives that, in a framework of equity and social justice, will benefit the development of the popular sectors;

(vi) the defense of national independence and sovereignty and the values of national culture.[29]

Thus, essential values of tolerance and reconciliation—within the overarching framework of democratic pluralism—would act to soften the ultramobilized militancy of years past. Envisioned as well was a much broader canvas for reporting and opinion-editorial contributions. An attempt would be made to reflect and promote not only the vigorous discussions taking place within the FSLN, but also the "debate . . . between Sandinismo and other social sectors," as the New Editorial Profile phrased it. In a practical sense, this meant that sources and contributors who were once anathema to *Barricada* now would be the paper's stock-in-trade. This new pluralism, perhaps more than any other aspect of *Barricada*'s new line, rankled opponents of the autonomy experiment, with consequences that will be explored later.

A sine qua non of the new editorial orientation was acceptance of the UNO regime's right to rule. "It would be wrong, totally wrong, for us to deny the legitimacy of this government," said Chamorro in 1991. "If we decide they don't exist, that they're a fraud, simply the sons of Yankee imperialism—well, what we'd have to do is organize a coup d'état or a military insurrection. But they exist, and we have to dispute their ideas against our ideas."[30] Acknowledging this legitimacy while maintaining a spirited tone of opposition to most government policies was "a difficult balance to strike," according to staffer Guillermo Cortés. As he outlined the dilemma, *Barricada*'s "opposition cannot be so strong that it causes the fall of the government, nor can it stop being an opposition [paper]." Cortés perceived the quandary to be "weighing on the newspaper" as of 1991. But for him—and for a clear majority of *Barricada* staff—the difficulties were more than offset by the professional opportunities opened to *Barricada* in its new role as an opposition daily. "It's easier to do journalism from the opposition," Cortés said.[31] His comment touches, simply but elegantly, on the watchdog role that is almost definitional to liberal-democratic conceptions of the press, and which had now become a core feature of *Barricada*'s project. The emphasis upon critically disputing ideas and policies, rather than taking to the mountains or staging a coup d'état, had a professional dimension as well as a political one, according to Cortés: "In a country where conflicts have historically been settled with bullets, the mass media and the journalists have been limited in their opportunities to practice their profession. Here in Nicaragua, if the rule of law and the role of civil society is going to be strengthened, then there will be greater opportunities for professional journalism."[32]

Integral to the acceptance of both peaceful political competition and the watchdog role was the idea of *Barricada* as a leader of public opinion. This concept made regular appearances in the New Editorial Profile. Politically, the status of opinion leader would allow *Barricada* to promote the interests of the Sandinista Front in the wider society. If traces of the old vanguardism remained, though, the professional aspect was also germane. The new orientation would serve as an antidote to the depersonalized, predetermined character of *Barricada*'s reporting in the 1980s. "In general," Chamorro argued in the profile, *Barricada* "has lacked opinion leaders on various themes. The reality of [relations with] the FSLN and the lack of a tradition has impeded the projection of a broad spectrum of opinions, even within Sandinismo." Accordingly, *Barricada* "must aspire to convert itself into a leader of public opinion. This supposes its aggressive involvement and the taking of positions in the national debate, not only in relation to political questions, but with regard to all the themes of interest to the population."

As a public-opinion leader, moreover, *Barricada* would be able to mitigate some of the inevitable constraints on a print medium in an underdeveloped country—at least when direct and indirect assistance from the government in power could no longer be counted on. *Barricada,* it was hoped, could play an agenda-setting role for Nicaragua's network of private radio stations. This would permit it to extend its political influence and professional identity by piggy-backing on broadcast media. These were vastly cheaper for the poor majority to access (compare the cost of a transistor radio and occasional battery purchases with that of a newspaper subscription); did not require basic literacy skills; and needed no infrastructure to disseminate their message beyond a transmitter and scattered (usually shared) relay stations. Sofía Montenegro, speaking in 1991, saw the combination of print and broadcast media as a harmonious one: "The news in *Barricada* is much more in-depth than anything you can do on the radio, and it serves to give guidelines to the radio stations themselves. The people who are on the radio *read* the newspaper. And if you can influence the directors and journalists of the radio stations, you can influence the wider population indirectly. . . . Maybe it'll come to the point that we distribute only ten thousand copies of the paper, but it'll be important and influential nonetheless."[33]

With new forms of cooperation went new forms of competition. One of the most striking developments of the postrevolutionary era was *Barricada*'s reorientation—in the marketplace of commerce rather than ideas, at least—from the perennial struggle with *La Prensa* to a new jockeying for position with its longtime political ally, *El Nuevo Diario (END)*. Since it arrived on the Nicaraguan media scene in 1980, *END* had sought to preserve something of the populist sensibility of the old *La Prensa*, where most of the paper's staff had once worked (see chapter 1). Though *END* was also a good source of intellectual commentary and criticism, it cultivated a generally "lighter" tone, and indulged in lashings of *periodismo amarillo* (yellow journalism) to bolster its mass readership. In a 1996 interview Carlos Fernando Chamorro expressed admiration for the balance *END* had managed to strike, and described it as influential on *Barricada*'s own autonomy experiment:

> We learned from *El Nuevo Diario* a lot about trying to make the newspaper more attractive. It was very difficult to compete with *El*

Nuevo Diario, because they move on a totally different logic, and their readers don't judge the newspaper by the same standards that they judge *Barricada* or *La Prensa*. You read *El Nuevo Diario* today as a kind of humor magazine, and tomorrow you read it as a newspaper, and then three days after it's a humor magazine again. It's very versatile [*muy versátil*]. And you don't care if they make mistakes, because they're supposed to make mistakes! They're *supposed* to be scandalous, they're *supposed* to be imprecise.[34]

Accordingly, the "qualitative evaluation" carried out by the editorial council in April 1992 spoke of the need to "lead the agenda of public opinion in the sphere of daily life, in order to have a greater impact and penetration in the popular sectors." It was now acknowledged that these sectors read *Barricada* not only for political and economic information and for a depiction of the "social crisis of the country, but also for recreation"—for coverage of the events of daily life that lay outside "the national political agenda." In practice, this meant tentative steps toward periodismo amarillo of the type *END* had long favored. *Barricada* began to pay greater attention to "crime, beauty contests, women's asses on the beach," as Max Kreimann unabashedly conceded in 1991. "The reality the majority of people here were born into—you can't change that in twenty years," Kreimann contended. "People like to read this stuff." *Barricada*, he said, sought to temper these *amarillista* elements with greater attention to professional values and craft: "We're a little yellower, and people like it. These were policies that didn't exist before. But I would say the little yellow journalism that's there is . . . *educated*. Educated in the sense that it's unlike *El Nuevo Diario*, which will say: 'So-and-so raped so-and-so,' give lots of details, names and surnames, and then three days later the people who are mentioned write letters saying it didn't happen. That shows a lack of respect for those people. We try not to print sordid things in a way that a child who reads them will think of them as somehow normal; we try to be more balanced and courteous."[35]

Editorial council member Sergio de Castro put the matter more bluntly still, in an interview conducted around the same time: "Look. People—revolutionary people—like to fuck, like to drink, to go to the beach. Why not? Who can imagine that if you're a revolutionary or a progressive, you're going to behave like a monk in a monastery? It's crazy. People are tired of war. They have been saturated with politics. We have to reflect the other aspects of normal life."[36]

The lighter-hearted page *De todo un poco* was one beneficiary of the new emphasis. A survey of 3,300 *Barricada* readers in 1990 had found it to be the most popular page among readers.[37] (The notion of a readers' survey itself aptly symbolized *Barricada*'s reorientation.) *De todo un poco,* accordingly, was expanded from one to two pages. Especially mocked by more traditional readers of the paper was the prominence *Barricada* gave to *The Horoscope of Madame Tousso;* it would now run weekly instead of monthly ("in response to numerous appeals from our readers . . . [expressed in] letters and phone calls," the announcement proclaimed).[38] For Carlos Fernando Chamorro, the horoscope, though patently silly, was nothing to get exercised about. "I don't personally like to read the horoscope. For me, it's totally idiotic. But a lot of people like it! What can I do? When I go and talk to the people who sell *Barricada,* they tell me I should have a horoscope every *day!*" It was, he said, "a concession" to popular demand.[39] Interestingly, even the ortodoxo heirs of *Barricada* found it advisable, after the defenestración, to retain the horoscope as a regular feature.

This sensational turn in *Barricada*'s coverage can itself be sensationalized. *Barricada* remained a serious, sometimes dour paper. The qualitative evaluation acknowledged "the strong competition" that *El Nuevo Diario* was able to give *Barricada* "based on its yellow strategy, which lends its news a high degree of sensationalism." (At the time, *END* was outselling *Barricada* by about ten thousand copies a day—forty thousand to thirty thousand.) But the editorial council pledged itself to avoid "descend[ing] to the extremes of *El*

Nuevo Diario." *Barricada* would not abandon its essential sobriety of outlook—the only appropriate tone, it was felt, given Nicaragua's impoverishment and perpetual political crisis. But "*serious* has a double connotation," Chamorro said in 1996. "One is a good one: it implies credibility. The other meaning is: boring. I felt we shouldn't be afraid of being perceived as a serious newspaper, but what we needed was more color, more balance, more of an equilibrium between what we call traditional news—politics, the economy, foreign policy—and [human-interest] news stories."[40]

Some sense of how the new emphasis on human interest translated to daily coverage can be gained from a nonsystematic glance through several months of *Barricada* coverage not long before the defenestración. In addition to stories on corruption, addressed separately below, the paper published an exposé on the mafiosi operating in Managua's markets; features on incest, AIDS, drug addiction, unemployment, and the energy crisis in Nicaragua;[41] a long meditation on the legacy of the Sandinista revolution, titled "The Children of the Change"; a four-part story on the return of Nicaraguan boxer Alexis Argüello to his home country; another four-part feature examining Nicaragua's claim to the Colombian islands of San Andrés and Providencia, as well as portions of Honduran territory and the Gulf of Fonseca;[42] a profile of a forensic scientist at work;[43] and a two-part, nonsensationalist story on transvestism.[44] During this period *Barricada* also introduced a new weekly computer section in *De todo un poco,* edited by the paper's resident techno-buff, Daniel Alegría.[45] There was little doubt that the paper's informational canvas and stylistic range had expanded greatly since the bland and predictable days of the 1980s.

The wider outlook was reflected too in the increased professional ties that the paper cultivated with regional and other international media. Beginning with the thaw of 1987–88, Managua's dailies had cooperated in arranging joint visits to Costa Rican newspapers. Now *Barricada* took things a step further, cosponsoring an innovative investigation into Nicaraguans working illegally in Costa Rica with the conservative San José daily *La Nación*.[46] Alfonso Malespín, a political reporter with *Barricada,* recalled that between 1991 and 1994 he had "had a chance to go to Germany, Florida, Honduras, Costa Rica, and Colombia" for tours of dailies in those countries, while other *Barricada* staff "went to Japan, Venezuela, Brazil, and Chile."[47]

The introduction of a Sunday edition in July 1993 was another first for *Barricada* and for Nicaragua as a whole. Carlos Fernando Chamorro cited it as evidence of the paper's desire to "offer to the reader polemical general-interest reporting, debate and diversity of opinions, and reading matter appropriate for [one's] free time," to meet the needs of an audience that was "ever more demanding and heterogeneous."[48] The same thinking apparently lay behind *Municipios* (Municipalities), a section introduced in August 1993 "to open space for the daily activities of local government, along with [local] residents, trade union representatives, producers, and all types of popular and trade union organizations."[49] Another new section, *Noticiero costeño,* debuted in February 1994, targeting Nicaragua's historically marginalized Atlantic coast communities—sectors that the FSLN and *Barricada* had alienated in the 1980s, but that were now seen as potential growth markets for paper and party alike.

One of the most interesting side-projects of *Barricada*'s autonomy era—for which it also served as harbinger—was *Gente* (People), a weekly supplement first introduced in 1989 under the direction of Sofía Montenegro. A long-standing thorn in the side of many Sandinista leaders (who considered her, she said, a loose cannon), Montenegro was appointed to direct *Gente* only after "a little internal battle" within the FSLN—this according to Chamorro, who waged the battle on behalf of Montenegro and the professional imperative of the paper. *Gente* was conceived as one of the projects that would allow *Barricada* to exploit the internal opening offered by concertación and the thaw of 1987–88. It would be "a publication not too tied to political demands, to the agenda of the FSLN"; rather, it would "deal with problems of everyday life, of culture in the broad sense of the word."[50] It would also, inevitably, bear the stamp of Montenegro's flamboyant personality, lending some much-needed unpredictability and flair to *Barricada*'s pages.

The project, though, quickly ran up against the mobilizing requirements of the front and its component institutions. This time, reservations were expressed not through the National Directorate per se, but through several of the mass organizations established before and after the Sandinista seizure of power in 1979. The independence of these organizations had been sharply curtailed over the course of the revolutionary decade, as the front's vanguardist character was intensified by war and economic meltdown.[51] But the mass organizations were still capable, in the late 1980s, of exerting influence over areas of policy in which they could claim a territorial interest. Once *Barricada*'s plans for the new supplement became known, said Chamorro, "We had to organize an internal lobby within the FSLN, because . . . everybody wanted to be the *owner* of that supplement. The Sandinista Youth [JS-19] wanted to have a youth supplement. The Sandinista women's movement [AMNLAE] wanted to have its own supplement."[52] According to Sofía Montenegro, it was AMNLAE that pressed its case hardest, even though "they were planning on putting people in charge who had no experience with journalism, communications, editing, or anything"[53]—shades of the political commissariats that had aroused such opposition early in *Barricada*'s life.

Barricada, though, had amassed enough institutional autonomy and credibility by this point to constitute its *own* powerful lobby within the FSLN. In Chamorro's words, "We said, *we* are the ones who are the professional journalists." A compromise was worked out, granting the mass organizations input "at the level of an editorial council," while "direct responsibility" for *Gente* would reside with the council itself—headed, for appearance's sake, by Chamorro. The National Directorate "said there had to be someone in charge to control me," Montenegro recalled wryly. She settled for the position of editor, and for the near total day-to-day control over the supplement's content that came with the post.[54]

After the trauma of 1990, the façade of the editorial council was abandoned and *Barricada*'s strategic control over *Gente* increased. "After the Sandinistas lost the election," said Montenegro, "it was obvious that the one who was really running the whole damn thing was myself. Besides, the representativeness of this editorial council was now in a state of crisis: you had people representing sectors that were themselves in a state of upheaval or disintegration. Finally we decided it was ridiculous to have a council that had no real say or significance. . . . That's when I became director [of *Gente*]."[55]

The fervent feminism and radical individualism that had alienated Montenegro from many Sandinista leaders—and from the more conservative "official" women's organization, AMNLAE—immediately became hallmarks of *Gente* when it first appeared in 1989. They proved enormously popular with readers. *Barricada*'s 1990 readers' survey found that *Gente* was preferred by an absolute majority (54 percent) of readers; only one other weekly supplement (*Revista de campo*) reached double figures.[56] Much of the appeal derived from *Gente*'s groundbreaking analysis of controversial social issues, especially those linked to gender and sexuality. The supplement dealt frankly—sometimes brazenly—with sexism, homosexuality, impotence, pornography. Its tonal range was impressive, ranging from "infotainment"-style gossip to long scientific treatises by noted professionals. The basic political line hardly varied from that of *Barricada* as a whole, but the style was dramatically different. "Our intention was to promote the self-affirmation of the individual and of individual experience," said Montenegro in 1991. "The Sandinista revolution had always spoken of *nosotros,* 'we.' 'We the people,' and so on. . . . The collectivist and communal mentality was very powerful. We wanted to fortify the 'I,' and at the same time stress the validity and necessity of not divorcing individuality from the collective."

Like the daily *Barricada,* Montenegro worked within certain pre-determined limits. But early on, at least, these responded more to the conservative strand of Nicaraguan culture than the political dictates of the Sandinista Front. Homosexuality, "the relationship between power and sex," incest, "other so-called weird behaviors like pederasty and voyeurism"—such issues had been touched on only "a little" in *Gente* as of 1991. Montenegro at that time said she was looking forward to pushing the boundaries further: "If you're a man who wants to dress up in women's clothes, if it makes you happy—beautiful!"[57] But as the autonomy experiment wore on and the forces of opposition to *Barricada* coalesced, *Gente* came under increasing fire from the National Directorate and others within the front. A special bone of contention was Montenegro's sometimes incendiary feminism. Some front leaders felt this was overwhelming the content of the supplement, and there were those within *Barricada* itself who agreed—to a point. "*Gente* was under scrutiny to change" by 1994, according to Daniel Alegría. He said many considered Montenegro "too narrow, too militant" in her approach.[58]

These criticisms would surface, rather opportunistically, after the *defenestración,* when *Barricada*'s new directors published the text of a letter written by Montenegro to Carlos Fernando Chamorro and other *Barricada* editors in late 1993, threatening to resign over the pressure placed on her to change *Gente.* "For years I have put up with condescending tones . . . , insinuations, jokes, mockery," Montenegro protested. "These things have greatly inhibited me, led me to censor myself and render myself invisible, to the point that I don't any longer allow myself to write. . . . I have always felt myself to be a citizen under permanent suspicion. . . . For these and other reasons I believe the most sensible thing, for you and for me, is for me to leave the operation." In 1996, though, Montenegro and other interview subjects downplayed the controversy, calling it a minor blip in *Barricada-Gente* relations—one blown out of proportion after October 1994 in order to embarrass Montenegro and the *Barricada* old guard in general.[59]

In retrospect, the *Gente* story seems central to any wider evaluation of the autonomy era at *Barricada,* and the fact that it was present at the creation of the autonomy experiment in the late 1980s
makes it appear more seminal still. Its significance, and the breadth
of its appeal, was acknowledged in an intriguing fashion by *Barricada*'s new leadership after the defenestración of October 1994.
Perhaps surprisingly, given Montenegro's gadfly status within ortodoxo sectors of the front, Comandante Tomás Borge and his senior
staff went out of their way both to praise and to preserve the *Gente*
project. *Gente* reappeared under new direction on 11 November
1994, mere days after Montenegro departed the paper. The intro-
ductory note to readers was titled "Same *Gente,* Different *Gente*"—
but few differences were evident, either in format or content. The
cover story was on homosexuality in Cuba. Inside could be found a
full-page feature on "The Pleasure of Masturbation," and a pledge to
"defend women" and "be, above all, an instrument to recover the
limited rights of the female sex." Borge himself made a point of prais-
ing *Gente* as an "indispensable" component of *Barricada.* "In its format," he said, it had been "very well done, though not so much in
some of its content." In the sixteenth-anniversary issue of *Barricada,*
the first since the defenestración, Borge was even more fulsome in his
praise, calling *Gente* "an extraordinary supplement . . . the best-loved
and most widely read weekly in the country."[60] Clearly, the enthusiasm *Gente* had evoked was not lightly to be trifled with, especially
with the post-1994 *Barricada* hemorrhaging readers and struggling
for professional credibility on all fronts.

Material Crisis, Institutional Response

No understanding of mass-media functioning, or of liberal-democratic
conceptions of professional journalism, is possible without attention
to the material side of press functioning. Likewise, a fuller grasp of

Barricada's autonomy project in the early 1990s requires consideration of the material crisis that afflicted the paper in the post-Sandinista era and the diverse means by which the paper sought to confront it.

Barricada entered the 1990s with its glory days behind it, at least as far as circulation was concerned. The inflated print runs of the mid-1980s had ebbed even before the FSLN fell from power, beginning with the Sandinistas' "hesitant turn toward the market." The subsidies on which *Barricada* (along with the other Nicaraguan dailies) depended were sharply cut back. Hyperinflation, meanwhile, attained levels not seen since Weimar Germany in the 1920s; all three Managua dailies were forced to boost their prices "almost every week" (in the words of former *La Prensa* director Pablo Antonio Cuadra).[61] All saw their circulations plummet: from over one hundred thousand for *Barricada* at its peak in the mid-1980s, to around thirty-five thousand for the newspaper in 1991.[62]

Beginning even before the Sandinista election defeat, *Barricada* was forced to introduce deep staffing cuts. The payroll plummeted 17 percent in 1988–89, to four hundred employees. Further cuts after the 1990 elections reduced total staff to three hundred fifty. Research in 1996 confirmed that a further staff cut of thirty-five or forty workers had taken place around Easter 1994—a downsizing that proved particularly difficult to negotiate, since those released included senior managers who demanded (and received) generous severance packages.

The damage to morale that accompanied these cuts can readily be imagined, but also, perhaps, overstated. Most of the "redundant" workers were on the production side of the operation. Senior editorial personnel remained comparatively immune from dismissal, until the *defenestración*. But this added measure of security carried its own dangers for the long-term viability of the autonomy project. It drove a deep wedge between remaining blue-collar staff, who were left to wonder whether each working week would be their last—while journalists and editors seemingly lived high on the hog. This institutional tension would have important implications at the time of Chamorro's dismissal, and during the brief interregnum between old order and new (see chapter 3). Even during the era of semiautonomy, staff reductions exacted "a political cost," according to Carlos Fernando Chamorro; this acted as a brake on further "changes that we wanted to introduce," presumably a reference to even deeper staffing cuts.[63]

The onset of true material crisis at *Barricada* dated from the inauguration of the UNO government in April 1990 and intensified with the regime's "maxi-devaluation" of March 1991. This virtually halved *Barricada*'s bank balance, which plummeted from $430,000 to $220,000, according to then business manager Max Kreimann.[64] In 1991 as well, existing stockpiles of cheap Soviet newsprint finally ran out, and all the Nicaraguan newspapers were forced to pay market prices for their most essential material resource. "I don't think the management team at *Barricada* was able to understand well the change in that variable," Carlos Fernando Chamorro recalled in 1996. "The paper was not organized or prepared to assimilate . . . [the fact] that you were buying paper at $350 per ton, and then from one day to [the next] you were paying $550."[65]

While the new economic environment sapped resources from the paper, so too did the new material relationship between *Barricada* and the Sandinista Front. With the FSLN starved for funds, its few still profitable institutions—like *Barricada*—were called upon to help the party out of its financial crisis. *Barricada* staffers may have taken a certain pride in the fact that the paper was now a donor to, rather than a drain upon, FSLN coffers. However this may have warmed their hearts, though, the subsidy denied the paper much-needed investment capital. Chamorro referred to the decision to contribute some $250,000 to the front over two years (1990–91) as "an error. It was too much. We needed that money for capitalization and for other purposes."[66]

Most features of the material crisis, as noted, were shared by the other Nicaraguan dailies. But the new era also brought challenges specific to *Barricada*. The most obvious was the collapse of the privileged relationship with the largest client for *Barricada*'s sophisticated publishing operation—the state. Shortly after it took power, the UNO government, "for explicitly political reasons" (according to Max Kreimann), declined to renew *Barricada*'s contract to publish textbooks for the Ministry of Education. Kreimann estimated the loss to *Barricada* at between $500,000 and $2.5 million annually.[67] There remains the question of how dependable Kreimann's financial estimates are, given the corruption scandal that eventually led to his departure from the paper (explored further below). I present the estimates without demur, for three reasons: there is little else to go on; Carlos Fernando Chamorro read Kreimann's comments without taking exception to them; and, most important, the corruption in which Kreimann and others were allegedly involved does not seem to have been on a sufficiently large scale to substantially offset the estimates. According to several sources at *Barricada*, the government turned to a publishing operation in Colombia, since *Barricada*'s was the only press in Nicaragua capable of handling the contract.

Life under UNO also meant a precipitous decline in state-sector advertising. This had constituted anywhere up to four-fifths of the paper's ad revenue in the 1980s, leading the paper to take a rather blasé and "idealistic" attitude (Chamorro) toward private-sector advertising: "I remember one time we may have rejected a page of advertising by a transnational corporation because we thought we had some ethical principles that were not to be sold on the market." That was changing even before the revolution lost power: in the latter half of the 1980s, *Barricada* "went to the street in competition for private advertising."[68] In the first half of the 1990s, though, the quest for such advertising became a matter of life and death. Granted, at the time of my fieldwork in 1991, state-sector advertising still constituted a significant *proportion* of ad revenue—around 30 percent. The figure could even rise for brief periods, when the UNO government introduced important policy initiatives with publicity campaigns designed to appeal to all social sectors, including *Barricada*'s (gradually diversifying) constituency. Still, this was 30 percent of a much smaller pie. From about five pages of ads per edition before the FSLN's fall from power, *Barricada* in early 1991 was publishing about two—a "below-survival level," in Max Kreimann's estimation at the time.[69]

A dramatic turnaround seems to have begun shortly afterward, however. As the autonomy project gathered steam, private advertisers began to show signs of accommodating to the former official publication of their political enemy. *Barricada* "did well in selling advertising" in the two years before the defenestración, contended Carlos Fernando Chamorro: "We were the number-two paper in ads in the country, after *La Prensa*. . . . And we had potential. That was the most important thing. You talk to the advertising companies, and they always told us that sometimes it was difficult for them to convince their clients to put their ads in *Barricada* because we were a Sandinista newspaper, and in the last analysis they thought they were giving money to the front. But they started to accept that we were a respectable newspaper, of even higher quality than the others."[70]

The most systematic internal appraisal of the autonomy experiment, the editorial council's Qualitative Evaluation, also put *Barricada* in second place nationally in terms of advertising, with an average of 6.5 pages daily. (The house organ of the business establishment, *La Prensa*, predictably soared ahead with 10.4 pages, while the downmarket, brashly populist *El Nuevo Diario* was the least favored by private-sector advertisers.) The rebound at *Barricada* permitted a remarkable expansion in the size of the paper—from a daily average of ten pages from 1988 to 1991, to between sixteen and twenty-four from 1991 to 1994. This gave *Barricada*'s professional project considerably greater scope as well—funding new editorial sections and the expansion of existing ones, and generally "making it possible to improve the attractiveness and quality of the publication."[71]

One explanation for the advertising turnaround was *Barricada*'s unique ability to print in color—something it emphasized to potential clients in April 1991 by publishing each day's edition in color, albeit at a considerable financial loss. The strategy was designed to lure readers, but also, in Max Kreimann's words, "to attract more advertisers—offering them color, giving it to them free as a promotion, and implementing a variety of features related to the fact that in Nicaragua there has never existed a newspaper that came out in full color every day." The paper also turfed the staff of its monthly overseas edition, *Barricada Internacional,* out of their commodious offices across from the main *Barricada* building. A beefed-up advertising department was installed in their place—another revealing indication of the new prominence of material, as opposed to strictly political, considerations in the paper's functioning.

Barricada's printing resources proved indispensable in two further respects during the lean years of the early 1990s. They allowed *Barricada* to bolster its design and presentation: in the (admittedly biased) estimation of the qualitative evaluation, *Barricada* could claim "the most modern system of graphic design of [all] the dailies and other periodical publications in the country." This made an important "contribution to the redefinition of the newspaper's personality." Similar advantage was taken by the publishing operation, Editorial El Amanecer, which now courted customers regardless of their political leanings. For anyone who recalled the ultrapolarized political scene of the mid-1980s, some of the new publishing arrangements could only raise eyebrows. *El Nicaragüense,* for example, was the weekly newspaper of COSEP, a business organization that had been one of the most persistent thorns in the side of the regime during the revolutionary decade. But COSEP decided the political differences that had surfaced with the UNO regime and its supporter,

La Prensa—where *El Nicaragüense* had been printed—were more intractable than those with *Barricada,* which at least was also critical of the new regime from its own, rather different perspective. An agreement was reached. Max Kreimann's summary of the changed mentalities offers particularly concise testimony to the new salience of market factors in *Barricada*'s material operations, and the corresponding de-emphasizing of political considerations: "[In addition to *El Nicaragüense*] we print thoroughly anti-Sandinista religious newspapers. And they all send in their advertising too. This didn't happen before, because the political factor predominated in business decisions. *Now you see more the business aspect of the newspaper, because it's more necessary;* if we don't [adopt this approach], we won't survive."[72]

Various other changes in design and marketing were implemented from 1991 onward. They included dropping the guerrilla-at-the-barricades logo, which the New Editorial Profile dismissed as "belong[ing] to another political epoch," and which inhibited *Barricada*'s attempts to secure a politically diverse readership and advertising clientele. The number of columns was reduced from seven to six, "permitt[ing] a cleaner design, a more legible publication, and a major improvement in graphic [capability]." New typefaces made the appearance of the paper's pages "fuller and stronger."[73] On the marketing front, when the Chamorro regime introduced its maxi-devaluation in March 1991, *La Prensa* and *El Nuevo Diario* both raised their prices from one córdoba to C$1.40. *Barricada* held back for a number of days, in an attempt to lure cash-strapped nontraditional readers. Then it raised its price to C$1.20. *La Prensa* dropped its price to match *Barricada*'s; *El Nuevo Diario,* with perhaps the most devoted readership and the greatest material dependence on newsstand sales, stayed put at C$1.40.

The overall effect of these diverse strategies was to preserve a semblance of material stability at *Barricada,* and as broad and diverse a constituency as was perhaps viable at a time when press readership was in free fall across the board. If institution-specific responses to the material challenges are to be considered, though, one should not gloss over actions and decisions that may have undermined or eroded the paper's competitiveness during the years of the autonomy experiment. The most damaging of these centered on a corruption scandal that ensnared, among others, Max Kreimann, the paper's general manager at the time of my fieldwork in 1991. Kreimann's resignation in April 1994 "to devote himself to private activities"[74] climaxed the worst internal upheaval at *Barricada* since the mid-1980s, when several senior editors were let go after a practical joke backfired (see chapter 1). His departure, and that of several dozen other employees in the paper's administrative division, resulted from an internal investigation into the management of *Barricada* and its associated publishing operation. The investigation uncovered "a lot" of corrupt activity, according to staffer Alfonso Malespín:

> There were several things happening at the same time. One of them was that since 1990, they thought that there would be an Ortega takeover of the newspaper. So some of the administrators began to create small enterprises, taking funds out of the newspaper and creating these small printing businesses. And then they got out of hand, totally. On the other hand, they were dealing cars, selling them at extremely high prices—paying around $1,000 for one and then selling them to journalists for around $3,500 or $4,000. Building houses, taking trips and vacations on *Barricada*'s funds, gambling—things like that. This was happening for a long time. We told Comandante Bayardo Arce about it. They never did anything, so finally, in 1994, when this situation was extremely hard, all this administration was asked to quit.[75]

William Grigsby, editor of *Barricada* at the time of field research for this book in 1996, went further still, alleging that a "coterie of thieves" had entrenched itself in the paper's administration during the early 1990s.[76] Others, though, suggested the extent of the wrongdoing was exaggerated by *Barricada*'s opponents to justify the defenestración. Chamorro depicts the administrative situation at the newspaper during the autonomy experiment as compromised only by "petty dishonesties . . . not anything significant":

> There was one guy who was in charge of advertising, who was taking personal advantage. . . . [Let's say] I sell advertising, but I can also exchange advertising for services [a time-honored practice in Latin American countries]. I'll give you an ad for your restaurant, and you give me dinner. . . . They were silly things, like going to a motel and not paying, or going drinking. It's not like anyone stole $50,000 or anything like that. Not big dishonesty. Obviously, in a situation of crisis, if you steal a pencil, everyone's going to say that's something really big, and I would agree with that. But you cannot explain the crisis [at *Barricada*] by saying some people stole $1 million, or $100,000, or $5,000.[77]

Chamorro and his editorial staff, it should be noted, were never personally accused of involvement in corrupt practices. In February 1998, a time of renewed crisis and transformation at *Barricada*, Comandante Tomás Borge went out of his way to exculpate Chamorro of any responsibility for practices that had, Borge claimed, sapped the resources of the newspaper he took over in October 1994.[78] Was Chamorro, though, asleep at the wheel as events unfolded? He acknowledged in 1996 that "somehow the management side went out of our control" during the years of the autonomy project, leaving *Barricada* "in a very vulnerable situation in economic and financial terms. . . . I knew very well by 1993 that we had an economic crisis and that it would take quite a few years to put everything in order."[79]

By the time of the defenestración, the paper was heavily in debt, though it is impossible to ascertain the precise extent of the burden. William Grigsby gave a figure of $2 million.[80] Alfonso Malespín guessed even higher, "around $3.5 or $4.5 million," though Carlos Fernando Chamorro considers this "highly exaggerated."[81] Sofía Montenegro's account also suggests considerable economic stress: "We were breaking our fucking backs, believe me, in order to keep the newspaper afloat." Montenegro added, though, that increased private-sector advertising helped to mitigate the administrative and "structural" problems of the enterprise.[82] It is apparently the case that economic difficulties, whether externally or internally generated, did not translate to a sense of day-to-day material crisis at *Barricada*. "The finances of the paper *were* shaky," said Daniel Alegría. "But the paper was running. I never felt it was going to close from one day to the next. I think we could have managed to survive. . . . And it would have been done in a professional way."[83] *Barricada* personnel indeed felt the pinch—but the suffering was limited almost exclusively to the paper's blue-collar staff, decimated by successive waves of layoffs.

The Politics of Barricada: *The Challenge of Opposition*

The 1992 Qualitative Evaluation of *Barricada* spoke of "two funda-mental reference points" that would "orient the new role of the news-paper: on one hand, the process initiated by the FSLN aimed at the organic and political recuperation of its forces—[the product of] the First Congress [in 1991]—and, on the other hand, the Sandinista opposition strategy toward the government":

> In its policies for news and opinion pieces, *Barricada* has privileged the actions and struggles of the popular Sandinista movement. . . . The overarching themes of the Sandinista agenda—property, disar-mament, privatization, defense of the Constitution, social conflict/political struggle and *concertación,* the consequences of "stabilization" and structural adjustment, the isolation of extremist sectors, hunger and unemployment, initiatives of the popular move-ments, and so forth—have been permanent features of *Barricada*'s agenda. . . . In covering the FSLN, understood as [the sum of] its organic structures: the DN [National Directorate], the Sandinista [parliamentary] bench, the departmental committees, the structures at the base—the dominant tendency has been to stress the discourse

of the National Directorate, in coverage of its political activities, or by means of interviews.[84]

The privileged treatment of FSLN policies, and the activities of the Sandinista leadership, contrasted markedly with the stance adopted toward the UNO government. Such, at least, was the claim of the newspaper's directorate. Whether this was actually the case during the era of semiautonomy remains a highly contentious issue. To arrive at some tentative conclusions, two separate cuts can be made in the paper's day-to-day coverage and wider editorial strategizing. One, the paper's coverage of its FSLN sponsor, is postponed for treatment later in the chapter. To the other—the paper's treatment of the UNO government led by Carlos Fernando Chamorro's mother—we turn now.

For those who decried the de-officialized incarnation of *Barricada,* the politics of the paper between 1990 and 1994 represented an about-face from the mobilizing imperative that had guided it from its birth. *Barricada* had abandoned its revolutionary principles and commitments, affiliating itself with a dissident social-democratic wing of the front that sought to undermine the revolutionary energies of the movement by diverting them into bourgeois pseudo-opposition. *Barricada,* the critics hinted or alleged, had indeed become *un periódico del sistema,* as Chamorro had envisaged back in the late 1980s—but a voice of the *new,* counterrevolutionary system that was struggling to entrench itself in the face of continued opposition from the FSLN leadership and militant base. By these lights, *Barricada*'s watchdog pretensions toward the Chamorro regime were farcical. Juan Ramón Huerta, one of the few staffers on the editorial side of the paper for whom the 1994 defenestración came as a relief and a vindication, described the newspaper's strategy under Carlos Fernando Chamorro as one of "loyal[ty] to the proprietors [*dueños*] and the bosses [*patrones*]"—that is, to the most reactionary and oligarchic forces in Nicaraguan society. William Grigsby likewise accused the custodians of the pre-1994 *Barricada* of maintaining "a very intimate involvement with the [UNO] government."[85] Daniel Ortega told a Cuban news agency after Chamorro's dismissal that *Barricada* "had been turned into a mouthpiece for neoliberal, imperialist, and right-wing politics";[86] pro-Ortega militants denounced the semiautonomous *Barricada* as "rightist, in the service of the government, and the exclusive redoubt of the renovationists."[87]

Clearly, many thousands of dedicated Sandinistas felt betrayed by *Barricada*'s new political line. How, amid all its talk of impartiality and pluralism, could the newspaper mobilize the revolution's remaining constituency to confront an uncertain and perplexing future? How could serious criticism of the FSLN be countenanced in the front's own newspaper? Most painful, it seemed, was the respect the paper now displayed for public figures it had once delighted in reviling—counterrevolutionary figures whose actions and policies could only further immiserate the poor.

Carlos Fernando Chamorro was a special target of the accusations leveled at *Barricada*. Often, the critiques contained implicit references to his aristocratic roots, and his family connection to the new president (as well as a number of her key advisors). Consider, in this context, Daniel Ortega's casually barbed comments to the Spanish publication *El País*, shortly after the defenestración: "It isn't the first time we've proposed changes in *Barricada*, and it always causes a stir. I don't think anyone in the FSLN is untouchable. The head of the Sandinista bench in Parliament was just removed from his position as well, but since Sergio Ramírez isn't from one of Nicaragua's great families, since he doesn't have a famous last name, nobody protested [!]. In the case of Carlos Fernando Chamorro, *I've heard it said that he can't be removed because he is a Chamorro, that he's linked to Doña Violeta, and so forth*. I don't think these are valid arguments."[88]

Chamorro vigorously rejected these charges of collusion, maintaining that the semiautonomous *Barricada* "was always critical of the government." Even during the period of *co-gobierno* (co-government, 1990–93), when the FSLN entered into a tacit alliance with more centrist elements of the UNO coalition, Chamorro argued that *Barricada* "didn't have a co-gobierno mentality, ever." Rather, it had pursued its new watchdog role diligently and professionally. *Barricada* was critical "simply because we were very conscious that we were a newspaper and that we could not be perceived as a pro-government newspaper. The government certainly never perceived *Barricada* as a friend or an ally." The reason for the complaints from ortodoxo elements within the FSLN, Chamorro said, pertained rather to the new *tone* of *Barricada*'s coverage. "Probably we were, let's say, more like a loyal opposition, in terms of being less rhetorical. We were not going to behave in an insulting way." Nonetheless, "The official editorials of *Barricada* were 80 percent of the time against the government."

For *Barricada*'s director, proof of the oppositionist stance was to be found in the paper's investigations of regime corruption and its stark depiction of the damage wrought by UNO's economic policies. "In general, I would say we had the best stories on corruption" of all the Managua papers, Chamorro claimed: "No one else had stories with more documents and evidence of the lack of transparency in some of the government operations. It's not that one big functionary stole a million dollars—but rather the [ongoing] traffic in influence, that sort of thing. I think on that topic we were very consistent. We always put the government on the defensive."

The FSLN "benefited from the type of journalistic work that we did," said Chamorro, even if "[ortodoxo intellectual] Mónica Baltodano and others probably wanted us to shout and use words like *Thief!*"[89]

Alfonso Malespín, an up-and-coming political reporter during this period (and an interesting holdover to the new, reofficialized era—see chapter 4), also cited the corruption investigations as proof that *Barricada* had avoided excessive coziness with the ruling authorities, though he was aware his opinion differed from that of the paper's post-1994 directorate:

If the Sandinistas were the opposition to the government, it was logical, from our perspective, to be an opposition newspaper. And in order to do that, we had to write a *lot* about the government. What did we publish? We published news that was uncovering corruption, theft, wrongdoing, all the things that were happening in the privatization process. And so perhaps they [interview subjects who accused the paper of close links to the regime] felt the government was very, very highly involved in the newspaper. But I think they are not right. . . . Mainly our news was about how the government was creating more unemployment, creating a new elite in the country, giving away almost free some very, very expensive enterprises around the country; how the government was creating a new class, in which the interests of the state and of private enterprise were mixed. Things like that.[90]

A nonsystematic perusal of *Barricada* from July to September 1994—the period immediately prior to the defenestración—found no shortage of examples to justify Chamorro's and Malespín's assertions. The paper tackled corruption in the customs service in June.[91] In July it published a three-part story on the flow of contraband through Honduras,[92] and in August an in-depth investigation of Minister of Agriculture and Livestock Roberto Rondónin. The minister, it transpired, was indebted to the tune of nearly C$20 million to the National Development Bank; he was later forced to remit C$3 million of the debt.[93] Perhaps most memorably, *Barricada* tracked down the former vice-minister of the presidency, Antonio Ibarra, a fugitive from Nicaraguan justice who had fled to the United States. The paper's reporting led to a formal government request for Ibarra's extradition.[94]

A similarly critical (though rhetorically restrained) stance appears to have prevailed in the vital area of government economic policy. In April 1994, as ortodoxo forces were marshaling for the decisive Special Congress of the FSLN, *Barricada* berated the government for its structural adjustment measures, accusing it of having "ceded fundamental economic levers to the control of international organizations." This, the paper editorialized, was tantamount to "a cession

87

of sovereignty. It is one thing to rely on advisors and the technical support of foreign experts; it is something very different when national decisions are totally subordinated to programs conceived and managed by international organizations."[95]

A further sense of *Barricada*'s posture vis-à-vis the UNO regime can be gleaned from a study of the paper's coverage during one of the tensest periods of postrevolutionary Nicaraguan politics: the massive transport strikes of September 1993. Taken as a whole, the coverage again appears to bolster contentions that *Barricada* adopted a strongly critical stance toward the government. But it also points to the paper's willingness to advance its own political and normative line, independent to some extent of the desires and pronouncements of FSLN leaders—notably Daniel Ortega, whose rhetoric was substantially more inflammatory, and who at the time was only a few months away from establishing his formal alliance with the ortodoxo current of the front.

The September strikes were a direct response to a new range of government-imposed taxes that hit the transport sector especially hard. In its early coverage of the strikes, *Barricada* laid the blame for the crisis squarely on the government's shoulders. "The protest of the transport workers and managers . . . was a mobilization without any party-political tint," read the first editorial on the subject. "No one is more guilty than the government of having provoked the unity of the transport workers."[96] Another editorial zeroed in on Minister of Finance Emilio Pereira: "As we have indicated on other occasions, the origin of the problem is that the government is faced with a dramatic decline in the collection of public finances. . . . Minister Pereira has refused to acknowledge this situation publicly, which is directly responsible for his failed negotiations with international bodies. As his only solution, he has opted to impose new taxes, which aggravate the situation of ungovernability in the country."[97]

Popular frustration soon boiled over into random violence and, eventually, deaths. *Barricada* lamented "unfortunate acts of violence" that nonetheless "should not obscure the civic character of the protests." But on 22 September, the paper published dramatic front-page photographs of the death of police commander Saúl Alvarez in a clash with an armed group of unspecified political affiliation. *Barricada* still stuck to its line of blaming the Chamorro government for "irresponsibly prolonging" the strike by refusing to negotiate with the protesters. But while Daniel Ortega was raging against "a murderous government" and directly accusing Violeta Chamorro and her key officials, Antonio Lacayo and Alfredo César, of responsibility for the officer's death, *Barricada* was drawing back from the brink. It acknowledged that the character of the protests had changed with the assassination; its support for the strikers softened accordingly. Reporter David Gutiérrez-López wrote on the same day, "The transport strike, which began . . . in an organized and relatively peaceful manner, yesterday degenerated into violence, anarchy, and vandalism carried out by groups of demonstrators." The following day, 23 September, an opinion piece appeared on the editorial page titled, "In defense of the police," wondering "why no one demanded that these 'workers' stop attacking the police."[98]

The paper's unwillingness, at this critical juncture, to climb on board with the more militant strand of FSLN opinion incurred the wrath of many within the front—especially Daniel Ortega. In retrospect, however, Carlos Fernando Chamorro was sanguine about *Barricada*'s coverage. "We simply put the facts," he shrugged, "and the front got very mad at us"—even though *Barricada* had compromised the objectivity of its stance by withholding information about "the degree to which certain elements of the front manipulated these strikes, provoking confrontations with the police and the death of certain people." What most angered the leadership, Chamorro said, was the decision to publish photos of the murdered Alvarez. At a September 1993 meeting of the Managua FSLN committee (discussed further in chapter 3), Chamorro was upbraided by militants who "wanted us to repeat Daniel Ortega's rhetorical speech saying, 'Saúl Alvarez was killed by President Chamorro'—something that didn't make sense. He was shot by someone on the other side who had a gun, and we had a picture of it. But they were very critical of that [editorial decision]. . . . My argument [at the meeting] was: even if the front decided from one day to the next to become ultraradical, *Barricada* should not necessarily follow as a newspaper. It should follow its *own* dynamic as a newspaper, not the front itself, because it was not a mirror of the party."[99]

We will see shortly that the paper was most likely to discount leadership preferences on the core issue of the legitimacy of violent struggle. Peaceful competition was the sine qua non of *Barricada*'s opposition strategy. Nonetheless, this shallow sampling of *Barricada*'s coverage in the early 1990s suggests that criticism of the ruling authorities *was* prominent in the paper's reporting and editorials. This evidence casts doubt on the more extreme ortodoxo depictions of *Barricada*'s posture during the years of the autonomy experiment.

A more general question remains to be asked. How did *Barricada*'s mobilizing origins, and the continuing close relationship with its FSLN sponsor, condition and constrain the paper's daily coverage and professional imperative? What trade-offs, both political and professional, were necessary in order to fulfill the enduring mobilizing imperative—to serve as a privileged space for the Sandinista Front and its leadership?

The Politics of Barricada II: Sandinismo and Self-Censorship

The defenestración of 1994 demonstrated vividly how fragile was *Barricada*'s position within the Sandinista Front. To maximize its autonomy vis-à-vis its sponsor, the newspaper was forced—or willingly chose—to subordinate the strict requirements of a professional imperative to the mobilizing role that remained central to its self-definition. Given the fractious internal politics of the front, this was a fine line to walk from the outset. It became increasingly delicate as the ortodoxo current of the front established unquestioned hegemony over the party apparatus in 1993–94. Most of the remainder of this chapter is devoted to an examination of the tradeoffs—the issues and policy areas in which *Barricada* plainly accepted mobilizing constraints; others in which its editorial policy was ambiguous, and which regularly attracted criticisms from the ortodoxo tendency; and one—the issue of violent struggle—in which the paper adamantly, perhaps fatefully, held to its own unswerving line while FSLN leaders and militants seemingly vacillated according to the perceived political requirements of the moment.

THE INTERNAL POLITICS OF THE FSLN

Upon its relaunching in January 1991, *Barricada* responded to criticisms of the paper's new orientation with a pledge "that we would not interfere in the internal affairs of the front," according to Carlos Fernando Chamorro. The basic editorial strategy adopted to balance mobilizing and professional imperatives in this sphere revolved around a distinction between formal editorializing, on the one hand, and opinions of individual writers and outside commentators, on the other. In an attempt to abide by mobilizing constraints while still cultivating "leaders of public opinion"—within the front as well as within the wider society—Chamorro and his editorial staff reserved the right to publish personal-opinion pieces that took strong stands in both the intraparty and the national debate. Several of these articles—like Chamorro's 1993 call for Humberto Ortega to resign as chief of the army—were as controversial as anything *Barricada* published during this period. In editorials, however, "It was clear that *Barricada* . . . would not make any comment" on the front's internal politics, according to Chamorro.[100] The Qualitative

Evaluation likewise stated that in the first year or so of the autonomy experiment, *Barricada*, "as a norm of editorial policy" (*como
norma de política editorial*), had "endeavored not to pronounce
itself on the question of the public debate of the FSLN."

One can certainly see the strategy at work in the period leading
up to the all-important May 1994 party congress. At that time, the
newspaper introduced a new section, *Congreso FSLN,* to orient
Sandinista militants for the debates to come. As its own contribution to the debate, though, *Barricada* pledged to work above all for
reconciliation among Sandinistas, and for a broad pluralism of
debate. The battle lines were as clearly drawn as they would ever be,
and the final showdown loomed; but even though senior *Barricada*
personnel were active on behalf of the renovationist current, the
paper was careful to preserve a formal neutrality in its editorials:
"We [at *Barricada*] are not a cathedral where dogmas are preached,
but a medium open to doubt, to intellectual honesty, constructive
controversy, the exchange of practical experiences to bring about
solutions. . . . The existence of distinct currents of opinion is a symp-
tom of the vitality of Sandinismo's democratization. *Barricada,* as a
medium of communication, has the responsibility to offer the reader
an exhaustive overview of this exchange of organized opinions."

"Finally," the editorial stressed, "we wish to inform the reader that
among the journalists and workers of *Barricada,* and members of its
editorial council, there exists a variety of personal opinions on the
subject of Sandinista debate, which they will express in the pages of
the daily under their own names. Only editorials represent the
official position of the newspaper."[101]

The reference to "a variety of personal opinions" among staff
merits closer examination. To my knowledge, at no time did any
senior *Barricada* writer actually take the opportunity to submit an
opinion piece that was strongly supportive of the ortodoxo current
within the front. True to its pledge, the newspaper regularly printed
the opinions of key ortodoxo activists and ideologues, such as Julio

López and Mónica Baltodano. But the ortodoxos could be forgiven for their belief that the sum contribution of *Barricada* personnel to the internal debate—notably the commentaries of Carlos Fernando Chamorro, Sofía Montenegro, and Daniel Alegría, all of whom were regular contributors to the op-ed page—tended strongly in a renovationist direction. The editorial council may have acknowledged as much. In the Qualitative Evaluation, it conceded that despite its best efforts, *Barricada* "could have given the impression" of taking an institutional stand in the intraparty debate. This subject deserves closer attention, which it receives in a separate section below.

THE PIÑATA

Of all the dubious actions that dogged the Sandinista Front through the early 1990s, none was pricklier than the *piñata*,[102] the term popularly attached to the outgoing Sandinista regime's stripping of state assets prior to the April 1990 handover of power. Sandinista leaders vigorously defended their actions—necessary, they said, to compensate thousands of militants who had worked for years with meager remuneration, or none at all. The piñata, argued leading ortodoxos like Rosario Murillo, was simply justice for services rendered:

> You had tens of thousands of people who were given the right to own the house they lived in, or the car they drove themselves around in, or the right to a piece of land to work when they were left without jobs. Those people came to you, pleading. . . . Mothers of martyrs; relatives of people that had given their lives for this revolution. They were asking for a freezer or refrigerator, so they could sell ice or *gaseosas* [sodas] from their houses, and earn some kind of living that way. We had buses to take them to Government House, where they were given something to help them provide for themselves. That's the piñata. Well, why not defend it?[103]

The Sandinistas anyway were forced to defend it, in the face of a sustained outcry from critics who pointed to numerous apparent abuses in the process—including the comfortable home in the upper-class Managua neighborhood of Reparto El Carmen acquired, for a token payment of $3,000, by Daniel Ortega and his partner—Rosario Murillo.[104] With the front's leadership constantly on the defensive over the piñata, *Barricada* was the very last quarter from which criticism would be tolerated. Carlos Fernando Chamorro, and others at the paper, got the message. Throughout the four years of the autonomy experiment, the piñata was an unmentionable subject—perhaps the most unmentionable of all. "We never had an editorial on the internal abuses of Sandinismo, nothing at all," said Chamorro. He called it "the most powerful concession I made to the front," but also an inevitable one. Coverage of the piñata was "unmanageable." Bayardo Arce, the National Directorate's representative to the recently formed editorial council, "would never have accepted it. It was a matter of him or myself. If I wanted *Barricada* to get involved in that issue, he would [have said] to me, 'Well, I quit, or you quit.' . . . It's not that we got to that point, but it was very clear that this was a kind of taboo."[105]

Once again, though, the line drawn between editorials and opinion pieces permitted an oblique reconnaissance or two of the mine-laden terrain. "We accepted some *opiniones* from others [outside the newspaper]," said Chamorro, "but they were always very, very costly. The front would get very angry if we accepted opinion pieces from critical Sandinistas saying, 'We have to discuss this openly, we have to clean up the problems.' I think that is the most important topic, and the most important limitation that we had, seeing ourselves as an institution that included, as one of its goals, helping in the transformation of Sandinismo."

THE OTHER ORTEGA

When Humberto Ortega—a founding member of the FSLN's Tercerista tendency during the 1970s, and chief of the army while his brother, Daniel, was president—was allowed to continue in his role into the era of Violeta Chamorro, it served as one of the most visible signs of concertación and co-gobierno. Ortega's leadership assured Sandinistas that the institutional legacy of the revolution would not be entirely dismantled under the UNO regime, and that the country's dominant left-opposition force would not be exposed to the kind of savage suppression by the national-security apparatus that was standard across Latin America. Throughout the early 1990s, though, right-wing calls mounted for Ortega's dismissal, and his replacement by a figure who would better reflect the postrevolutionary reality as the FSLN's critics—and some within the front—perceived it. Confronted with this mounting opposition, the National Directorate closed ranks. Their position, said Carlos Fernando Chamorro, "was that if [Ortega] wanted to stay on for ten more years, fine. If they had a different view, they would never say it in public."

The sensitivity of the subject again prevented *Barricada* from engaging with it as fully and openly as Chamorro and other staffers might have preferred. "We had very careful editorials about the army," Chamorro acknowledged. This, though, was not enough to preserve *Barricada* from criticism. "Just by covering the facts!" Chamorro protested. "Just by covering the facts you could have a problem with the front, with Daniel Ortega, and with the army." In August 1993, as calls for Ortega's dismissal grew in volume, Chamorro went a step further. He published a personal-opinion piece, "The Exit of General Ortega," in which he argued that Ortega "should make way for the choice of a new chief . . . in the interest of the military" as a national institution.[106] (Ortega eventually stepped down in 1996, to be replaced by Joaquín Cuadra—another former Sandinista.) The article predictably provoked a fierce response from ortodoxo ranks.[107] It could also be expected to rouse the ire of Humberto's brother, whose role in truncating the autonomy experiment would prove decisive a year later.

HUMAN RIGHTS

The revolutionary past and oppositionist present of both *Barricada* and its FSLN sponsor drew the paper naturally toward an editorial stance aimed at promoting and defending the human rights of all Nicaraguans. The political and professional imperatives that guided the new *Barricada* were founded on a defense of constitutional freedoms—those enshrined, of course, in the constitution the FSLN itself had drafted in the latter half of the 1980s. Nonetheless, *Barricada*'s zeal in pursuing the subject during the years of semi-autonomy seemed a little pallid, compared with its vigorous investigations into corruption and economic mismanagement under the UNO regime. The reason, according to Chamorro, was that "human rights are very politicized here, and there's one side of the story, which is Sandinistas violating human rights." The taboo against delving into the FSLN's own behavior placed *Barricada* in an awkward position when it came to the actions of the UNO government. The paper, said Chamorro, was "more or less consistent in trying to find a balance" on the human rights issue. But *Barricada* never succeeded in becoming a point of reference—a public-opinion leader—in this area.

The issue of the legitimacy of violent struggle in postrevolutionary Nicaragua, which arose with such urgency during the transport strikes and at other key junctures, marked one point of divergence between *Barricada* and certain FSLN leaders (not to mention a good portion of the front's militant base). The subject receives more detailed treatment below, but is worth touching on here as an example of the mobilizing constraints that operated in the area of human rights coverage. Asked if he had been aware of links between the FSLN and armed groups within Nicaragua, especially the so-called *recompas* in the northern countryside, Chamorro responded: "Yeah. We were aware, we had perceptions, but we did not investigate that. Probably we unconsciously didn't want to find out some ugly things."

"LET'S PUT IT this way," said Chamorro of these taboo subjects. "We were conscious that these were not our main topics. We did not hide them, but we did not pretend to be the 'owners' of these topics. We covered our appearances. If anyone wanted to accuse you of hiding the truth, we would say, 'No, we're not hiding the truth. Here it is.' [But] probably you could say, 'Well, why don't you dig more deeply?' That's another question." The answer would likely say a great deal about the complex trade-offs involved in balancing *Barricada*'s enduring revolutionary obligations with the professional agenda that its staff was now working to implement and deepen.

On no occasion were these complexities cast in such stark relief as when *Barricada* broke the story of the Buzón de Santa Rosa—perhaps the greatest scoop the paper could claim in its two decades of publication. "That was a big story," Chamorro said proudly in 1996. At issue was a large cache of weapons and forged documents uncovered in a suburban Managua neighborhood in May 1993. The cache's existence was not the story—it had been revealed by police. What was *not* known, until *Barricada* published the details, was the complicity of El Salvador's Fuerzas Populares de Liberación (Popular Forces of Liberation; FPL) in stashing the arms—in collusion with the terrorist forces of the Basque ETA.[108] When *Barricada*'s star investigative journalist, the late Noel Irías, traced the web of complicity to its source, *Barricada* became "the first medium, [whether a] newspaper or radio station, to talk about the existence of the network and all these false documents." The next day, Chamorro remembered, "we had dozens of telephone calls—from Mexico, the United States, everywhere. Everybody wanted to know about our story. We did it very well."

But whatever professional pride *Barricada* staffers felt when the news broke on the paper's front page, it was hardly shared by the FPL—which still maintained close ties with the FSLN leadership. Salvadorean representatives paid a visit to the newspaper at the behest of leading ortodoxo intellectual (and *Barricada*'s future subdirector)

Julio López. In Carlos Fernando Chamorro's recollection: "I had a private meeting with representatives of the FPL, who asked me not to create problems for them. I said, 'Listen, this is a public investigation. Everybody else is looking for it. We're not going to do extra damage to you; but it's better if *we* do it than if others do it.' They were upset, obviously. They thought that because we were political friends, we were supposed to hide their problems. And we said, 'We cannot hide this.'"

The FPL were not the only ones to take umbrage at *Barricada*'s coverage. For many Sandinista ortodoxos, the former official organ was rubbing salt in the wounds of revolutionary movements throughout Central America. The reporting was further proof that *Barricada* had betrayed the mobilizing imperative that gave it birth.

In the case of the buzón saga, *Barricada* chose to emphasize professional considerations over mobilizing ones. When the chips were down, though, this was rarely the case. The off-limits areas laid down by the FSLN leadership were largely respected. The quid pro quo that Carlos Fernando Chamorro demanded in return for abiding by these constraints was the front's respect for *Barricada*'s own institutional identity and professional agenda—a recognition that the paper, in turn, required concessions from the leadership. Said Chamorro in 1996: "I was very conscious that it was one thing to be a political party dealing with the government, and another thing to be a newspaper that was being judged every day by public opinion. We had to take stands at different moments of the conflictual relationship between the party and the government, and we did not always follow the front's line, the official line."[109]

The FSLN, Violence, and Barricada: A Closer Look

On no subject did *Barricada* hold more adamantly to its own editorial line, regardless of feelings within the front, than on the legitimacy of violent struggle. "I developed a very strong conviction," Chamorro said simply, "that one could not make any concessions on that issue." The paper, here, was exploiting—but also implicitly denouncing—the leadership's uncertain stance on the issue, which Chamorro characterized as riddled with "ambiguity [and] double standards . . . saying one thing but doing another." Such equivocation "probably made me much more suspicious of the leadership. . . . I was very careful in the newspaper that we should not follow the front on that."[110]

Nonviolence was central not only to the pluralistic political project favored by nearly all *Barricada* editorial staff, but to the very conception of the newspaper as a public-opinion leader for the wider society. *Barricada* had a responsibility to "help establish a certain tone for political discourse," Sofía Montenegro argued in 1991, as the paper's new profile was first being presented to readers. "If *Barricada* lowers its voice and seeks to encourage tolerance, it creates pressure on others to follow suit."[111] Around the same time, Guillermo Cortés also spoke of Nicaraguan "society as a whole . . . moving toward a new way of being, of resolving problems—of talking *to* each other, not shooting *at* each other." The only appropriate political *and* professional response, he suggested, was for *Barricada* to promote the trend.[112]

Violence was so fundamental an issue because it so palpably threatened to tear Nicaragua apart during the early 1990s. Its ravages, moreover, remained vivid in the collective consciousness of the population. In the space of a decade and a half, Nicaragua had known the thuggery of the Somoza dictatorship, the civil war of the 1970s, and the protracted siege and contra war of the 1980s. Since the fall of the Sandinista regime, numerous small-scale clashes had occurred between armed groups of recontras and recompas—and between both groups and the security forces of the UNO government.

Against this backdrop, a powerful lobby within Sandinismo called on the FSLN to renounce any use of violence to contest or regain power. Early on, in fact, with concertación and co-gobierno all the rage, this came close to being a consensus position—at least for public consumption. The consensus was spelled out at the FSLN's first postrevolutionary gathering, at the aptly named town of El Crucero (The crossroads) in June 1990. Sofía Montenegro describes the dominant strand of opinion at El Crucero this way: "One decision was that we would abide by the law and the rules we ourselves implanted in the country: to respect the results of the elections, and also [to reject] recourse to violence. Another decision was that we should be a critical opposition, but not a destabilizing opposition. And finally, we would begin to democratize the party: to reorganize the elections and the leadership; to replace the [traditional] leadership with an emerging leadership; and to recompose the force of the front."[113]

With hindsight, though, it seems clear that from the outset of the post-Sandinista era, a minority of Sandinistas never reconciled themselves to the surrender of power. They shared the view of most Sandinistas (and this author) that the 1990 elections had been skewed against the FSLN by a U.S. government in intimate alliance with domestic forces of reaction. Montenegro again:

> There was a big discussion as to whether the Sandinista Front would resort to armed struggle or not, immediately after the election. There was a minority that said at that meeting [El Crucero], and the [July 1991] congress after that, that armed struggle shouldn't be renounced. The hard-liners said, We should never give up the weapons; there is a reason still to believe in armed struggle in Nicaragua. The majority of the [Sandinista] Assembly voted no. . . . This the minority accepted, because they were *in* a minority at the moment of voting; but they never really accepted it in their hearts.[114]

The perils of co-gobierno allowed plenty of opportunities for this minority viewpoint to surface—sometimes violently, but more often obliquely or clandestinely. The more bellicose strand of Sandinista thinking gained strength as concertación and co-gobierno eroded between 1991 and 1993. On 11 July 1993, the Group of 29—the first organized expression of ortodoxo thinking within the front—issued its call for the FSLN to return "to lead[ing] the popular struggle, distancing itself clearly from the government."[115] Finally, in September 1993, in the wake of the violent transport strikes of that month, the FSLN leadership fired what seems in retrospect to have been the first salvo of the 1996 election campaign. It formally renounced the policy of coexistence and in no uncertain terms distanced itself from the economic and social policies of the Chamorro regime. The policy shift was accompanied by a ratcheting-up of rhetoric on all sides of the political conflict, bringing the question of violence once more to the fore. Earlier in the year, Daniel Ortega had "reject[ed] all involvement with armed groups" (April)[116] and joined the business organization COSEP in stating that "all types of armed activity in the countryside are inadmissible" (July).[117] Now he issued his call for Nicaraguans to "struggle" against "a murderous government" (*un gobierno asesino*)—not a direct endorsement of armed struggle, by any means, but a highly inflammatory outburst nonetheless.[118] At the end of the year, he was quoted telling *El Semanario* that "the Sandinistas are capable of making a new revolution, of rebelling if necessary."[119]

As a new conflagration loomed, *Barricada* remained staunch in its condemnation of violence, whether perpetrated by forces of the left or right. Any number of examples can be cited to bolster the assertion of a basic consistency in the paper's political line; the language varies little. Typical was the editorial page condemnation of tit-for-tat kidnappings and armed assaults by leftists and rightists carried out in August 1994. *Barricada* denounced all such actions "with the same energy," arguing that "violence only engenders more violence, and this spate of armed kidnappings carries with it the risk of bringing the country to the brink of anarchy."[120]

Barricada's coverage of two of the most serious outbursts of violence, both orchestrated by leftist organizations, provides further evidence of the paper's conviction that the issue transcended the mobilizing imperatives of the front. In July 1993 forces of the Revolutionary Worker-Peasant Front (FROC), led by an ex-major of the Sandinista People's Army and consisting mostly of demobilized Sandinista soldiers, launched an armed attack against the northern city of Estelí. Forty-five people were killed in the fighting, and nearly a hundred others injured, mostly civilians. *Barricada* angrily derided the "lamentable tragedy, in which an insensitive and pseudo-revolutionary [FROC] leadership sought to carry the war to the cities, and ended up confronting their ex-comrades-in-arms [the Sandinista-dominated police and armed forces] with whom yesterday they defended together the institutions of the country."[121]

The other controversy related to the actions of the Punitive Forces of the Left (FPI). The strategy of this shadowy organization, Carlos Fernando Chamorro bluntly contended, "was not popular violence, it was terrorism": "They came out with leaflets saying they were going to kill all the rightists—with a list, you know, like those death squads in Guatemala. At first, it looked really crazy. You could say, 'Well, maybe this is an invention of the CIA,' or whatever. But after a certain period, they killed a rightist—he was the head of the Asociación de Confiscados [an organization founded to represent those whose land or other holdings had been confiscated by the Sandinista government during the 1980s]."

Chamorro took for granted the existence of links between the FPI and senior figures within the FSLN. "It ended up that the head of the FPI was a lieutenant-colonel of the army. . . . These groups were paramilitary forces created by the front with the approval of Daniel and Humberto Ortega. It was clear." And "the official position of the front," in Chamorro's view, "was some kind of silent complicity with these groups." The point was driven home forcefully when Chamorro reiterated his opposition to violence at a meeting of the Sandinista Assembly, to which he was a delegate. "When I'd finished, someone came to me—I will not tell you who—and said, 'I think you shouldn't say this type of thing. These compañeros are fighting to defend the popular interest.'" Chamorro allowed that his interlocutor was "someone at the leadership level of the front."

Rather than bending to such pressure, Chamorro said he chose to write articles that decisively distanced *Barricada* from the FPI's actions, "criticiz[ing them] from a left point of view":

I took it personally, as something I thought was very dangerous for the front. And if Daniel Ortega did not want to distance himself from it, I said, "OK, that's his problem. That's the front's problem. But I'm going to make it clear to the public that this newspaper, as long as I am the editor, is not going to conciliate with these groups." OK? Daniel never condemned it. The National Directorate made a decision that the front should take a stand very strongly against [violent struggle]. [Ortega] took the communiqué and put it in a drawer. The public never saw it.

Whether Ortega was truly prepared to champion violence as a means of regaining struggle, or whether he was merely displaying the political opportunism for which he had long been renowned, is impossible to say. Even if his ambivalence was merely opportunistic, however, the comandante appears to have grown increasingly chagrined at *Barricada*'s failure to follow his example—a subject explored at much greater length in chapter 3.

The Autonomy Experiment: Summary and Evaluation

How, in closing, to measure the appeal of this hybrid model of pro-revolutionary journalism implemented during the years of semi-autonomy? A question that has lapped at the edges of the analysis so far concerns the allegations of sectarianism and intraparty favoritism that dogged *Barricada* from the moment it began to move out from under the FSLN's shadow in mid-1990. *Barricada*'s critics claimed the autonomy project was a thinly veiled attempt to direct the revolutionary impetus of Sandinismo in a renovationist—hence counterrevolutionary—direction. Was the balance and professionalism that *Barricada* now claimed to be pursuing only a chimera, an excuse to abandon the interests of the popular classes and advance the cause of reaction? Was *Barricada*'s "neutral" editorial stance in the internal party debate simply a façade to disguise the renovationist hammerlock on the FSLN's media flagship?

The character of such charges was evident very early in the post-Sandinista era; only its constituency widened as the ortodoxo strand gained ascendancy in the intraparty struggle. Indeed, one of the most virulent attacks against the paper was launched even before the parameters of the autonomy experiment became clear in early 1991. In September 1990 the paper's tentative new editorial approach—especially its soliciting of a broader range of sources and op-ed commentary—brought a blistering denunciation from Rosario Murillo (who at the time actually edited *Barricada*'s weekly cultural supplement, *Ventana*). Murillo published her broadside in *El Nuevo Diario*, under the Zolaesque headline: "I Accuse the Sect!" *Barricada,* she alleged, had fallen under the control of a "Fourth Power . . . which has for a long time been granting itself exclusive property rights over criticism within the Sandinista Front; [and] which has made use of the Sandinista Front's media, funded by the FSLN, for the purposes of personal projection, both at the level of ideas and currents and at the level of appointing themselves alternative figures of the revolution." Both the daily and Sofía Montenegro's supplement, *Gente,* she asserted, had

> been used . . . to promote hatred of women toward men [an apparent reference to Montenegro's feminism], antiparty feeling, and disrespect for the revolution's symbols. . . . The "independence" our media outlets demand from the Sandinista Front is used to attack and discredit the Sandinista Front. . . . Sandinista leaders are relegated to the inside pages of those media outlets while either the ruling family is highlighted [an indirect dig at Carlos Fernando

Chamorro], or those the sect is interested in highlighting, for ends that are not only not in the FSLN's interests but are often harmful to them. . . . What merit is there in having been promoters, from media outlets paid for with Sandinista blood, of popular rejection of the Sandinista Front, of disunity in the Sandinista Front, from the leaders to the grassroots, of the weakening of Sandinista policies, of the discrediting from beginning to end of the Sandinista Front's heroic effort to survive the confrontation with the [U.S.] empire . . . ?

"I am in favour of the Revolution's media playing an active role in criticism of our political action in all areas," Murillo wrote. "But criticism is one thing and discrediting and destruction another."[122]

Many observers dismissed Murillo's comments as sour grapes: a reflection of the fact that *Ventana* was perhaps the most opaque, and apparently the least popular, of *Barricada*'s weekly supplements, while Montenegro's *Gente* substantially boosted the paper's circulation on the day it appeared. (*Ventana* would eventually be closed due to lack of funds, after the 1991 FSLN congress.) But her visceral outrage at the notion of a privileged Sandinista space being defiled by reactionary content and commentary[123] became a touchstone for ortodoxo objections in the years leading up to the defenestración. One can see it reflected in a letter published in *Gente* just before Chamorro's dismissal, signed by the executive secretariat of the Committee for Solidarity with Cuba. The letter criticized *Gente*'s publishing of an article, written by a Cuban journalist in exile, that was strongly critical of Fidel Castro's regime: "Nicaraguans have seen a 180-degree turn in the positions taken by *Barricada,* which proclaims that it exists to serve the national interest and pretends to [have] an objectivity that is absolutely false, as evidenced by the fact that in twelve pages of the aforementioned weekly [*Gente*], three— that is, 25 percent of the total content—were dedicated to . . . a very dignified treatment [*una crónica muy digna*] of an article by a member of the Cuban exile community."[124]

In *Barricada*'s pages immediately following the defenestración, supporters of the paper's new directorate echoed these viewpoints. On the editorial page of 9 November 1994, Juan Carlos Sarmiento inquired of a cross-section of respondents in the city of Matagalpa what they thought of *Barricada* before the defenestración. Respondents from the "popular sectors," he reported, referred to *Barricada* as "rightist, in the service of the government, and the exclusive redoubt of the renovationists." He concluded that *Barricada* under Carlos Fernando Chamorro "had ceased to place emphasis on coverage of the popular sectors." Instead, it had buttressed the informational agenda of the UNO regime (*se mantenía la dinámica informativa con gobierno*), and sought support from the business class and anti-Sandinista political parties. "The popular sectors were reduced to the municipal page and, on rare occasions, to other pages. . . . Opinion pieces were not published in a balanced way; rather, in the pages devoted to these, more room was granted to the writings of those who today are renouncing the FSLN."[125]

Implicit in this line of criticism, from Murillo's opening salvo on down, was a rigid mobilizing conception of Sandinista mass media. "If the [former] director of *Barricada* was committed to those [reno-vationists] who renounced the FSLN," proclaimed Daniel Ortega in March 1995, "the decent thing to do would have been to give up his position, but he insisted on keeping it." Ortega's argument seemed somewhat circular—Sergio Ramírez did not resign from the front until a couple of months after Chamorro's dismissal (chapter 3). What is interesting, though, is the tacit assumption that the director of *Barricada* (and thus the newspaper as a whole) should reflect the leanings and wishes of the dominant opinion within the front. Tomás Borge was similarly blithe in this regard, stating in an interview published shortly after he took over as *Barricada*'s director, "If you had to find a compañero with professional journalistic qualities, with the popular touch [*don de gente*], and other virtues, you'd have to say that person is Carlos Fernando Chamorro. If instead you sought a driving force [*conductor*] for the newspaper identified with the revolutionary objectives of the FSLN, in harmony with its projection of power and its programmatic lines, in the present conditions that person is not Carlos Fernando Chamorro. It's a shame that both characteristics didn't coincide."[126]

Was the link between *Barricada* and the renovationist forces as intimate as the paper's detractors contended? The extent to which true diversity of opinion existed at *Barricada* is a subject of continuing dispute. Borge claimed after the defenestración that *Barricada*'s autonomy project had led it to an "align[ment] with a fraction of the FSLN," at which point it "began to abandon national interests in order to place itself at the service of a minority group." Some evidence that this was indeed the case has already been cited: the public involvement of several senior staff in the renovationist bloc; the paucity of pro-ortodoxo commentary penned by *Barricada* writers themselves from 1990 to 1994. But if few staffers chose to back the ortodoxos, this does not mean that *Barricada* was institutionally bound to an organized renovationist wing. For one thing, that "wing" is at least as much the creation of outside observers as of any coherent force within the front. For most commentators, the renovationist tendency was linked to Sergio Ramírez's Movimiento de Renovación Sandinista (MRS), which contested the 1996 elections independently of the front, attracting a derisory proportion of the overall vote. But there is no significant evidence of collusion between *Barricada* staffers and Ramírez's nascent political party. Nor did my research turn up any indication of significant pro-Ramírez commentary in the paper, apart from op-ed pieces submitted by Ramírez himself (who was, after all, among the most prominent Sandinista figures: vice president under Daniel Ortega in the 1980s; leader of the FSLN parliamentary bench from 1990 to 1994; and a leading poet and novelist in a nation—and revolutionary movement—of poets and novelists). "Look, I'm not a *ramirista*," said Daniel Alegría, the senior editor at *Barricada* who would replace Carlos Fernando Chamorro for a brief period after the defenestración. "Neither is Roberto [Fonseca], neither is Sergio de Castro"—Chamorro's seconds in command during the early era of semiautonomy.[127] Chamorro's own evaluation is congruent. "I would say that a majority of the people on the *Barricada* staff did not take sides with anyone," he argued in 1996. "A few people sided with the [renovationist] *corriente de las mayorías,* others with the other [DL] group. But the majority did not take sides, for whatever reasons."[128] Probably the most outspoken and activist of *Barricada*'s senior editors, Sofía Montenegro, was so famously icono-clastic that it was difficult to imagine her seeking the embrace of *any* organized political party.

We are left, then, with a range of opinion and commentary by *Barricada* staff that tended in a broadly renovationist direction, along with four signatures appended to the seminal "mayorías" proclamation of early 1994. If this indeed constituted a bias on the newspaper's part, did the concept of impartiality integral to the new professional imperative offer any meaningful counterweight? There is evidence it might have. First, *Barricada*'s coverage of the key 1994 party congress suggests no pronounced tilt against the ortodoxo current. The paper seems to have stuck scrupulously to a neutral line at precisely the time one might have expected it to come down firmly on one side or another. (If not quite a foregone conclusion at the time of the congress, the defenestración was certainly a palpable possibility as the balance of forces within the front became clearer.)

There is the further fact that numerous think pieces by leading ortodoxo commentators did make it onto *Barricada*'s op-ed page in the early 1990s. Julio López, Mónica Baltodano, Daniel Ortega, and other architects of Chamorro's dismissal all put in regular appearances.[129] When the declaration of the ortodoxo Group of 29 was made public in July 1993, *Barricada* responded not with an editorial refuting the proclamation, but with a front-page headline noting rather blandly that the document had "reopen[ed] debate in [the] FSLN." It published two pages of diverse opinion pieces, both pro and con; four days later, it turned over the entire *Debate* page to dueling representatives of the ortodoxo and renovationist currents. Lastly, it should be noted that field research, including interviews with noted ortodoxos, turned up neither evidence nor allegations that opinion pieces submitted by adherents of that current were ever rejected, even for ostensibly professional or space reasons.[130]

If a preponderance of op-ed commentary in *Barricada* nonetheless followed a broadly renovationist line, it is fair to ask whether this might partly reflect the self-imposed constraints of the ortodoxos themselves. Carlos Fernando Chamorro expressed frustration that arrows were slung at *Barricada* from ortodoxo quarters more commonly than opinion pieces were actually submitted for publication. The ortodoxo perception of *Barricada* as one-sided may have had a self-fulfilling dimension. As well, Chamorro pointed out, "probably the people who were more used to writing for newspapers were [in general] more critical of the front's official line at that point. Not many people write in newspapers, or write articles with a certain quality—not simply letters or declarations." The Qualitative Evaluation of 1992 also touched on this point, acknowledging that "intellectual sectors" of the population were disproportionately represented in *Barricada,* and noting that such sectors were generally more "critical of the process of institutionalization in the FSLN"—that is, sympathetic to the broadly renovationist strand (with its emphasis on the internal democratization of the front) versus the more "vanguardist" ortodoxos. The evaluation argued, though, that this was merely "a natural expression of the lack of a tradition of debate among FSLN cadres, together with the greater interest and possibility of expression of these [intellectual] sectors."[131] A class variable may also have made its influence felt here. The ortodoxos were more likely, as events proved, to command the allegiance of Sandinista militants at the base. Most Sandinistas in the popular sectors—like most Nicaraguans—were too preoccupied with the daily struggle for survival to write opinion pieces for *Barricada,* in the unlikely event that they had developed a facility for it.

The appraisal of the uniquely positioned Alfonso Malespín (see chapter 4) allows greater purchase on the controversy that swirled around *Barricada* in the early 1990s, resulting, finally, in the orto-doxos' vetoing of the autonomy experiment. "What happened was not so much that [*Barricada*'s directors] were involved with the MRS," said Malespín, "but rather, they had made the decision to make a professional newspaper." Ortega and the ortodoxos, meanwhile, "wanted a newspaper that was clearly identified with the [dominant] political line of the party."[132] In this sense, the old feminist maxim that the personal is the political can be dusted off and slightly revised. For both *Barricada* and its enemies, the *professional* was the political. Any Sandinista institution that claimed for itself the right to determine an appropriate blending of mobilizing versus professional considerations could not help but align itself, in some sense, with the current of Sandinista opinion that recognized such a right. Likewise, it could not but clash with the increasingly dominant strand that sought to reimpose greater central control over key front institutions. I will show in the next chapter that this struggle for hegemony over the party apparatus, including *Barricada,* was the defining feature of ortodoxo strategy between 1991 and 1994. The beliefs almost universally held by *Barricada* staff in these years were not consistent political ones per se, but derived from a common commitment to the autonomy project and the professional imperative that underpinned it.

If doubt remains on this score, consider the statement signed by thirty-seven *Barricada* staff members in September 1994, just before the defenestración. The statement included an overview of the paper's recent evolution and presented a clear vision of "jour-nalism in a democratic society":

In January 1991, *Barricada* ceased to be a party-political institution. It is [now] a journalistic enterprise, where positions are filled accord-ing to professional merit, experience, and responsibility for one's work [*responsabilidad laboral*].

We *Barricada* journalists are united in our commitment to profes-sional and ethical journalism, dedicated fundamentally to [the needs

of] readers, stressing from a Sandinista perspective the right to freedom of expression, respect for diversity of opinions, the democratization of society, the defense of national interests and service to the
community.

These rights that we stress for all society, we also stress for ourselves:
the existence of a plurality [of ideas] and the right to express our own
political opinions, as a result of which we consider any attempt to
restrict us unacceptable.

. . . It is for this reason that we consider the autonomy of the daily
must be extended even further, insofar as Nicaraguan society in its
totality demands greater informational objectivity and impartiality in
recording the facts.[133]

Beyond the question of factional affiliation, it remains to consider
Barricada's success, during the years of semiautonomy, in establishing itself as a leader of public opinion for the wider society. This is
naturally impossible to gauge with any certainty: "You don't measure
that by doing a poll," Carlos Fernando Chamorro acknowledged.
Nonetheless, Chamorro and other staffers claimed a high degree of
success, in purely professional terms, for *Barricada*'s autonomy project. "We were number one in [national] influence," said
Chamorro,[134] a verdict echoed by Daniel Alegría: "*Barricada* perhaps wasn't the most-read newspaper, but it *was* the one with the
most credibility. It really made opinion, formed opinion. It was a reference point, more than the other papers." As evidence, Alegría cited
the fact that "when we took people, ministers, to task, things would
happen. . . . Things would actually change. And other papers would
then pick it up."[135] Chamorro said he observed signs of *Barricada*'s
growing influence among constituencies that had once shied away
from the paper:

We were offering stories that were deeper than the others. We were
always proposing topics in advance of the other newspapers, and we
were setting an agenda—not the agenda of the country, but we had
a[n agenda-setting] capacity that the other newspapers didn't have.

... The U.S. embassy is not my point of reference for making a good or a bad newspaper. But when foreigners came to Nicaragua and went to the U.S. embassy, they were always told: "The best newspaper in this country is *Barricada.*" Professionals, people from the private sector, would say, "Well, it's a pity, but I have to tell you that *Barricada* is a better newspaper than *La Prensa.* I have to accept that. The fucking Sandinistas are making a better newspaper than *La Prensa.*"[136]

A number of turning points appeared to assist *Barricada* in establishing professional credibility among these nontraditional sectors. An early, dramatic example was the article by Victor Tirado, a member of the National Directorate from its inception, published in *Barricada* on the anniversary of the Sandinista revolution in 1991. Tirado placed the FSLN's election defeat in a wider, indeed global, context. "We have completed the anti-imperialist cycle of revolution," he wrote, "in which the main method was armed struggle and the aggressive use of political and diplomatic philosophy toward imperialism with the aim of destroying it definitively.... Revolutions of this kind cannot sustain their economies and militarily defend themselves all alone; now [i.e., in the wake of the collapse of the Soviet bloc] there is nobody to subsidize them."[137] As an apparent obituary for the forces of revolutionism, at least as traditionally conceived, Tirado's piece confounded some Sandinistas in the same way the National Directorate decision to open negotiations with the contras had staggered many believers in 1987 (see chapter 1). Another seminal moment also occurred not long after the formal relaunching, when *Barricada* commissioned and published the results of an opinion poll that, in Chamorro's words, "made it quite clear that Arnoldo Alemán"—then mayor of Managua, subsequently Nicaragua's president—was not only "a rising figure," but was actually more popular with Nicaraguans than FSLN leader Daniel Ortega. Many readers and critics, according to Chamorro, had presumed that, given longstanding mobilizing constraints, "no Sandinista media would dare to publish a poll in which Daniel Ortega was not the leading figure."[138]

Perhaps the most significant turning point was *Barricada*'s unveiling of Salvadorean guerrilla involvement in the Buzón de Santa Rosa, detailed earlier. *Barricada*'s coverage here does seem to have set the agenda domestically and even internationally, despite the strong objections voiced by one of the Sandinistas' closest allies and by many within the front itself. The emphasizing of professional over mobilizing considerations, Chamorro indicated, impressed outside observers more than any piece the paper ran: "Probably that is the story that more or less made quite clear—to the Americans, to the diplomatic community, to people in Costa Rica and Mexico—that we were a real newspaper, and no longer a propaganda newspaper."[139]

The professional bonds established with the conservative San José daily *La Nación*, leading to the joint investigation with *Barricada* of Nicaraguan emigrants to Costa Rica, likewise bolstered *Barricada*'s standing in the eyes of nontraditional constituencies. According to Chamorro, the joint venture impressed many among the Nicaraguan bourgeoisie and diplomatic community. It was also a nicely timed professional stab at *Barricada*'s right-wing rival *La Prensa*, which considered itself, with reason, the likelier partner for such a venture.

If these evaluations seem overly subjective, we do not entirely lack firmer evidence of *Barricada*'s strategic successes during this period. Two small-sample reader surveys were conducted during the era of semiautonomy—both in 1994, the second only a few months before the defenestración that brought the autonomy experiment to a close. The first survey was not commissioned by *Barricada*, but by its new rival on the newsstands, *La Tribuna*—which may lend it an added measure of interest. In May 1994, J. R. Castillo y Asociados, a business consultancy firm, carried out one hundred interviews with respondents from "all sectors of society" in the capital city—though the fact that many respondents seemed accustomed to reading more than one newspaper suggests a more upmarket sampling. The results were as follows:

Daily newspapers customarily read
[*que acostumbran más leer*] by respondents

La Prensa	64%
Barricada	60%
La Tribuna	32%
El Nuevo Diario	32%
El Semanario (weekly)	2%

Readers' preference [*la preferencia de los
lectores encuestados*] among daily newspapers

Barricada	37%
La Prensa	34%
La Tribuna	15%
El Nuevo Diario	12%
El Semanario	2%[140]

A still smaller, but more in-depth survey was commissioned by *Barricada* itself and carried out by M and R Consultants in August 1994.[141] It is tempting to see it as an effort to marshal evidence for presentation to the National Directorate, in a last attempt to head off the impending coup against *Barricada*. If so, it was a futile endeavor; but the survey does offer some insight into the thinking of *Barricada*'s regular and nontraditional constituencies alike. It sampled the opinions of four distinct groups of readers (though only nine or ten respondents in each): Newspaper readers who didn't read *Barricada* (subdivided into middle and popular classes); and regular *Barricada* readers, all defined as middle-class, but subdivided into Managua and regional respondents. The questions asked of each group were: "What are the changes that we could introduce in order to increase our market influence, and what are the principal strengths and weaknesses of the newspapers with the greatest market share?"

The survey found that nonreaders of *Barricada* still associated the paper with "the image of the official organ that the newspaper had before 1991." *Barricada* was perceived as a *partidista* publication, one that still "accommodated itself in every aspect of its functioning to the interests of the party." The propaganda stigma was clearly hard to shake. By contrast, "In general, the regular readers of the *Barricada* daily view the paper very favorably; they are satisfied with the newspaper. Among the major suggestions they make is that the current process should continue, of transforming the publication into a genuine instrument of information, education, and recreation for readers." Readers who preferred *Barricada* to the other dailies based their preference on the following, according to the survey:

1. It is very professional and high quality, both in its informational content and its presentation. Possibly the best journalists [in Nicaragua] are to be found at this newspaper.

2. It is seeking independence. It is moving from being a propaganda organ to [being] a serious daily. . . . There is still a long way to go, but progress is being made.

3. It is varied, well balanced, with a little of everything [*de todo un poco*].

4. It is attractive and well presented.

The favorite sections of the newspaper, for the regular readership, were: "1. the front page, 2. *De todo un poco,* 3. the horoscope, 4. international news, 5. sports, [and] 6. departmental [regional] news." (As a weekly supplement, *Gente* was not included in this survey, but was cited as being "regularly read" by respondents.)

Barricada's market share, the survey's authors opined, was "small but solid." Further outreach was required among readers of *La Prensa* and *El Nuevo Diario.* In order to "make incursions" into these constituencies, the firm recommended that *Barricada* "deepen the process of political autonomy," preserving a "critical and self-critical" editorial line. "*Barricada*'s main competitor," the researchers wrote, "is not *La Prensa* or *El Nuevo Diario,* but the stigma of THE PAST [*LO QUE FUE;* emphasis in original]. . . . *Barricada* carries the slogan 'IN THE NATIONAL INTEREST.' What is missing is an effective demonstration to the marketplace of readers in this country that this slogan has been put into practice."

Again, the sample size of both surveys is small, and the results of the latter may partially offset *Barricada*'s claim to have won significant credibility among nontraditional constituencies. Still, neither sample gives reason to doubt that *Barricada,* as of 1994, was holding its own with the other Nicaraguan dailies, and that most of its readers appreciated the degree of autonomy the paper had established from the FSLN's mobilizing agenda. Indeed, they may well have wanted to see that autonomy deepened and extended—an opinion likely shared by those (non)readers who considered the "new" *Barricada* little changed from the ultramobilized organ of the 1980s.

What neither survey reckons with is those readers, especially poorer ones, who might have given up on *Barricada,* not only because they could no longer afford to buy it—a phenomenon that affected all the Nicaraguan dailies, as noted—but also because they felt alienated by the paper's new attempts at professionalism, and by its move away from strict adherence to a mobilizing agenda determined elsewhere and by others. One could argue, though, that if readers abandoned *Barricada* in large numbers on political grounds, they would have returned to buying the paper in the wake of the defenestración. Clearly, the directorate installed after 1994 was counting on precisely that. Their hopes were drastically misplaced, as chapter 4 explores. If there *was* a disaffected corps of militant readers, the ortodoxo version of *Barricada* introduced after October 1994 did not have what it took to regain their custom.

One point that has perhaps been implicit in the previous discussion, but which should be stressed, is that the autonomy strategy at *Barricada* relied for its successful implementation on a professional corps extending well beyond the directorial levels of the newspaper. No scholar could refuse the opportunity to spend dozens of hours in conversation with sources as engaging, insightful, and well informed as Carlos Fernando Chamorro, Sofía Montenegro, and Daniel Alegría. But the resultant emphasis on their thoughts and perspectives may leave an impression of excessive *protagonismo* on the part of these actors in the drama. This would be particularly misleading in the case of Montenegro, whose *Gente* operation was distinct, editorially speaking, from the *Barricada* daily, and who was not closely involved with the post-1990 transformations in the daily's coverage. Chamorro, for his part, emphasized that "between 1991 and 1994, *Barricada* . . . put together the best journalistic staff in the country. We combined experience with new talent, and attempted to specialize in information in every field."[142] For example, *Barricada*'s sports coverage—which naturally occupies a somewhat peripheral position in this analysis—was widely recognized to be the best in Nicaragua. The impressive sense of institutional cohesion and identity that *Barricada* staffers displayed prior to and immediately following Carlos Fernando Chamorro's *defenestración* (chapter 3) attests to a broad commonality of professional vision at the paper, and a near unanimous conviction that implementation of the autonomy project offered the best way forward for the FSLN's former official organ.

The author's own perspectives on *Barricada*'s autonomy experiment have likely been apparent at various points in the discussion. I considered the project for the most part worthwhile, even exciting. The paper's attempts to depolarize political discourse in Nicaragua, to give space to a greater diversity of views and sources, to undertake new forays into investigative journalism and more penetrating and stylish feature reporting—all seemed extremely promising, not only in the context of national journalism, but as an example for Latin American media as a whole.[143]

The project was not without serious missteps, as the miniscandal over administrative corruption suggests. The massive layoffs that were a cornerstone of *Barricada*'s institutional restructuring in the early 1990s might well have been less severe, and evoked less bitterness among remaining blue-collar staff, if the resources drained from the paper by shady dealings had instead been available for salaries or retrenchment packages. But these were secondary features of the era of semiautonomy, at least as far as its long-term viability was concerned. What undermined and eventually capsized the autonomy project was not maladministration or poor labor-management relations, but a concerted campaign by core elements within the Sandinista Front, many of whom opposed it almost from the start. The disarray and dislocation in Sandinista ranks initially diminished the power of the forces that would later regroup as the ortodoxo Democratic Left, and opened vital space for the autonomy experiment to flourish. By 1994, the ortodoxos had regained the upper hand. They used it to close the space that had opened to dissident elements in the immediate postrevolutionary era. The next chapter aims to fix *Barricada* more firmly in the internal power struggle that consumed the Sandinista Front in the first half of the 1990s. It was a struggle in which political programs, ideologies, and powerful personalities all clashed. It climaxed with the purging of the renovationist wing of the front, and the destruction of the young but promising project underway at the FSLN's media flagship.

Chapter 3

Chronicle of a Coup Foretold

UNRAVELING THE EVENTS that led to the upheaval at *Barricada* in October–November 1994 can lead the analyst years into the past— perhaps as far back as the 1960s. Consider one chain of correlation if not causation: the May 1994 Special Congress, the *defenestración* of Carlos Fernando Chamorro several months later, and the wider endgame to expel renovationist forces from the front marked the climax of a sectarian division that had grown increasingly obvious since the electoral catastrophe of 1990. The particular configuration of forces assembled for that ortodoxo-versus-renovationist confrontation was in part the outgrowth of conflicts that had been latent during the 1980s—notably those involving then president Daniel Ortega. Those conflicts, in turn, can be seen as a variant of the factionalism that had always lain behind the democratic-centralist façade that the FSLN had managed to cobble together in 1978–79 and maintain throughout the revolutionary decade.

The debates in which the different currents (*corrientes*) were caught up in the 1990s, furthermore, bore certain similarities to those that consumed the front in the late 1960s and early 1970s. Slowly emerging tendencies crystallized with the splitting of the FSLN in October 1975, when the current known as the Proletarian Tendency (Tendencia Proletaria) chose to go its own way.[1] In response, the group that then constituted the core of the FSLN—the guerrilla forces based in the mountains of northern Nicaragua—formed itself into the Prolonged Popular War tendency (Guerra Popular Prolongada, GPP).[2] The third and final faction was the Tendencia Insurreccionel, or Insurrectional Tendency. The Insurrectionalists were popularly known as the Terceristas, since they promoted a "third way" of achieving revolutionary victory via broad-based popular insurrection. Assembled mostly by Sandinista leaders in exile, including Daniel Ortega (from his base in Cuba), the Terceristas called for a coalition that transcended class affiliations. To a considerable degree, it was this current's mediating role that brought about the eventual reunification of the front in early 1979—a necessary precursor to the final, successful offensive against the regime.[3] The more moderate rhetoric of the Terceristas also helped to mollify middle-class and elite elements within Nicaragua, as well as Somoza's traditional backers in the United States. When it came time to ratify the revolution in the national elections of 1984, it was the Tercerista leader, Daniel Ortega, who was chosen to run as the FSLN's candidate. His candidacy was held to symbolize the influence and indeed predominance of a pragmatic approach to revolution making.

Ortega's apparent transformation from moderate to champion of the ortodoxo current in the 1990s struck many observers as counterintuitive. It is possible, though, to see it as merely the latest expression of Ortega's political pragmatism—and personal ambition. This issue will be considered further when we examine Ortega's role in the machinations surrounding *Barricada* in the early 1990s. The point to bear in mind as we begin our analysis, though, is that the revolutionary solidarity that impressed so many outside observers (including this one) in the 1980s was far from the norm in the long history of the Sandinista Front. In the 1960s, 1970s, and again in the

1990s, the movement was riven by the kind of ideological, strategic, and personal conflicts common to left-revolutionary movements the world over. What was missing in the critical years of 1993 and 1994 was any overriding impetus for unity, such as had existed in 1978–79 and throughout the revolution's years in power. There was, instead, a growing desire to settle accounts and purge party ranks of dissident elements—though the differences would be handled without violence, another theme that had characterized relations among Sandinistas since the movement's birth in 1961.

Barricada *and the Struggle for Sandinismo*

On 11 July 1993, twenty-nine Sandinista militants, including deputies to the National Assembly, mayors, political secretaries, and union leaders, issued a call for the FSLN to "distanc[e] itself clearly from the government" of Violeta Chamorro, and "to lead the popular struggle" anew, beginning with the fourteenth anniversary of the Sandinista revolution on 19 July. Among the key figures of the Group of 29 (as it was quickly dubbed) were René Vivas, the former police chief of Managua; Mónica Baltodano, a former guerrilla leader who had served as minister of municipal affairs during the revolutionary decade; her husband, Julio López Campos, the future brains behind a revamped and reofficialized *Barricada;* Victor Hugo Tinoco, the FSLN's political secretary in Managua; and Mirna Cunningham and Lumberto Campbell, two prominent Sandinistas from the Atlantic coast. All but López were members of the FSLN National Directorate at the time, or would be appointed to the expanded twelve-member directorate at the May 1994 Special Congress. The signatories included three more Sandinistas (Doris Tijerino, Orlando Núñez, and Carlos Fonseca Terán) who would be drafted to the directorate when its three remaining renovationist members resigned in February 1995.

"The greatness of our party," proclaimed the Group of 29, "has been, and must continue to be, its stand alongside the people, and not on the side of the structures of power that oppress them." The signatories avowed the legitimacy of the FSLN's decision in 1990 to pursue concertación and co-gobierno with the UNO regime. They argued, though, that the time for such cooperation was past, given Nicaragua's enduring social horrors and the regime's apparent determination to aggravate rather than alleviate them:

> After three years of neoliberal policies, the economic and social results could not be more eloquent[ly clear]: poverty and social decomposition, unemployment and lack of access to education and health care, delinquency, prostitution, the total abandonment of Nicaraguan children and of the Atlantic coast. Administrative corruption, the surrendering of national sovereignty, noncompliance with political agreements, and the hoax of promises made to the people have become the institutionalized policy of the government. The socioeconomic achievements of the revolution, in particular all those that benefited thousands of Nicaraguan peasant and worker families, are on their way to extinction.[4]

As *Barricada* noted the next day in a sober front-page headline, the Group of 29 declaration "reopen[ed] debate in [the] FSLN." That was putting it mildly. The manifesto was the first coordinated salvo fired by the ortodoxo current of the front, which now felt itself sufficiently strong to challenge the renovationist sentiment that had briefly gained the upper hand after the catastrophe of 1990. In February 1994 a second seminal ortodoxo proclamation, the "Propuesta desde la izquierda democrática sandinista" (Proposal of the Sandinista Democratic Left), formalized the alliance between the Group of 29 and its new leader—Daniel Ortega. The so-called Pikín Guerrero manifesto emphasized the FSLN's self-definition "as a revolutionary party, whose fundamental objective is to struggle and work, in the short and medium term, for the establishment of the rule of law and social justice, and for a humanistic and democratic socialism."

The renovationist wing of the front was always more chimerical than its ortodoxo counterpart. It had mustered no formal response to the Group of 29 proclamation. The consolidation of the alliance with Daniel Ortega, however, could not pass without comment. A formal renovationist response finally came on 10 February 1994, less than a week after the Democratic Left announced its existence. It was titled the "Propuesta por un sandinismo de las mayorías," and—crucially— it was codrafted and signed by the director of *Barricada,* Carlos Fernando Chamorro. Three other prominent figures at the newspaper also appended their signatures: Onofre Guevara, Darwin Juárez, and Sofía Montenegro. The call "for a Sandinismo that returns to the majorities" appealed for "a new vision of change and renovation" within the front, and the development of party structures that were more "open, participatory, and creative." While the renovationists echoed the ortodoxos' rejection of neoliberalism, they urged the front to "proclaim without doublespeak [*dualidades*] our respect for private property and all other legitimate kinds of property," and to "declare our rejection, now and in the future, of any kind of confiscation." Most emphatically of all, the "mayorías" document rejected violence as a means of struggle: "Sandinistas cannot sponsor, defend, justify or excuse any type or method of armed or violent struggle in Nicaragua."[5]

The battle lines were now drawn for the Special Congress scheduled for May 1994—although given the rhetorical abstractions of the opposed manifestos, it was necessary to expend at least as much energy reading *between* those battle lines to determine the ideological and personal core of the dispute. One of the most insightful analysts of the FSLN's internal divisions in the 1990s was Guillermo Fernández Ampié, feature writer for *Barricada Internacional.* Writing in the aftermath of the May congress, Fernández succinctly depicted the ortodoxo and renovationist currents as

revolv[ing] around the way each group has analyzed the 1990 electoral defeat, their different proposals for regaining power, and even different opinions about the party's fundamental nature. . . . Those belonging to the current "For the majorities" [i.e., the renovationists] fought for modifications to a number of statutory and programmatic concepts which had previously been fundamental to the FSLN, in order to "adapt to changing times." These included discarding the concept of a "vanguard," anti-imperialist party as well as the practice of classifying members in two categories, as activists or affiliates. Furthermore, they rejected and openly condemned all forms of armed struggle and violence in the popular fight for political and economic objectives. . . . The Democratic Left, although proposing some changes of their own, argued that following the other group's recommendations would "destroy the revolutionary essence" of *Sandinismo*. . . . The dispute between the tendencies was also influenced by the personal struggle between [Sergio] Ramírez and Daniel Ortega for political control of the party, apparently motivated by the 1996 general elections, for which there [then was] still no designated Sandinista presidential candidate.[6]

In the immediate wake of the 1990 election debacle, renovationist sentiment enjoyed what seems in retrospect to have been its high-water mark. As late as July 1991, at the FSLN's historic first party congress, virtually no one dared—or bothered—to speak against the need for renewal and internal restructuring. Nonetheless, with so much of the front in disarray, there seemed little point in making precipitous changes that might only weaken the FSLN further. In a decision that now appears fateful, congress delegates swallowed whatever misgivings they may have felt and gave their backing to a "sunset clause" aimed at preserving continuity at the leadership level while the expected deeper renovation was carried out. All sitting members of the National Directorate were allowed to retain their positions as a single slate; only Humberto Ortega declined, in order to remain as chief of the army under the UNO regime. Even Sofía Montenegro, who had perhaps the rockiest relationship with the directorate of any Sandinista alive, supported the compromise: "In order not to make waves and create upheaval, or more distrust and confusion, in such a situation, there was a transaction—which was wise. You don't wipe out, from one day to another, a whole leadership. So what we did was [say], 'We won't wipe you out completely in this first cleaning-up, but you *will* have to share this position and power with more people. To make the National Directorate *again* a collegial body, with more people inside to control Daniel.' Because already Daniel was out of control."7

Correlating with the relative strength of renovationist sentiment, but related also to the separate and intense internal lobbying of the past year, *Barricada*'s editorial staff won important official confirmation of the paper's new line. Surveying the course of postrevolutionary Nicaraguan politics in 1998, Carlos Fernando Chamorro cited the congress seven years earlier as a vital foundation for *Barricada*'s controversial explorations and editorial policies between 1992 and 1994. At the congress, said Chamorro,

> We lobbied to introduce in party documents our own thesis on the autonomy of the press. Not many people were interested in discussing this matter, but we had a particular interest. Onofre [Guevara], Sofía and myself were party delegates. Finally, the congress adopted our proposal, and therefore the autonomy concept became legalized as the official party line by the maximum authority.
>
> There was little significant debate in the congress. One of the few important issues that provoked controversy had to do with freedom of opinion. There was an article on the rights of militants, saying you had the right to defend your own opinions until the party made one decision. We fought hard to establish the principle of freedom of opinion, which meant that even though the party had taken a decision, you had the right to maintain your own opinion as an individual, even though you had to apply the party decision. What this meant for those who understood the significance was [providing] the platform for the idea of permanent debate, promoting opinion leaders, and eventually corrientes of opinion in the party. People like William Ramírez, Julio López, and Bayardo [Arce] himself were in the opposite camp. And the result was tremendously important for us.

Another thing was that the results of the congress elections in the Sandinista Assembly were very favorable for us. I got elected with a relatively high percentage of votes—in the first 22 out of 90, while people like Rosario Murillo, our main detractor, were not elected at all. Julio López also was not elected. In general, the correlation of forces was very much in keeping with the mood of the El Crucero document.

So it was like winning the first battle with *Ventana* [i.e., Murillo] and Ortega's opposition. It was like the political legitimizing of the decision to cease being the official organ, and making *Barricada* a paper open to Sandinista debate. This explains why, when Ortega came to *Barricada* to meet with staff, we not only had institutional or journalistic strength, but also political strength.[8]

Only three years later, though, the ortodoxo current and Daniel Ortega had succeeded in stalling what enthusiasm there was for the autonomy of Sandinista institutions, let alone more sweeping transformations in that direction. At the next party congress, in May 1994, Ortega and his Democratic Left counterparts—including Murillo and López—played their hand and won, inflicting a decisive defeat on the diffuse renovationist wing of the front.

The period between the two congresses, during which the ortodoxos and Ortega established and consolidated a firm hold over the party apparatus, is murky indeed. There was no doubt about the results, however. As Daniel Alegría noted in 1996, the May 1994 showdown left the ortodoxos with "the keys, the seals to the party. They have the apparatus, and it works. It still works like a well-oiled bulldozer, although it's missing a few parts now."[9] Certainly it worked well enough to bulldoze the renovationist tendency out of the Sandinista bench in the National Assembly, out of the National Directorate—and out of *Barricada*.

In this struggle for the party apparatus, Sandinista-owned communications media were one of the most prominent arenas of conflict. The jewel in the crown was the FSLN's former official organ.

This requires explanation. Why should *Barricada,* a newspaper with a circulation at the time of the defenestración of around twenty thousand copies, be seen as the biggest prize of all, and "for many the most important political test for postelection Sandinismo"?[10] In a country where broadcast media are far more popular than print as a source of news and entertainment,[11] *Barricada* might have been viewed as a poor cousin to, say, the FSLN-controlled TV Channel 4, or Radio Ya, or Radio Sandino. Sofía Montenegro, for one, declared herself perplexed by the preoccupation of the most powerful Sandinista, Daniel Ortega, with the newspaper she had helped to found. "I don't know—he had television, radio. Why did he want *Barricada* so much? Why was the printed press so important to him? . . . This obsession with the newspaper I still don't understand."[12]

An explanation may lie in the traditional centrality of print to Nicaragua's political elite, along with the lure, for revolutionaries, of controlling the longtime official organ. In my view, though, a factor of equal if not greater importance was the enduring grudge harbored by Daniel Ortega against *Barricada,* its director, and the autonomy experiment initiated without Ortega's formal approval in 1991. When the comandante's personal antipathy combined, in 1993–94, with the more ideologically based opposition of powerful ortodoxos like Julio López, Tomás Borge, and Mónica Baltodano, an alliance was forged that *Barricada* as an institution was helpless to withstand.

"The Frente Danielista"

Daniel Ortega,[13] the leader of the Sandinista Front (confirmed in his post at the party congress of May 1998), is also the movement's most enigmatic figure. In the final years before the revolution, and during the revolutionary decade itself, Ortega was widely viewed as a moderate figure, as we have seen. Key Sandinista policy initiatives of the 1980s—the decision to leave a majority of the economy in private hands; to reach out to "patriotic producers" among Nicaragua's agrarian elite, even at the expense of landless peasants; to impose, after 1987, economic prescriptions that varied little from the neoliberal norm; and to cultivate contacts and supporters internationally well beyond the East Bloc links that the FSLN's critics focused on— all seemed to suggest that the pragmatism of the 1978–79 insurrectional strategy had carried over to the new regime. Ortega, elected president in 1984, was the bastion of that pragmatism.[14]

Is it in this understanding of Tercerista ideology and Ortega's personality as essentially pragmatic that the explanation for the comandante's actions in the early 1990s is best sought? Even some of Ortega's sharpest critics found the idea persuasive. Sofía Montenegro averred that Ortega "hasn't been a hard-liner ideologically, or a purist. He's been a pragmatist on power and politics."[15] For Montenegro, that pragmatism paved the way for the formation of the Democratic Left coalition in 1994. Ortega, she claimed, saw the coalition as the best means of preserving his personal power and influence— to which all ideological considerations were subordinated.

Another line of argument, though, points to persistent ortodoxo-style elements in Tercerista thinking and policymaking. Phil Ryan, for example, contends that an emphasis on the pragmatic component begs the larger question of the ideological position from which that flexibility was extended. For Ryan, the ideological foundation of *all* the major Sandinista currents was an "orthodox Marxism," albeit a belief system that could be easily reconciled with the tactical pragmatism required to seize and retain power:

> To say that the Sandinistas were influenced by orthodox Marxism does not mean that they did not demonstrate flexibility. Ideological commitments need not imply dogmatic rigidity. In fact, the Sandinista leaders demonstrated a remarkable capacity to reflect upon their fundamental project and modify it on the fly. But flexibility must always *start* from somewhere: it is not enough to say that FSLN leaders were

flexible, one must also identify the framework within which that flexibility operated. Just as the position of a moving object depends upon the direction and speed of its movement *as well as* its starting position, so too did Sandinista ideology at any given moment reflect not only its "movement" or flexibility, but also its starting point.[16]

The Tercerista strand in particular—what Ryan calls "the Ortega tendency"—"had strong reasons for cultivating confusion" about its ideological predispositions, "since ambiguity was essential to its political strategy." But he argues that Ortega and his fellows were united with other Sandinista currents in their commitment to basic pillars of Sandinista strategy, including seizure of state power, mobilization of "an organized and socialist-oriented mass," and above all the need for a revolutionary vanguard. "So long as the level of development of the people lagged behind the vanguard, the latter represented something like the 'essence' or 'soul' of the Nicaraguan people. . . . This immediate identification of the people and its vanguard meant that the people held power because the vanguard held power."[17]

Did ortodoxo-style ideological leanings indeed lubricate Ortega's alliance with the Group of 29, and the formation shortly thereafter of the Democratic Left current? Was his commitment to a verticalist and vanguardist model of party organization—one of the central issues dividing ortodoxos and renovationists—a constant in his strategic thinking? If so, and if we further integrate the personal dimension that is never absent from politics (least of all Nicaraguan politics), perhaps deeper insights can be gleaned into Ortega's fractious relationship with *Barricada*, both during the revolutionary decade and into the postrevolutionary era.

One thing is certain: Daniel Ortega did not have to be dragged kicking and screaming into the ortodoxo campaign of the early 1990s against the front's former official organ. In fact, no National Directorate member had had so volatile a relationship with *Barricada* as Ortega. None had clashed so openly with the paper during the

1980s; none other had absented himself from the critical directorate deliberations over *Barricada*'s autonomy project in December 1990; none had leveled the kind of accusations and innuendo against *Barricada* that Ortega did when the autonomy project was implemented. Thus by the time the intraparty conflict reached its climax in 1994, Ortega's animosity toward *Barricada*'s staff and his suspicion of their evolving professional imperative had been building for nearly a decade.

The first substantial conflict between *Barricada* and then president Ortega was discussed in detail in chapter 1: the joke gone wrong that led to the dismissal of Xavier Reyes and Marcio Vargas. On that occasion, Ortega appears to have been drawn into the controversy more as a reflection of his status as Nicaraguan president and first among equals on the National Directorate. The affront was apparently felt in a similar way by his fellow directorate members: according to Carlos Fernando Chamorro, in fact, it was Humberto Ortega who pressed hardest for sanctions against Reyes and Vargas.[18] It was not long before Ortega clashed again with *Barricada*, though, and this time the conflict was a good deal more personal. Also in 1987, a national assembly of Sandinista women was convened, and Ortega was invited as guest speaker. His speech to the assembly was followed by some aggressive questioning from the audience. Among the delegates was Sofía Montenegro, who recalled the events in 1991:

> Some of us [delegates] had already been holding meetings at the base in which we began to question the approach of AMNLAE. At the meeting, some of us stood up to point out to the movement—and to Comandante Ortega—that women were dying from backstreet abortions; there were as many women dying for lack of decent medical care in such situations as there were men dying in the war [against the contras]. You couldn't fool around with this shit and pretend nothing was happening. . . .
>
> I just stood up and wagged my finger and said all that to Comandante Ortega. Many others stood up too, but because he knew me, he directed his comments to me personally. He said the

views I was putting forward were those of petty-bourgeois women; the women from the *pueblo* [common people] were asking for other things entirely. He derided my qualifications, angrily, in front of three thousand women.

Ortega's comments, according to Montenegro, were at odds with the official Sandinista line on women's issues, as set out in a seminal FSLN declaration, "Women and the Sandinista Revolution," released just before the conference. The document was the result of years of lobbying by the nascent Nicaraguan women's movement, the representatives of which were understandably distressed to hear Ortega reverting to a position that struck many as classically *machista*. *Barricada,* editing Ortega's speech for print, "decided it couldn't 'officialize' [Ortega's] words," said Montenegro. The feeling at the newspaper was that was that Ortega "wasn't giving us the official position of the National Directorate, but rather his personal opinion. He wasn't behaving like a president or a revolutionary, but like a chauvinist who understood nothing of women's problems. . . . So they cut out that portion of the speech when they reprinted it in the paper."

Ortega then "went on the radio and said the same damn thing, just to spite us. Once again the version of his words that appeared in *Barricada* were censored. That hurt his pride even more." The events led to Montenegro's receiving an indirect warning from Bayardo Arce to avoid writing about women's issues for the time being. Carlos Fernando Chamorro persuaded Montenegro to abide by the edict—no mean feat.[19]

Interesting though they are as harbingers of the later conflict between Ortega and *Barricada,* however, it is difficult to explain his antipathy toward *Barricada* on the basis of such isolated events. In fact, it was not until after the election fiasco of 1990 that the extent of Ortega's hostility toward *Barricada* became clear. At first, in the recollection of Carlos Fernando Chamorro, Ortega seemed fairly amenable to granting *Barricada* greater independence from the FSLN leadership. In the chaotic interregnum between the election defeat and the swearing-in of Chamorro's mother, Violeta, as Nicaragua's new president, Chamorro fils said he arranged a meeting between Ortega and various Sandinista and pro-Sandinista journalists. At the meeting, Ortega was "quite open in terms of saying, 'OK, we don't want to have any control over what you do. We're simply going to give you information, and everybody can do what he wants, with his own ideas and lines.'"

After the meeting, Chamorro approached Ortega to discuss the autonomy project specifically. "I went up to Ortega and said, 'Don't you think it's time now for *Barricada* to stop being an official organ of the FSLN? There's no reason for it now.' He said, 'Yes, it's a good idea. Why don't you make a proposal?'" At the time, Chamorro said, Ortega seemed to share the opinion of other National Directorate members that "something had changed" in the wake of the FSLN's fall from power: "It was no longer a question of principle whether *Barricada* was the official organ or not."[20]

Whatever Ortega's original enthusiasm for the project might have been, however, it rapidly dissipated. In September 1990 came the first public denunciation of *Barricada* from what might be called the Ortega camp: Rosario Murillo's broadside, detailed in chapter 2, against the "sect" that had allegedly seized control of the FSLN's media. Murillo, of course, was Ortega's longtime companion; it was tempting to read, in her references to "Sandinista leaders" being relegated to the inside pages of *Barricada* and "the ruling [Chamorro] family" being given preference, an expression of Ortega's own frustrations with the direction taken by *Barricada* and other Sandinista media.[21]

By the time of the critical National Directorate meeting to approve *Barricada*'s autonomy experiment (December 1990), Ortega's ambivalence had apparently intensified: he was conspicuous by his absence. In an interview conducted several months after the February 1991 relaunching of the paper, Chamorro confirmed that opposition to the autonomy project had been voiced at the directorate level. He declined to name names, but in retrospect Ortega was almost certainly the leading critical voice.

At last, in February 1992, Ortega openly joined the fray, delivering what the *New York Times* called a "frontal attack" on the new incarnation of *Barricada*. He openly expressed opposition to the directorate's approval of the autonomy project: had he been in the country at the time of the vote, he said, he would have opposed it. Ominously, he now said he wished to see the decision overturned. Ortega also accused *Barricada* of placing excessive emphasis on "commercial" considerations at the expense of political ones.[22] This charge seemed to derive, proximately at least, from the paper's decision to publish a full-page political advertisement from a protorenovationist grouping dubbing itself Sandinistas por un Proyecto Nacional (Sandinistas for a National Project). As with Murillo's 1990 polemic, though, Ortega's deeper concern was apparently *Barricada*'s willingness to solicit comments and op-ed pieces from a broad cross-section of Nicaraguan politics and society, and to court the advertising revenue of the mostly conservative business community. As Carlos Fernando Chamorro remembered the dispute, Ortega "basically said that *Barricada* was becoming a mouthpiece for the rich . . . that you had to pay in order to express your own opinion. That was a misunderstanding," Chamorro added. "I understood later his argument, but obviously the way he went about it was very confrontational."[23]

The implication that *Barricada* journalists were in the pockets of the powerful—and thus had descended to the corrupt level of prerevolutionary journalism in Nicaragua—immediately drew *Barricada*'s staff into the controversy. The "Declaration of *Barricada* Journalists," published on the editorial page on 6 March 1992, protested Ortega's attack on the grounds that it "contain[ed] insinuations that could injure the personal and professional dignity of our collective."[24] Chamorro, for his part, published a rare front-page riposte under his own signature, titled "The *Barricada* That We Need." In the measured tones from which he rarely departed in print,

Chamorro reminded Ortega of the decision of the July 1991 FSLN congress to "support and respect the autonomy of the revolution's communications media."[25]

In the wake of Ortega's incendiary attack, a meeting was arranged between the comandante and *Barricada*'s editorial council, the institution that best exemplified the goals of the autonomy project. According to Carlos Fernando Chamorro, Ortega at first refused to meet with the council. "He did not want to recognize the existence of the editorial council, OK? He said that I, as director, was the source of power in the newspaper, and he had to solve things personally with me. I always tried to stress that he had to accept the existence of the editorial council." In the end, Chamorro said his arguments were successful in persuading Ortega to meet with the council, "but in a formal way." Ortega seemed to view the proceedings as only minimally interesting and relevant. Instead, according to Chamorro, Ortega concentrated his lobbying efforts on a "long night meeting, five or six hours, with all the staff—the journalists and myself." Chamorro described the exchange as "very frank [and] direct";[26] political reporter Alfonso Malespín similarly recalled it as "long and controversial." In Malespín's 1996 recollection, Ortega

> had a couple of complaints. One was that he thought *Barricada* was no longer a Sandinista newspaper. He thought it was not publishing news that would benefit Sandinista interests. And the other complaint was that we were wearing two hats—that's how he said it. When we wanted, we wore the journalist's hat, and when we wanted, we switched and wore a political one. He said that *Barricada* was becoming an excellent newspaper, a very good newspaper, but that it wasn't the newspaper the Sandinistas wanted and needed at the moment. He said that it [change] needed to happen before the second congress.[27]

Ortega's attempts to sway *Barricada* staff to his views had little effect, as far as Chamorro was concerned. "The problem for him was that the staff at that time was very much cohesive. He could not open any windows or fractures. . . . At the end of the discussion we ended up much more consolidated. We felt that people had lost their fear of discussing [things] openly with Daniel Ortega, and telling him to his face: 'You are wrong, we are right.'"[28] But it proved a pyrrhic victory.

Endgame, 1993-94

If Daniel Ortega had been isolated in his opposition to *Barricada*'s autonomy experiment, or if that opposition had extended no further than Rosario Murillo and a handful of other FSLN intellectuals, the project might well have survived. In 1993, though, it became clear that a bloc was forming to confront *Barricada* and other perceived renovationist forces within the front. The confrontation with this bloc began, in Carlos Fernando Chamorro's estimation, at a meeting of the FSLN's Managua committee in September 1993, as increasingly violent transport strikes were paralyzing the capital city and other major centers. The meeting was the first strong evidence Chamorro had seen that the ortodoxo "project of reorganizing the party apparatus in Managua" had spilled over to a campaign aimed directly at transforming *Barricada* as an institution. Chamorro had already attended meetings of the Managua committee in which ortodoxos had "said they were listening to a lot of complaints about *Barricada* . . . that *Barricada* was not Sandinista enough, not radical enough." Now, with Chamorro in attendance, the meeting moved from a discussion of the strikes to what Chamorro remembered as "a kind of trial process against *Barricada*": "I think Mónica Baltodano took the lead in the attack. She said, 'Well, the front has decided to change its political line, so it's very simple. *Barricada* was conceived for another period, and that period—of peaceful coexistence with the government—is finished. Now we're going to another period. So we must change not only the editorial policy of *Barricada,* but also the director of *Barricada.*'"

135

Then Daniel Ortega rose to lend support to Baltodano's statements:

> What Daniel said that night was very interesting. He said, in a few words: "Well, when I talk to people from the diplomatic sectors—you know, foreigners who come to Nicaragua, very selective readers—they tell me *Barricada* is the best newspaper in this country. It's the most interesting, the most influential, and the most professional. . . . But," he said, "the problem is that I believe *Barricada* has lived past its time. It's a newspaper for another period—probably for the next ten years. But at this point in Nicaragua, we are very polarized, and as long as we don't solve the fundamental problems of property [ownership], I believe we need a combative newspaper. We don't need a newspaper like *Barricada.* It's very nice, very pretty, but we need a combative newspaper. That is my personal opinion, and I am not going to make any decision [by myself]; this decision will be made by the party."

The comments received a mixed response from delegates, according to Chamorro. The ortodoxos apparently were seeking "a resolution condemning *Barricada,* and ordering an investigation of the editorial line of the newspaper." But other representatives said, "'Hmmm, there's something weird here. This is a kind of ambush.'" Chamorro, of course, spoke out strongly in the paper's defense. In the end a resolution criticizing *Barricada* was voted down. But Chamorro was left in no doubt as to the meeting's import. Ortega's statements "established the agenda very clearly. By saying, 'I'm not going to organize a coup d'état, but we need a change in the correlation of forces.' . . . From that day on, everything was more clear. We were heading toward a confrontation. . . . It was quite clear that we were in separate camps."[29]

If the ortodoxo arguments had been received with lukewarm enthusiasm at the meeting of the Managua committee, the balance of power evidently shifted over the following months. Between September 1993 and the May 1994 Special Congress, though, the public face of the intraparty conflict moved from *Barricada* to the National Assembly. There, in November 1993, news broke of divisions between the Sandinista bench, led by Sergio Ramírez, and the FSLN National Directorate—in particular Daniel Ortega, who had begun jockeying with Ramírez for the FSLN's nomination for the 1996 presidential elections. The immediate cause of friction was the introduction of the Law to Regulate the Privatization of Public Services. Ramírez and a majority of bench members supported the law. The Sandinista Assembly, Daniel Ortega, and a probable majority of the National Directorate opposed it. Tensions boiled over; several FSLN parliamentary deputies reported death threats, while Ortega called loudly for a national referendum on privatization.

The conflict simmered until the end of January 1994, when the National Directorate and the FSLN bench reached a broad (albeit temporary) agreement on constitutional reform. The accord recognized the Sandinista Assembly's resolution as "the fundamental political document" determining the FSLN's stance in negotiations, but acknowledged that "documents or plans presented by the other groups or benches must be recognized as the legitimate positions of the other sides [*partes*]." Ortega declared optimistically that "whatever difference [existed] between the bench and the National Directorate has been completely overcome."[30]

The cease-fire lasted just two days. On 26 January it became known that the agreement had been in fact been reached four days after a far more significant one at the Escuela Pikín Guerrero outside Managua, where Daniel Ortega and the ortodoxo Group of 29 together forged the Democratic Left current of the front. Participants in the gathering reportedly agreed on the broad outlines of a campaign against Sergio Ramírez and his parliamentary supporters and also examined the possibility of purging dissident members of the National Directorate. It is unclear whether changes at *Barricada* were also discussed.[31]

Ortega tried to shrug off the significance of the Pikín Guerrero gathering, denying it had been "clandestine" in nature and calling press coverage "an overreaction." But the appraisal of William Grigsby—later to become *Barricada*'s editor in chief—seems more accurate in retrospect. Grigsby proclaimed that the Sandinista Front was "facing what could be its worst crisis since the division of 1975."[32] His comments had a self-fulfilling dimension. Grigsby had been present at Pikín Guerrero, and the day after the news of the gathering broke, his outspoken radio station, La Primerísima, joined with the FSLN-owned Radio Ya to issue a blistering denunciation of Sergio Ramírez. Carlos Guadamúz, director of Radio Ya, accused Ramírez of forging "ties with sectors of the right in the name of the FSLN," of "pursuing personal interests," and of a "total betrayal of the FSLN and the people." The attacks were so harsh that even some members of the Group of 29 felt obliged to distance themselves from the "inappropriate" tenor of the comments.[33]

On 4 February 1994 the second *ortodoxo* proclamation appeared and the Democratic Left was officially born. That prompted, as noted, the first—and only—coordinated renovationist pronouncement, the document "Propuesta por un sandinismo de los mayorías." Among the signatories were Carlos Fernando Chamorro and three other senior *Barricada* figures. How was their decision to sign the "mayorías" proclamation received by other staff at the newspaper? Daniel Alegria recalled a meeting with Chamorro in which "he read us this thing about the ramirista document":

> He said, "Look, I've helped write this document. I'm going to sign it. I want to see what you guys think of it." And more or less we all said the same thing to him: "Go ahead and sign it. It's up to you. Just don't bring it into the paper. But also be aware that if you sign it, you're out."[34]

Chamorro, for his part, described the announcement as provoking rather greater controversy. "Some of [the staffers] said this was a big mistake, that this would be used as an argument against

Barricada, and that it was kind of violating our internal rules. . . . But there was no big crisis."[35] "There was a big confusion in the staff," concurred Sofía Montenegro, who also signed the "mayorías" proclamation. "Some were saying, 'I think this will link us with the [renovationist] current.' . . . Then, once the thing came out, Daniel started accusing us of being part of the current." Montenegro said she pressed ahead nonetheless, because in her view *Barricada* was "already doomed. . . . We knew that we had a sword of Damocles hanging over our necks, that they would cut our heads off."[36] Chamorro too had few illusions about the likely effect of his actions:

I took the personal decision of supporting the "mayorías" document, knowing that it implied several risks, that people could use it as an extra argument to attack me or to attack *Barricada.* But for me it was very clear. It didn't matter whether I signed that document or not. They [the ortodoxos] had taken a decision [to change *Barricada*], and they were just waiting to accumulate strength. So I said, "Well, I'm going to do something because I feel, personally, in my conscience, that this is the way I would like the front to go." If [William] Grigsby has the right to his own personal opinion, if [Carlos] Guadamúz has his right, why not me? I'm not going to involve *Barricada,* I'm not going to make an editorial in *Barricada* on this topic; but I'm going to sign it. And I'm going to do some discreet campaigning on these issues, internally in the front, and I did.

I took some time to explain to the people on our staff that no matter what I did, they [the leadership] had already taken a decision. That decision was going to be focused on me. But it was a decision that implied much more than removing one person. It was a problem of conception: it was a problem of a structural vision of what the newspaper was, and the role that it played in society. The way we had conceived *Barricada,* starting in January 1991, was not compatible with the new correlation of forces being organized.[37]

"The new correlation of forces" was apparent as the FSLN's Special Congress of May 1994 opened. *Barricada*'s reporter announced what was plain to all observers—that the congress would be "an open struggle." The ortodoxo-Ortega alliance, though, all but ensured it would be a lopsided one. And while *Barricada* bravely proclaimed, in its best cheerleading fashion, that a "sentiment of consensus and unity still predominates among Sandinista ranks,"[38] hostilities rapidly spilled over. Sofía Montenegro and other renovationists felt thoroughly frozen out of the proceedings: "Tomás Borge, for example [who presided over the congress] . . . always behaved like he never saw us. He didn't give us the floor until the second day, third day, at two o'clock in the morning when there was nobody there to listen to what we had to say. And when we talked, they began to make noises, so everybody in the Olof Palme [convention center] wouldn't hear. They'd grunt like monkeys when we stood up and it was our turn to talk."[39]

In the final balloting for the new Sandinista Assembly, the ortodoxos secured an impressive 75 percent of delegate support. Ortega was reelected general secretary by an equally convincing 287–147 margin over Henry Ruíz, who presented himself as leader of an "anticurrent" current. "From that day on," said Carlos Fernando Chamorro, "I knew perfectly well that [the defenestración] was just a matter of time. The whole question was if they were willing to pay the political cost to do what they did. And they *were* willing to pay the cost, and they did it."[40]

A temporary lull followed the congress, as Sandinistas absorbed the implications of the new balance of forces. The renovationists had a chance to mount one final stand. The two main arenas of conflict were now the National Assembly—and *Barricada*. The final crisis broke in the assembly in August 1994. Sandinista deputies under Sergio Ramírez joined other deputies in backing the constitutional-reform project that had generated internal controversy in December 1993. The compromise worked out at the time, granting the bench a degree of autonomy in its designated sphere, now collapsed. The ortodoxo-controlled Sandinista Assembly elected at the Special

Congress withdrew the permission it had extended for Ramírez's bench to follow its own course. The parliamentary delegates, for their part, refused to recognize the legitimacy of the order, and continued to back the legislation.[41] This was as direct a challenge to established mechanisms of FSLN policymaking as could be mounted, given that the Sandinista Assembly was formally the preeminent Sandinista decision-making body. On 9 September the assembly voted to dismiss Ramírez as chief of the parliamentary bench and replace him with a delegate from the minority tendency on the bench—Daniel Ortega himself. The parliamentarians responded on 12 September by accepting Ramírez's dismissal—but also by contending that it was their right to select a replacement. They elected Dora María Téllez, a prominent renovationist on the FSLN National Directorate. The National Directorate denounced this "new [act of] disrespect"; Daniel Ortega called the action "precipitous," and immediately set about trying to have it overturned.[42]

A temporary truce was hammered out. Ortega and the bench agreed "to restabilize political communication and seek agreements of consensus that will contribute to resolving the crisis within the FSLN."[43] Finally, the bench bowed to the inevitable, accepting the decision of the Sandinista Assembly to seat Ortega in Ramírez's place. On 11 October, Ortega took his place at the head of the bench.

The same September meeting of the assembly that saw motions passed to replace Ramírez also witnessed renewed calls for the National Directorate to take over direct control of *Barricada* and dismiss Carlos Fernando Chamorro as director. Still displaying uncertainty on this count, though—or wishing to devote its energies to the bitter parliamentary conflict—the assembly resolved to postpone consideration of the issue for thirty days. It called on the FSLN leadership, instead, to solicit submissions on the desirable future course of *Barricada,* and to draft a proposal along these lines for the assembly's consideration.[44]

The clock was now evidently ticking on the autonomy project.

Staffers at *Barricada* decided to seize the initiative, preparing a sub-mission of their own to the directorate. On 19 September a number of staffers gathered for a 10 A.M. press conference at the office of the Union of Nicaraguan Journalists (UPN), seeking to explain their posi-tion on the *Barricada* project and "the implicit will to silence and cen-sor us." A document signed by thirty-seven staffers, titled "Un periodismo para una sociedad democrática" (Journalism for a demo-cratic society), was presented at the press conference and published on the *Opiniones* page on 20 September. This was the document quoted at length at the end of chapter 2, calling for "the autonomy of the daily [to] be extended even further," declaring the paper's staff "united in our commitment to professional and ethical journalism," and pro-claiming "any attempt to restrict us unacceptable."

Behind the scenes, a more formal submission to the directorate was also being prepared by the members of *Barricada*'s editorial council. The document that resulted, "Ajustes en la estrategia edito-rial de *Barricada*" (Adjustments to the editorial strategy of *Barricada*), was hardly designed to assuage those FSLN leaders and militants—now apparently a majority—who supported the reasser-tion of directorate control over the former official organ. As staffers had done in their open letter, the council members called quixotically not for a diminution of the paper's autonomy, but for that autonomy to be increased.[45] Given the now-or-never atmosphere of the pro-ceedings, the final text of the "Ajustes" declaration was agreed to only after protracted discussion by the council's diverse member-ship. "It was important to keep this group united," stated Carlos Fernando Chamorro in 1996:

> You had to take into account their opinions, and it was a very difficult balance to keep everything together. But we were successful in gen-eral, I think. . . . Bayardo [Arce] was the one who put on more pres-sure, saying, "Well, maybe we are wrong. Maybe they are right. Maybe what we need is a party newspaper." Probably he didn't say it like that. But what I'm trying to say is that we were open enough at

that point to think like the devil's advocate: to say, "Maybe we're all wrong, and what we need is something totally different. So let's discuss *this* possible scenario." And whenever we started with that reasoning, we ended up saying, "No, this is not wrong. This is the correct way of transforming a party newspaper into a newspaper institution. This is what Nicaragua needs. If they like it, fine; but we are not going to make an accommodation to the new balance of power within the front."

Remarkably, at no point did the final text actually refer to *Barricada* as a Sandinista or revolutionary institution. The emphasis throughout was on the paper's "Sandinista and non-Sandinista" constituencies—and potential constituencies—alike. (Indeed, non-Sandinistas were seen as the most promising avenue for future expansion.) If *Barricada* was to extricate itself from its economic dire straits, the authors asserted, it would have to further strengthen its autonomy from the partisan interests of the FSLN. This was the thrust of a full section of the "Ajustes" document titled, "The Political Factor: Autonomy or Party Affiliation [*partidismo*]?" Among non-readers, the document contended there "exist[ed] a strong political prejudice toward *Barricada*," based on a feeling that the daily was "excessively party affiliated and biased." The editorial council buttressed this contention with a reference to M and R survey data (see chapter 2) indicating that 75 percent of readers considered *Barricada* the most "professional" and "credible" of the Nicaraguan dailies, but only 38.5 percent thought of it as the "most independent." "On the question of the *Barricada*—FSLN relationship," the council members wrote, "the majority of our subscribers would like to see a greater editorial and informational autonomy in the newspaper's dealings with the party." There followed the most barbed passage in a generally moderate document: "These aspirations run contrary to the demand of sectors of the base and leadership inside the party structure of the FSLN, who demand a greater degree of support [*protagonismo*] for their political activities in the newspaper's pages, together with a 'militant' editorial policy favoring the official positions of the FSLN."

This vision the editorial council categorically rejected. Instead, it urged "consolidat[ion of] . . . the daily's professional discretion": "The newspaper decides the relevance of the news. News value is the fundamental criterion in considering whether news coverage is fair or not. News judgment cannot be placed at the service of subjects, sources, or groups, but [only at the service of] the broader public, and of what the audience considers vital. The newspaper must administer this criterion with total autonomy." Accordingly, *Barricada* reaffirmed "the principle of the separation of information and opinion" and declared its desire to publish a still "greater diversity of opinion, Sandinista and non-Sandinista, in order to sponsor a genuinely national debate."

In retrospect, the document reads partly as a deposition to the directorate, partly as an elegy for the autonomy experiment that was shortly to breathe its last. "I think we were trying to sell the project without being much convinced of our ability to do so," Chamorro stated. "We thought it was our responsibility to put it in words, put it on paper, and say, 'OK, this is our editorial strategy. Don't ask us to change it, because we don't think it has to be changed. What we can do is to make some adjustments that are not necessarily political adjustments—like what kind of supplements we have, whether we are going to be more popular or less popular, if we are going to be more integrated in our approach to advertising and news.'"

Chamorro said he was more straightforward still in a letter he wrote to accompany the document's submission to the National Directorate, "saying: After the congress, we recognize that there has been a change in the balance of power of the front, and apparently the front now do not feel comfortable with *Barricada*. So this is our [proposed] strategy. If you take it, you take it, and we ask you to support it. If not—well, make the changes that you want [at *Barricada*]. . . . You have the right to make the changes you want. But we want to tell you that we think *this* is the best way to orient the newspaper."

Inevitably, the arguments counted for little. The document was submitted to the directorate on 21 October 1994, but "was never discussed at all," said Chamorro. "They had already made their decision."[46] Four days later came the defenestración.

Coup and Interregnum

The first that Carlos Fernando Chamorro heard about the precise timing of his defenestración came as *Barricada* headed into its final weekend as a semiautonomous publication. Senior editor Daniel Alegría had received a call from Tomás Borge, whom Alegría had served as both bodyguard and speech writer in the Ministry of the Interior during the 1980s. Apparently perceiving Alegría as one of the few sympathetic figures within the newspaper, Borge sought to persuade him to serve as *Barricada*'s editor for a period of transition to follow Chamorro's departure. Eventually, and evidently grudgingly, Alegría agreed. Then he phoned Carlos Fernando Chamorro to tell him the boom was about to descend.[47]

In its front-page headline of Monday, 24 October, *Barricada* brashly reported the "Agreement to Dismiss the Director" of the publication. The same day, Ernesto Cardenal, a defrocked Catholic priest and former Sandinista cabinet minister, announced his resignation from the front. "Since the last congress," Cardenal contended in his open letter (also published in *Barricada*), "a small group headed by Daniel Ortega has taken over the FSLN," imposing *"caudillismo* [strongman tactics], verticalism, and authoritarian control."

The next day—Tuesday, 25 October 1994—*Barricada* printed Carlos Fernando Chamorro's lengthy "final reflection" (quoted in the introduction), together with an article aptly titled "The Hour of Truth," by second in command Sergio de Castro. The current impasse had arisen, de Castro angrily alleged, because *Barricada* "has been ever less inclined to use our pages for political maneuvers that respond to the power interests of individuals or groups, at the expense of the institutions created by the revolution, of which we consider ourselves a part, and which we have sought to strengthen. . . . The National Directorate and Sandinista Assembly . . . have offered nothing new to Sandinismo or to Nicaraguan society, [only] reiterating at every stage methods and political styles that stress control by the apparatus of power."

The morning's edition also divulged news that three members of *Barricada*'s editorial council—Alejandro Martínez, Rodrigo Reyes, and Emilio Baltodano—had tendered their resignations.[48] As *Barricada* readers were digesting this reportage and commentary, the Sandinista Assembly was meeting at the offices of CIPRES, a research institute near Managua's Universidad Centroamericana

Figure 3.1. *Barricada* director Carlos Fernando Chamorro writes a final letter of protest to the FSLN over his impending dismissal, 25 October 1994. *Photo: Oscar Cantarero. Courtesy IHCA, UCA archives.*

headed by Group of 29 member Orlando Núñez. At the request of the National Directorate, delegates voted—narrowly—to dismiss Chamorro as director of *Barricada,* and to reestablish party control over the newspaper.[49] Finally, just before three o'clock, Tomás Borge and Lumberto Campbell made their trek across town to the *Barricada* plant, assembly resolution in hand. There, they formally divested Chamorro of his post and began the arduous process of restructuring *Barricada* as a journalistic and revolutionary institution.

As the defenestración unfolded, no one, perhaps, felt in a more awkward position than Daniel Alegría. The boyish-looking editor now had the unenviable task of guiding *Barricada* through the most contentious editions the paper had ever published. "When Carlos Fernando resigned, publicly, the other editor—Roberto Fonseca—quit immediately," Alegría recalled in 1996. "Right then. He just put his stuff in a box and left. And Sergio de Castro . . . was sick in bed with the flu. So I was the man!"

Perhaps only the edition *Barricada* prepared the day after the 1990 election defeat can compare with the atmosphere of dislocation and uncertainty spawned by the defenestración—and staffers were at least able to bring a sense of *institutional* cohesion and solidarity to their coverage of the electoral fiasco. The behind-the-scenes negotiations and disputes that eventually produced the edition of 26 October 1994 were thus sui generis in the newspaper's experience. As Chamorro steered his Jeep Cherokee away from the throngs on the *Barricada* steps, Alegría was already beginning to map out the next edition. The top story was never in doubt: "Obviously, we were news that day. That wasn't the problem." The difficulties began to arise when Alegría carried proofs of the paper's front page to the spacious office that several hours previously had been occupied by Carlos Fernando Chamorro. There he found Tomás Borge, Lumberto Campbell, and a considerable retinue of ortodoxo supporters. "There were people there that didn't have anything to do with the paper; they had a lot to do with the party," said Alegría. "It reminded me of a gathering of pirates that had taken over somebody else's ship, with their feet on another guy's desk, smoking cigars! Just living it up."

Alegría showed Borge the proofs, with the banner headline: "DN se toma *Barricada*" (National Directorate takes over *Barricada*). "He takes a look at the headline, and just crosses it out," Alegría recalled. There was, of course, a deep familiarity underlying Borge's apparent brusqueness:

> You have to remember that I used to be a speech writer for him. So he's very used to this style with me—I'd give him a speech proposal and then he'd cross that out and put his own stuff in. That's totally acceptable. But this was different, although he didn't realize it.
>
> He wanted to change the title. He disagreed with "DN Takes Over *Barricada*." He wanted something like "*Barricada* Is Back with the FSLN." I told him that wasn't the truth. . . . A whole discussion began, and then everyone else in the room started, you know, attacking my position. So I said to Tomás, "Look, can we meet elsewhere? . . . I want to talk to you and Lumberto [alone], otherwise we'll never get anywhere. And if you don't like it, I've got no problem with leaving."

The trio moved to the *Barricada* library, where they were soon joined by the flu-ridden Sergio de Castro and Sofía Montenegro. More haggling ensued over the headline. "He [Borge] was disagreeing. Finally, he said, 'OK, I'll give in, but change the title to "AS" ' "— to suggest that the paper was being taken over by the Sandinista Assembly, rather than the National Directorate. In Alegría's recollection:

> I said, "OK, that's a reasonable compromise, although the story's all about the DN and not the AS. And that, I'm *not* going to change." Then Tomás said, "Daniel, don't be unreasonable. This paper is *vomiting* against us. Everything in this [edition of the] paper is against the DN and against the decision to take over *Barricada*." He

didn't want Roberto Fonseca's opinion piece in there. But we kept the paper as it was, and it was a pretty strong paper.

The outlines of a compromise were emerging, but the immediate controversy would drag on well past midnight. Alegría left the library to inform anxious staff of developments. "It was a very tense moment," Alegría said. "I'm not accustomed to public speaking, and people were looking at me and going, 'Who is this guy? All of a sudden he's starting to call the shots here.'"

I explained to them: "Look, we decided to change the headline from 'DN' to 'AS.' Are you going to back me up on this, or what? Because I don't want any more quibbling." The thing was, the guys in the print shop were saying, "Look, Daniel, whatever you say. If you say we go, we go. If not, we won't. We're not paying attention to anyone else right now, you're the man—at least until tomorrow, until things are defined." There were some people saying, "Ah, let's just not bring out the paper. Let's take the *planchas* [plates] to *El Nuevo Diario*, and they'll publish it for us."

The controversy over the wording of the headline continued. Around 11 P.M., Borge called a meeting with senior staff "to try to explain his position," and to persuade them that the heading should be less confrontational. "That was the really hard meeting," Alegría recalled. One of Borge's most vocal critics, predictably, was Sofía Montenegro. Borge's basic argument, according to Montenegro, was that

it wasn't the National Directorate [that had taken control of *Barricada*], but the Sandinista Assembly. We told him, "The Sandinista Assembly is a bunch of puppets. Don't avoid your historical responsibility for what has happened today. The Sandinista Assembly is doing what *you* decided to do, a long time ago." We decided that we would tell the whole story [of the defenestración in the paper]. . . . We were there until two o'clock in the morning, because Tomás wouldn't permit the paper to go out with this [content]. At the end, we had a meeting within the staff and decided, "What is more important, that it says 'Sandinista Assembly' or 'National Directorate' [or that the rest of the content appears]? So we decided not to give a fuck. We changed it, in order to have the rest go through. We said, "We will permit you to change the front-page headline. But you cannot pull out one single word of the rest of the newspaper." We fought inch by inch, for the text, the photos.[50]

When at long last the 26 October edition was put to bed, recalled Daniel Alegría, "We all met over at Carlos Fernando's place. Everybody was there. We had a blast." Alegría described the experience as "my fifteen minutes of fame."

The mutual acrimony and tense negotiations of 25 October set the tone for the extraordinary three-week interregnum that followed. Some sense of the scale of the transition engineered at the paper during this period can be gleaned from *Barricada*'s masthead, which in the final (25 October) edition of the semiautonomous *Barricada,* published on the day of the defenestración, looked as follows:

Editorial Council
President: Bayardo Arce Castaño
Carlos Fernando Chamorro B., Emilio Baltodano C.,
Alejandro E. Martínez Cuenca, Sergio de Castro, Rodrigo
Reyes P., Roberto Fonseca L.
Director: Carlos F. Chamorro B.
Subdirector: Sergio de Castro
Editor: Roberto Fonseca L.
Subeditor: Daniel Flakoll Alegría
Gente Supplement: Sofía Montenegro

Sections
Art and Design: Mario A. Castro Mora
Events: Juan José Lacayo
The World: Vilma Areas

Sports: Edgard Tijerino
Economy: Roberto Larios
Opinion: Darwin Juárez
Readers' Forum: Onofre Guevara
De todo un poco: Mildred Largaespada
Municipalities: Juan Ramón Huerta

Administration
General Manager: Ronaldo Gómez R.

Three weeks later, of those listed above, *only Juan Ramón Huerta* remained on the masthead. The staffing hemorrhage was reflected in the very first edition following the defenestración, where the decapitation at the senior editorial level was graphically plain: it seemed there had not even been time to adjust the dimensions of the masthead. A blank space appeared where the names of *Barricada*'s editorial council once had been. Lumberto Campbell was formally listed as *Barricada*'s director, although his replacement by Tomás Borge on 1 November caught few observers by surprise. Bayardo Arce, for the time being, was still president.

It is worth pausing briefly to examine the roles—in Arce's case, the continuing role—of these three actors in the *Barricada* drama (Borge will receive additional attention later in the chapter). Like Daniel Alegría, Lumberto Campbell, who hailed from Nicaragua's Atlantic coast, was destined to play a transitional role in the *Barricada* drama. He was selected in large part because he represented the most acceptable public face of the FSLN leadership, in Carlos Fernando Chamorro's estimation:

> They knew Campbell was the right person to [take over the paper], in the eyes of the apparatus, because Campbell is a member of the National Directorate; he's in charge of propaganda and education; and he's a nice person—like anyone from the Atlantic coast, he's very soft and doesn't shout and smiles. He has a good image. He doesn't have the image of someone repressive or bad. So he lent his name and

his moderate image, so that [others] would do all the dirty jobs, eliminating people in *Barricada.* Then Julio López or Grigsby will come in three or four weeks and take control.[51]

Campbell, though, had no prior journalistic experience. "Lumberto didn't even know how to work a computer," said Daniel Alegría, who felt obliged to take the comandante under his wing: "I said to him, 'Look, you and I are the fall guys in this. Because neither you nor I are going to stay; we're just here for a transition period, and we're taking all the shit, without the real power of decision. But if somebody more hard-line than you had come here, this paper [the 26 October edition] wouldn't have come out. So let's just stick with each other, but remember what I'm saying: that you and I are just here for a period, and we're not really going to make or break this paper.'"[52]

From the start, the power behind the scenes at the new *Barricada* was Tomás Borge, the only surviving founding member of the Sandinista Front. Borge's route to the directorship was a complicated and circuitous one. When the Sandinista government fell in 1990, Borge was forced to abandon the Ministry of the Interior, which had become something of a personal fiefdom over the long years of national emergency. The comandante—who was, like many in the Sandinista leadership, an accomplished writer and intellectual—had seemed somewhat rootless since. For a while, he worked as a columnist for *El Nuevo Diario,* but fell out of favor when that paper began increasingly to favor the renovationist wing in the intraparty debate. The Special Congress of May 1994 was meant to cap Borge's decades of service to the revolution by creating for him a new, largely symbolic position in the party hierarchy, that of FSLN president. For reasons that can only be guessed at, though, delegates voted against creation of the post. Borge remained a legend without a portfolio.

There were several other reasons why Borge seemed a good candidate for the post of *Barricada* director. For one thing, during and after the Sandinista era, Borge had channeled his entrepreneurial energies and political connections into a close involvement with the

Mexican state-owned paper giant, PIPSA, serving as its Nicaraguan representative.[53] Significant in the National Directorate's calculations, in the view of Carlos Fernando Chamorro, was "the idea that if they gave [Borge] responsibility for *Barricada*, he would be able to mobilize resources in Mexico and other parts [of the region] that would be very important to the newspaper economically." In addition, there was likely a perceived (and self-perceived) symmetry between Borge's intellectual pursuits and directorship of the front's flagship. Again according to Chamorro, "It's like if I tell you one of my dreams is to have a house on the beach—well, one of [Borge's] dreams is to say he's the director of a newspaper. Probably he considered that it fit in well with his image of an intellectual."[54]

If Daniel Ortega was now in a position to dispense such largesse, he had good personal reasons to reward Borge. Despite a sometimes conflictive relationship between the two over the years,[55] Borge had swung his support firmly behind Ortega and the ortodoxo cause as the party rift deepened in 1993 and early 1994. It is also possible that the two shared a material interest in *Barricada* as an enterprise. In the aftermath of the defenestración, the Managua daily *La Tribuna* reported "strong suspicions" that Borge and Ortega were in fact the largest shareholders in the paper, and that Borge had demanded his shares be increased to 30 percent in return for taking over as director (and perhaps securing sources of key supplies through his business involvements). There is no firm evidence to support these assertions, however.[56]

Lastly, there was Borge's relationship with Daniel Alegría, which provided the architects of the defenestración with access to a figure who might be able to mediate between the directorate and an openly hostile *Barricada* staff. Borge, said Sofía Montenegro, was something of "a father figure" for Alegría;[57] it is true that as late as 1996, Alegría struck a conciliatory tone in evaluating the role Borge had played in the defenestración and the new incarnation of *Barricada* implemented in its wake.

A formal transfer of *Barricada*'s presidency from Bayardo Arce to Tomás Borge occurred one week after Chamorro's dismissal and marked Arce's departure from the commanding heights of the paper. Arce's absence from the account so far may seem surprising, given his important role as the directorate's representative to *Barricada* during the late 1980s and early 1990s. But though he displayed a willingness to defend the paper's autonomy project between 1991 and 1994, Arce kept about as low a profile during the defenestración as was possible: for reasons that remain obscure, he was out of the country when the National Directorate and Sandinista Assembly voted to dismiss Carlos Fernando Chamorro and reestablish direct control over *Barricada.* He returned to Nicaragua only to offer his resignation as president of the editorial council. The letter walked a tightrope between defense of the project he had helped to implement and an apparent desire not to burn his bridges with the new order. "Since I have not participated in the elaboration of [the] different concept of the newspaper," Arce wrote, "it does not seem appropriate for me to continue as head of the board of directors of Editorial El Amanecer and the editorial council of *Barricada.*" He reiterated his opposition to the defenestración, but emphasized that he did not deny the right of the paper's sponsor to administer the enterprise as it saw fit. Arce, in fact, went further: he claimed *he* had proposed that Borge take over presidency of the editorial council, since "in these new conditions, the presidency should be in the hands of the National Directorate."[58] By stepping aside gracefully, Arce secured himself a continuing role at *Barricada,* though one with little practical significance (see chapter 4).

To Carlos Fernando Chamorro's mind, Arce's actions during the 1994 transformations at *Barricada,* and his more general positioning in the Sandinista internal debate, reflected a politics of personal survival. Arce "confronted Ortega at certain points when he had to," according to Chamorro, but by the time of the May 1994 Special Congress, he was marginalized within the leadership and "in a very weak political position." The ortodoxo element by this time had clearly gained the upper hand—and Arce's relationship with leading ortodoxos was uncertain at best, given his sometimes spirited defense of *Barricada*'s autonomy. Thus, according to Chamorro, Arce "made an agreement with Daniel Ortega two days before the congress to be reelected a member of the directorate":

> He came out of the congress elected [to the directorate], but weak, because it was obvious to everyone that he was there as the result of a last-minute agreement. His behavior after the congress was to always try to tell me to shut up: that I should try to manage this crisis in silence, and that he was going to deal with it. That I should trust him. [He claimed] he was powerful enough to deal with Daniel Ortega, to deal with the rest, and to manage the crisis. But the condition was that we should make some concessions and not make too much noise. I never thought that was really realistic.

When Arce left the country on the eve of the defenestración, the comandante shrugged off Chamorro's concerns. "I [asked] him, 'Why are you leaving? They [the National Directorate] are going to take a decision on *Barricada* next Tuesday!'"

> He said, "No, don't worry, I will talk with Daniel. They won't make the decision when I'm outside the country." Obviously, they did. So when he came back, he played the role of saying, "Well, this is a disaster. I'm trying to convince Daniel to preserve the editorial strategy." I said to him, "You're totally naive. That's absolutely not possible." They said they didn't accept the new editorial strategy [presented to the directorate just before the defenestración]; they didn't accept it with us [the existing staff] or without us. So Bayardo quit, but said he was still there to help them if they needed anything from them. And six months later, he showed up as an advisor to the editorial council. But their editorial council doesn't work.[59]

WHILE THE LEADING actors in the defenestración were getting accustomed to their new powers, reduced powers, or total divestiture of power, *Barricada* staff were fighting for control of the paper's editorial content with scarcely less intensity than they had displayed on the day of Chamorro's dismissal. The 26 October edition arrived on the streets with its banner headline duly amended to emphasize the role of the Sandinista Assembly. Also on the front page was a statement by Lumberto Campbell, defending the directorate's decision against mounting criticism within the institution, in other Nicaraguan media, and around the world. *Barricada* "belongs to the FSLN," Campbell declared, and would "defend the interests of the FSLN, within the framework of popular interests and national interests." Criticism of the front would be countenanced; but "we must not confuse the self-criticism necessary within the FSLN with the shame and guilt [*vergüenza y culpabilidad*] of falling into a vulgar anti-Sandinismo." Coolly, he thanked Chamorro for "his efforts" at *Barricada*.

But Campbell's was the only defense of the *defenestración* published in *Barricada* that day, or for three days afterward. With a couple of ambiguous exceptions, to be noted, no alterations were made to articles and commentary that were at the very least plainspoken in their depiction of the preceding day's events, and often bitterly critical of the directorate's actions.[60] The most prominent note of dissent in the 26 October edition was a statement titled "Autonomía vs. partidismo," signed by seventy-four journalists and administrative staff at the paper. "The dismissal of our director is more than just the dismissal of an individual," the staffers wrote. "It is the liquidation of an entire journalistic project."[61] In particular, it represented a rejection of *Barricada*'s efforts to forge an "investigative, quality journalism" that would subject all those in "positions of public responsibility" to scrutiny, "independently of the party to which they belong." "These principles and criteria," the signatories asserted, "respond to the necessity of providing greater objectivity and impartiality in our media." They were indispensable if *Barricada* was "to gain credibility and esteem in the eyes of the public."

The staffers further condemned "the situation of instability and labor uncertainty" that prevailed in the wake of the *defenestración*. They referred to "the provocations, the veiled threats, [and] the defamation of the corps of writers and editors" that issued from ortodoxo quarters. These were "placing us, as journalists and workers, in danger." The document closed with a call for the directorate to "respect our physical and moral integrity," and for *Barricada*'s new directors to "respect the ethical and professional principles that, as journalists, we are obliged to abide by and defend."[62]

Still serving as caretaker was Daniel Alegría, who found himself, the morning after his protracted negotiations with Tomás Borge, coordinating the 27 October edition together with Lumberto Campbell. Borge was absent—receiving a dressing-down, Alegría claimed, from directorate members unhappy with the extensive and negative publicity the *defenestración* had generated. "At two o'clock [on the twenty-sixth] I meet with Lumberto and we talk about what stories should go where. He was in agreement on some things; on others, not." Alegría said he began to perceive the first signs of a new political agenda shaping *Barricada*'s content:

> I started seeing some political *clientelismo*. That day, somebody calls Lumberto and says, "Well, now that you're the editor, you can carry this on the front page." And he said, "Sure, no problem." It was some news that I'd already put on the international page, about Lumberto having visited somebody in a Spain a few days previously. . . . I said, "Look, to me that's not news. That goes on page four. You register the fact, but this and this and this are much more important. If you start doing favors like that, then you might just as well turn this into a rag and let people pay you for what they want you to publish. That isn't a newspaper."[63]

The events at *Barricada* slipped from the front page on 27 October, but the controversy within the institution—and in the wider society—abated not a bit. On 28 October Nicaragua's usually partisan journalists staged the first united protest in their history, in front of the building that housed the secretariat of the FSLN National Directorate. They proclaimed their blanket rejection of the defenestración at *Barricada,* and the measures taken simultaneously against the Sandinista radio programs *Sucesos* and *Perfiles.* Most of the protesters wore black armbands.[64] *Barricada* carried news of the protests on its front page on 29 October.

The day of the protest, though, was also the point at which a counterattack began to be mounted by ortodoxo elements within and outside the paper. Fifteen *Barricada* writers, led by Juan Ramón Huerta, responded to the declaration on "Autonomía vs. Partidismo" by calling for the decision of the Sandinista Assembly to be respected. *Barricada,* they contended, should abandon its pose of objectivity and neutrality and serve as "a privileged space for the popular sectors."[65] Most of the signatories were regional correspondents who had had little involvement with the day-to-day operations of the paper during the autonomy experiment.

The 28 October edition marked the final appearance of the supplement *Gente* under Sofía Montenegro's direction. Montenegro, as was her wont, chose to go out with a bang. "In three days of working day and night, I changed all the content [of the issue]. They couldn't stop it, because I had taken measures that in case they stopped the edition, all the negatives and everything would be with *El Nuevo Diario;* they would publish it instead." On the cover was a picture of a bemused-looking Carlos Fernando Chamorro, with the headline, "Scenes from a Dismissal." Fully half the content was devoted to the defenestración, including a two-page interview with Chamorro. "The assault on *Barricada,*" Montenegro wrote, "is no better in moral terms than the burning of *La Prensa* by Somoza" in the final days of the dictatorship. The cover would prompt a riposte from ortodoxo commentator Berenice Maranhao on 2 November, mocking *Gente* for putting the "sexy photo of its orgasmic director on the front page."[66]

The rift within the National Directorate over the defenestración reached *Barricada*'s pages along with Montenegro's final *Gente*. Four comandantes opposed to Chamorro's dismissal—the directorate's renovationist minority—published a quarter-page ad claiming Chamorro's dismissal had been plotted by "a sector of the FSLN that controls a majority of the directorate structures," and had used them to advance their agenda of "political intolerance, the repression of all manner of critical thinking, sectarianism, and verticalist imposition."[67] But the balance of power within *Barricada* itself was shifting. The renovationists' proclamation brought a response in *Barricada* the following day, written by Comandante Mónica Baltodano, long one of the most vocal critics of *Barricada*'s autonomy experiment. In her 29 October contribution, she bluntly charged the dissident DN members with "falling into an anti-Sandinista position."[68] Four days later, Berenice Maranhao (in her critique of *Gente* —see note 66) accused *Barricada* of constructing an "invented spectacle" reminiscent of both Nazi propaganda under Goebbels and the magical-realist writings of Gabriel García Márquez. The Nazi comparison was also implicit in the title of Maranhao's piece: "Lie, Lie, Some Will Believe."[69]

The battle behind the scenes was no less intense. "I had harsh words with Tomás [Borge] every night," said Sofía Montenegro. "I told him . . . I had appreciated him as a leader, but now I didn't see any difference between him and any vulgar foreman of a banana plantation. That really got his goat. . . . We remained there until two or three in the morning every day, and we fucked him up, because he had to stay there fighting us until whatever hour."[70]

"Every day it was a struggle," Daniel Alegría remembered. "Every day, [we argued] over what should go in and what shouldn't go in. But I could see how the paper was changing." After four days of working "from ten in the morning until two in the morning," Alegría came down with the flu and retreated to his home. There he received a phone call from Tomás Borge—just appointed president of *Barricada*'s publishing operation, and of its editorial council.

Tomás calls and says, "Look, I'm sending you an article that I want you to read, to publish on the front page." I read the article. It's an *auto-entrevista* [self-interview], done about Tomás by some Mexican [writer]. . . . He calls me back and says, "What do you think?" I said, "I think it's awful!" "Why?" I said, "Because it goes nowhere. . . . It's not front-page news." "But that's my opinion." I said, "Well, great." And then he said, "I want you to sign it. . . . You're somebody on the *Barricada* staff that people know. It's very different if you sign it than if this Mexican guy who nobody knows signs it." I said, "Well, if you want me to sign it, I'll do an interview that might be publishable on the front page, but it will have some other questions." He said, "It's too late. I wanted it for tomorrow." I said, "Well, I'm sorry, I'm not signing it."

Then he calls me and says, "Can you come here and discuss it?" . . . And so at six o'clock I go there and I see the proofs of the page, and [*Barricada* staffer] Juan Ramón Huerta had signed the article. . . . I said, "I think this is bullshit. I think it's really bad for Juan Ramón Huerta. He's going to be a laughing-stock." Because he published *everything*, even the fucking typos, and put his name to it! And then Juan Ramón Huerta says, "No, I only edited it." I said, "Look, it's so easy. If you would make a lead saying, 'In an interview done by so-and-so for such-and-such, in such-and-such a context, Tomás Borge . . .' And then you can sign it; I have no problem with that. But if you take out his name and pretend *you* did the interview, and you don't change anything, I think that's terrible."

For Alegría it was the final straw. "I was paving my way out. I said, 'If that's the way this paper is going to be, I'm quitting.' . . . Tomás tried to convince me to stay, but that was my way out. I knew I couldn't go on this way. Basically, they'd swallow me up and I'd have to eat shit for the rest of my life, or leave with my tail between my legs. I said, this is where I'm burning my bridges."[71]

The "interview" with Borge appeared on 2 November.[72] On 3 November, *Barricada* published Alegría's letter of resignation. In it, Alegría claimed he had agreed to serve as editor "for a brief period" in order to preserve some degree of continuity and normalcy in an institution he cherished. "But from the very day Carlos left, the political pressures began . . . every day in the editorial room little battles took place." The decision to take over the paper, Alegría contended, was realpolitik at its most naked: "The 'Democratic Left' needs a propaganda organ for the next electoral battle, and *Barricada* couldn't play that role. Now the owners want to go back down that road [*desandar el camino*]. . . . That's fine; they have every right to do so. What I don't agree with is the subterfuge and duplicitous behavior."

Alegría concluded his letter with a curiously wistful warning: "For a professional, it is sad to have to fall so far and violate the most elementary norms of journalistic ethics. But, well, everyone has to make his own bed, and lie in it. . . . If I'm wrong, and if *Barricada* does not degenerate into a party pamphlet, my resignation will stand as one of the worst errors of my life, because I will have left behind a project I believe in. But to be right would be even worse—since I would never feel it as a victory."[73]

As Alegría and Montenegro, two more of the paper's senior figures, were preparing to exit, cloudy but intriguing evidence was emerging of censoriousness among *Barricada*'s new directorate. *La Tribuna* reported the claim of *Barricada* staff writer Silvia Torres that an article she had written on 2 November had been rejected for publication by Lumberto Campbell. Torres said the article had taken to task fellow staffer Juan Ramón Huerta for attaching his name to the now notorious autoentrevista with Tomás Borge. Several days later, Mildred Largaespada, who edited *Barricada*'s popular page *De todo un poco*, likewise told *La Tribuna* that a column she had written for publication on 5 November had been censored. The column, she claimed, asserted that Mónica Baltodano had obtained "the object of her desires"—*Barricada;* according to Largaespada, Baltodano was "the big winner in this crisis." In a 1996 interview Largaespada repeated her contention that "The husband of this woman [Julio López, shortly to be named *Barricada*'s subdirector] censored me and told me that the newspaper was going to defend the Sandinista

Front." She said she was told that no further articles would be published on the internal crisis at the paper.[74]

These allegations, if true, revealed something of the mind-set of the new guardians of *Barricada*. But they should not be allowed entirely to offset the remarkable degree of freedom that opponents of the defenestración received during the trying days of the interregnum. It may seem clear, in retrospect, that the notion of decapitating the semiautonomous *Barricada* by dismissing Chamorro and perhaps a few other recalcitrants, then building a more "loyal" institution around remaining middle-ranking staff, was always unworkable. But the orchestrators of the defenestración could be forgiven for thinking that some compromise arrangement was possible. After all, Ortega, Borge and a number of the other directorate members (including the chameleonlike Bayardo Arce) had once cast a benevolent eye over the operations of a *Barricada* that appeared very similar to the model they were now seeking to entrench—and scant years earlier, to boot. That highly mobilized incarnation of *Barricada* had, in turn, been guided by more or less the same core group that staffed the paper in 1994. During the revolutionary decade, even those *Barricada* staffers most determined to increase the paper's autonomy—figures like Carlos Fernando Chamorro, Sofía Montenegro, Sergio de Castro, and Onofre Guevara—had accommodated themselves (with varying degrees of friction) to the vanguardist model of party-paper relations. Could *Barricada*'s staff not be swayed to the new party line, especially given the difficulty of finding other jobs in Nicaragua's shattered economy? The idea was not absurd in itself, especially once Daniel Alegría had agreed to play the role of interim editor. Alegría's resignation, and the more general cohesion among those who remained at the paper—vividly manifested in the protest letter signed by seventy-four staff, and again in the mass exodus that ensued in late October and early November—may have come as an unwelcome surprise to the ortodoxos. According to Sofía Montenegro, the leadership "believed the journalists didn't have a mind of their own: that there was somebody, a godhead [Chamorro], pushing them into this position. Their logic was, 'If we cut off the heads, the remainder will quiet down.'"[75]

Some tradeoffs and compromises would surely be necessary to implement this strategy—but no one in the Sandinista Front was a stranger to such negotiations. If the result was a *Barricada* that was perhaps not all the ortodoxos wanted, there would be a number of offsetting advantages. The most significant was institutional continuity. The proponents of the defenestración certainly understood the material challenge of keeping the paper going in an environment in which resources, both personal and material, were hard to come by. Key to the new project's survival would likely be the preservation of as much of *Barricada*'s existing readership as possible. Could a constructive balance not be struck between the mobilizing requirements of the front's leadership and the wishes of the paper's staff (and doubtless many readers) for a degree of editorial independence? At a number of points in the autoentrevista of 2 November, Tomás Borge appeared to be pursuing just such a compromise, seeking to assuage concerns about the professional identity of the new *Barricada*. In particular, he paid magnanimous homage to the professional character of the autonomy project and its custodians. Borge described Carlos Fernando Chamorro as "a compañero with professional journalistic qualities, [and] with the popular touch"—though Chamorro was an inappropriate director "for a newspaper identified with the revolutionary objectives of the FSLN." Weekly supplements like *Gente* were "indispensable" to the paper, and Sofía Montenegro's publication "ha[d] been, in its format, very well done."[76]

As October turned into November, though, it was plain that whatever positive inducements the paper's new directorate could offer would not wash with most *Barricada* staff. The trickle of resignations became a flood.

The "Negotiated Exit"

At some point about a week into the interregnum, the FSLN leadership seems to have decided the following:

- that *Barricada* staff were too united in their opposition to the new project to serve as a foundation for it;

- that the political costs of the defenestración and subsequent outcry had largely been borne, and there was now little to lose by wiping the slate clean;

- that even if *Barricada*'s circulation and influence were decreased by an exodus of readers, this could be overcome in time to mobilize the paper effectively for the 1996 elections;

- that the circulation of the paper might even increase in the wake of the defenestración—there were, after all, 350,000 registered FSLN militants in Nicaragua, who mostly supported the ortodoxo line and might be prevailed upon to support the new version of *Barricada*; and

- that even if none of these strategies worked, and *Barricada* declined in both circulation and influence, the material deficit would be offset in the larger scheme of things by a new harmony of interests between the paper's directorate and the now dominant ortodoxo current of the front. More efficient coordination, for example, would now be possible among the FSLN's various print and broadcast media—and the Sandinistas' prospects in the 1996 elections correspondingly enhanced.[77]

The circumstances of the top-to-bottom transformation of *Barricada*'s staff that ensued remain the subject of bitter controversy. All that can be said with confidence is that the situation prevailing after Chamorro's dismissal—the clash of mobilizing and professional imperatives that seemed to occur at every editorial gathering—was ultimately untenable for either side. Who among *Barricada*'s staff jumped ship, and who was pushed? Tomás Borge offered a paradoxical assessment that may also be the most accurate one: the staff "chose to leave," he said, but "we formally fired them because they asked us to do so."[78] Whatever the mechanism, the human underpinnings of the semiautonomous *Barricada* rapidly disappeared. As early as 1 November, *Barricada* reported on its front page that sixteen journalists, among them Sofía Montenegro and Onofre Guevara, were seeking a "negotiated exit" from the paper.[79] *La Tribuna* published Sofía Montenegro's contention that *Barricada*'s new directors had "told us that we do not believe in their proposals [for *Barricada*], and that there exists a mutual lack of confidence. They suggested we wouldn't want to cause damage to the enterprise, and that we could negotiate . . . as gentlemen, or seek legal redress. . . . Over the course of the rest of the week an agreement was worked out, and they will be free to look for their [own] journalists."[80]

One sector of *Barricada* staff, though, was isolated entirely from the wrenching upheavals taking place in the editorial division. Despite the earlier references to the solidarity that largely prevailed among the paper's journalists and editors, a clear distinction must be drawn between this sector and the blue-collar staff who ran the presses in Plant B of Editorial El Amanecer. The blue-collar workers displayed a much more sanguine—often a supportive—attitude toward the events of 25 October. According to Daniel Alegría, relations between plant and editorial workers at *Barricada* had never been close: "There has never been that sort of link between journalists and printers. I mean, not here, not anywhere. You know the guys, but they do one thing, you do another. Even your working hours do not coincide."[81] More important, it was the blue-collar side of the operation that had been gutted in the layoffs and downsizing of the early 1990s, while the editorial staff remained largely unscathed. "How many *compactaciones* [downsizings] have there been here?" demanded Frank Avilés, a *Barricada* photomechanic, shortly after the *defenestración*. "Nobody ever said anything when workers were fired. Nobody kicked up a fuss. They fired people without so much as a thank you for all the years they worked here. Well, now it's their turn." Another protested to *Barricada Internacional,* "They [the journalists] never did anything for other workers when they were laid off; they used to justify it, saying the paper was falling apart."[82]

Given the precariousness of their employment at *Barricada,* it was also the plant workers who felt most affronted by instances of corruption and mismanagement at the newspaper—during the same years that hundreds of *Barricada* workers experienced painful defenestraciones of their own. On the very day of Chamorro's dismissal, the workers in Plant B issued a declaration of their own in *Barricada,* accusing Bayardo Arce of being "the main one responsible for the chaotic financial state in which this enterprise finds itself." They called for the resignation of *Barricada*'s senior management together with Arce: all stood accused of resorting to "Somocista administrative measures that injure the interests of the workers."[83]

The schism between plant and editorial staff ruled out the formation of a truly common front at *Barricada* in the days and weeks following the defenestración. Had the plant workers struck—as they would in late 1997, with decisive results—a serious opposition to the new order might well have been mounted. So long as the presses and the delivery trucks kept rolling, however, resistance was largely symbolic. Whatever obstacles confronted *Barricada*'s new directorate, it would at least be able to rely on continuity at the level of production. The schism among staff also gave *Barricada*'s new guardians one of their few advantages in the court of public opinion. They were quick to exploit it: at one point Tomás Borge even claimed the defenestración had taken place "only for this reason"—that is, to demonstrate a proper "admir[ation] and respect [for] the work of those in the area of production."[84]

Barricada's directorate now moved to replenish *Barricada*'s depleted editorial corps. Within days of the defenestración, the two leading ortodoxos at the paper's Managua office—Juan Ramón Huerta, editor of the *Municipios* section, and reporter-photographer

Pablo Emilio Barreto—had been promoted to leading roles at the paper. Now they were designated journalistic recruiters (*reclutadores de periodistas*). Their early efforts bore little fruit. Mario Fulvio Espinosa, a veteran editor at *El Nuevo Diario,* agreed to move to *Barricada.* But at least three other journalists who were offered positions refused—including Silvio Mora, an assistant to Tomás Borge. Alfonso Malespín, a journalist unaffiliated with the Sandinista Front who had been brought in to buttress the "objective" tone of *Barricada*'s political reporting in the early 1990s, agreed to stay on. By mutual agreement, however, Malespín's position at the newspaper was changed from the sensitive one of political correspondent to editor of *De todo un poco,* the leisure-and-entertainment page. Malespín thus carved himself out a new niche at the paper, becoming something of "a case apart," in Sofía Montenegro's words. His perspective on *Barricada*'s experience in the 1990s is a unique one, and receives closer attention in chapter 4.

Many regional correspondents—the one generally pro-ortodoxo sector of *Barricada*'s editorial staff—offered to move to Managua to help fill the yawning editorial gaps. Among those who made the move were Marta Marina González (Estelí), Tatiana Rothschuh (Chontales), and Pedro Vindell (Granada). The focus of outside recruitment shifted to target a disproportionate number of Tomás Borge's assistants at the Ministry of the Interior during the 1980s: Fernando Solís, Mayra Reyes, José Reyes Monterrey, and Judith Ruíz among them. Many of these figures had little if any prior journalistic experience.[85] As Alfonso Malespín told *El Semanario* at the time, "The problem [the new directors] have is that they want to change the newspaper, but they don't know how to do it, because they haven't brought in anyone technically capable of introducing the changes they want."[86] This lack of professional experience would prove one of the most debilitating factors in the early months of the new *Barricada.*

A smoother transition was effected at the leadership level. On 4

November, Sofía Montenegro and subdirector Sergio de Castro disappeared from *Barricada*'s masthead. Julio López, a presence at the paper from the day of the defenestración, formally appeared as de Castro's replacement.[87] López was a former Baptist preacher and sociology professor with a law degree from the University of Lausanne. One of the "political temporary directors" installed at *Barricada* before Carlos Fernando Chamorro arrived as editor, he had also substituted for Chamorro at *Barricada* for a brief period in 1980, before moving on to work at the FSLN's Department of International Relations. Along with his wife, Sandinista comandante Mónica Baltodano, López had established himself as a leading ortodoxo voice in the intraparty debate of the early 1990s. He and Baltodano, as we have seen, were among the few ortodoxos who chose to contribute opinion pieces to *Barricada* during the years of the autonomy experiment.

On the same day as López was confirmed in his new position, an altogether more enigmatic figure was installed as *Barricada*'s new editor in chief. William Grigsby's appointment ended days of speculation that had seen a number of prominent Sandinistas bandied about as candidates, including Jaime Wheelock (the former minister of agriculture) and Miguel D'Escoto (foreign minister in the revolutionary government). At first glance, Grigsby seemed an unlikely choice for editor in chief. He was a former journalism student who had worked first with the state news agency, Agencia Nueva Nicaragua, and subsequently as a reporter with *El Nuevo Diario* for most of the 1980s. His professional credentials were thus considerable. In February 1987, though, Grigsby commissioned an interview with Alan Bolt, leader of a Matagalpa-based theatre group. Bolt strongly criticized the front's growing verticalism and called for a more democratic distribution of power: for "discipline without hierarchy . . . well-being for all, but without special privileges." The criticisms echoed Grigsby's own.[88] In light of his previous infractions, Grigsby was expelled from the FSLN. He promptly published a piece in *El Nuevo Diario* signed by him personally and titled "The Fear of Democracy." It riled front leaders "because of its honesty," Grigsby explained in 1991, "and because it was a challenge to the official line."[89] Among other things, it accused Daniel Ortega and his brother Humberto of maintaining unacceptably high standards of living. In May 1987, *El Nuevo Diario*—possibly bowing to pressure from the FSLN leadership—fired him. Grigsby moved over to the radio station La Primerísima, and quickly climbed the ladder to become director and host of the station's most popular program.

Throughout my interview with him at La Primerísima in February 1991, Grigsby appeared agitated, answering questions in curt bursts. A .45 pistol was parked prominently on his desk, with a full clip of bullets adjacent. Death threats had apparently become common as, after the election defeat, Grigsby renewed his populist attack on selected FSLN leaders, especially the Ortega brothers. A few months before the interview, in September 1990, La Primerísima's transmitters had been bombed. The station was knocked off the air and forced to seek international aid to get back on its feet.[90]

Grigsby's considerable popularity among listeners derived from his persona as voice of the impoverished Sandinista majority. While the poor fought the UNO regime's attempts to roll back the revolution's gains, Grigsby proclaimed, the FSLN leadership was betraying the people by engaging in concertación with the government. He denounced the piñata, which some within the front had used to bolster their own resources—notably Daniel Ortega, with his mansion in Reparto El Carmen. His most vituperative criticism, though, was reserved for army chief Humberto Ortega. In conversation in 1991, he accused the ex-comandante of "an overbearing nature, arrogance, and ambition, which prevent him from being a genuine revolutionary." As the military, still under Ortega's command, was slashed from seventy thousand to twenty-eight thousand troops, Grigsby opened La Primerísima's phone lines to disenchanted, disoriented career soldiers, who suddenly found themselves kicked out with few severance benefits and even sparser job prospects. When Humberto Ortega threw his support behind the UNO regime's suppression of strikes during the near insurrection of July 1990, sending in soldiers to dismantle the street barricades, Grigsby was apoplectic. How could a self-proclaimed Sandinista institution adopt a posture of neutrality or even active opposition in the face of massive popular discontent? Soon after, La Primerísima was bombed; Grigsby openly accused Humberto Ortega of complicity in the attack.[91]

There was also the matter of Grigsby's vendetta against Rosario Murillo.[92] In 1991, Grigsby had ridiculed Murillo, Daniel Ortega's partner, for her public statements, which stand in retrospect as one of the earliest expressions of the ortodoxo tendency within the front. He argued that her "purist" ideological pronouncements, directed against *Barricada* and others, were part of an intricate strategy to bolster the status quo within the front, and with it the power and influence of Daniel Ortega. To advance these ambitions, Murillo and her allies—including, implicitly, Ortega—were prepared to compromise revolutionary principles and betray the sectors for which the revolution had been waged. "An event to purge the ranks" was needed at the party congress of July 1991, Grigsby said a few months before the congress convened. It should be followed by "a national process of consultation" aimed at returning the front to its roots and "recover[ing] credibility among the Sandinistas and the people as a whole." Murillo's response to Grigsby's broadcast charges was to accuse La Primerísima's director of being a CIA agent.[93]

Given this background, one might sooner have expected Violeta Chamorro to be named *Barricada*'s new editor than William Grigsby. Perhaps, though, the above account offers clues as to why Grigsby was chosen. In a sense, few had taken a more militant or ortodoxo line than Grigsby in the years following the Sandinista defeat. His criticism of the policies of concertación and co-gobierno that the increasingly ortodoxo leadership would themselves abandon in mid-1993 seemed ahead of its time. Likewise, the accusations the ortodoxos would direct against *Barricada* and other perceived renovationist forces in 1993–94—of compromise with conservative forces, of a fickle revolutionary commitment, of personalism and clientelism—were precisely the charges Grigsby had been leveling at various Sandinistas (including more than a few ortodoxos) since 1990. Furthermore, if the front's leadership saw Grigsby as somewhat irascible and unpredictable, his combination of solid journalistic experience and pugnacious populism could help invigorate the new *Barricada*. Perhaps Grigsby's presence would garner the paper credibility among longtime readers who feared *Barricada* would become merely the house organ of Tomás Borge and Daniel Ortega. Borge himself hinted at a number of these factors in a 1996 interview: Grigsby was chosen, he said, "because of his professional capacities. Because of his journalistic efficiency and his basic identification with the front. He's a compañero with very independent criteria; he says what he thinks, and doesn't submit himself to arbitrary authority. But at the same time, he's very disciplined."[94]

In an interview conducted around the same time, Grigsby denied any dissonance between his past stands and his responsibilities as chief editor. To the contrary, he said, he had actively pursued the editor's position *"como trabajo militante"*—as his revolutionary duty. "The front knew that my thinking on many issues" varied from many in the leadership, he added; "but I don't bring my own opinions to bear on the newspaper. . . . *Barricada* might take a different position than mine, but here I respond to the needs of the paper." Did the arrangement allow him less freedom than he enjoyed at La Primerísima, the radio station he continued to direct? "Of course," Grigsby answered—then backtracked slightly. "Not less freedom, but . . . what I say here at *Barricada* has political consequences for the Sandinista Front. I have to think about how something I publish will affect the front. It's a totally different level of operation."[95] Grigsby's presence, though, lent a volatile ingredient to the postdefenestración mix—one that eventually proved impossible to reconcile with the new vision of the paper that Borge and the others were working to entrench. At the time of my fieldwork in 1996, there were hints that Grigsby's attempts to preserve a degree of professional autonomy for the paper were drawing him into conflict with Borge and his other immediate superior, Julio López. By the time *Barricada* breathed its last, in January 1998, Grigsby was long gone.

Aftermath

While *Barricada* struggled to find its feet under the new *dirección*, the displaced veterans shifted their strategy to other fronts. First they attempted to cast doubt on the legality of the *defenestración*. During the period of the interregnum, some disaffected staffers went so far as to contend, "The FSLN is not the owner of *Barricada*" (to quote a headline of the time in *La Tribuna*). Rather, according to *La Tribuna*'s report, "an anonymous society composed of prominent Sandinista leaders, among them Bayardo Arce and Joaquín Cuadra Chamorro, may be the [real] owners . . . and not the Sandinista Front as a party." The journalists said Ronaldo Gómez, who became *Barricada*'s general manager after Max Kreimann departed under a cloud of corruption allegations, had shown them documents indicating that Joaquín Cuadra Chamorro[96] owned 96 percent of the shares in Editorial El Amanecer, *Barricada*'s publishing enterprise. The remaining 4 percent allegedly was shared by Bayardo Arce and Carlos Fernando Chamorro. *Barricada*'s publishers issued a denial, and no credible evidence was found that might have permitted a serious legal challenge to be mounted.[97]

Another convoluted blocking maneuver was attempted, this time on procedural grounds. The board of directors of Editorial El Amanecer was the body formally empowered to appoint *Barricada*'s director and editorial council. According to ex-*Barricada* staffer Guillermo Cortés, writing in *El Semanario* after the *defenestración*,

"The Sandinista Assembly made a political decision [to dismiss Carlos Fernando Chamorro], but this has to be approved by the board of directors, whose president—just by chance!—was at that moment in Spain."[98] The president of the council, of course, was Bayardo Arce. He had indeed been absent when the boom was lowered on *Barricada*. Did that mean the board as a whole had not approved the defenestración? Was the status of the takeover thus in question? Apparently not, for this line of attack quickly fizzled as well and was forgotten.

The dispute then moved to the National Assembly. On 7 November 1994, seventeen recently departed *Barricada* staffers—among them Onofre Guevara, Sofía Montenegro, and Juan José Lacayo—made a submission to the assembly's Commission on Human Rights. They accused *Barricada*'s new directorate of violating their "constitutional and human rights," including the "minimum right of free expression." The new regime, they claimed, had "imposed censorship of opinion upon the journalists," "kidnapped articles," and created "a psychological atmosphere inappropriate for work" through "the presence of bodyguards and people linked to the new management." Now they were "trying to attack the right to information by publishing headlines and texts as news, when in reality they are simply political opinions." In an interesting turn of phrase, the submission accused the directorate of "practicing a policy of flattery, pressure, [and] moral and economic blackmail" against staff—again an indication, perhaps, that the new guard was offering blandishments to staff in an attempt to persuade them to stay on at *Barricada*.[99]

Rebuffed by the parliamentary commission, the ex-staffers carried their campaign to the courts. In the severance arrangements reached or imposed after the defenestración, *Barricada*'s directorate had offered only the minimum compensation required by the new Nicaraguan labor code—basically resuscitated legislation from the era of Somoza. The FSLN, of course, had vociferously opposed the code.

Barricada staffers now demanded much more generous severance benefits, along with 40 percent of the shares in Editorial El Amanecer.[100] But the legal avenues of redress likewise proved fruitless. Three consecutive judges ruled against the suits by *Barricada* personnel. Again the split between plant and editorial workers at the predefenestración *Barricada* reared its head, to the detriment of the former staff. Representatives of the printers' union were brought in to testify about mismanagement of the enterprise under Chamorro's direction, among other issues.[101]

There was little more that could be done, and finally all staffers except Sofía Montenegro accepted the terms of financial compensation offered by the front in the wake of the court defeats. Life went on. Mid-1996 found Montenegro working at the Center for Communications Research (CINCO), a social-scientific institute established by Carlos Fernando Chamorro not long after the defenestración. In her work at CINCO, and through her other involvements, she maintained a high profile in the Nicaraguan and Central American women's movement—which she said proudly had become "the biggest, strongest, most territorially extensive movement in Central America, and one of the strongest women's movements in Latin America." It was also, she said, "the only women's movement in Central America that has broken completely with the political parties"—as she herself had done after the coup at *Barricada.* Montenegro considered her "personal role" now to be that of "an independent investigator, a journalist, and—as Gramsci would say—an organic intellectual. For me, this is the role of the feminist in society." Her basic confidence in the future gave her backbone, she said. Gesturing from her sitting room toward her "garden of rage," a small but vibrant shrubbery she had begun to cultivate after leaving *Barricada,* Montenegro drew on a botanical metaphor to express her thoughts about the movement to which she had devoted her adult life: "Wherever people see destruction, I see, out of this chaos, the flowers [blooming]. I see the revolution in these things. The flowers are blooming a posteriori and self-conducted. They are not flowers that were born by decree. But they've gone through the fire. They are strong plants. Hybrids, good hybrids. I feel this country is like a greenhouse, like my garden of rage. Out of pure fucking rage, something so beautiful came out. An entire microclimate."[102]

Daniel Alegría, meanwhile, remained his buoyant self. He moved on to a position as regional project officer for OXFAM, after serving a stint at the monthly *Pensamiento Propio* before it folded. "It looks like everywhere I go closes down!" Alegría cracked. He spoke candidly of the political disaffection he, like many reform-minded Sandinistas, felt in the wake of the 1994 congress and the destruction of *Barricada*'s autonomy experiment:

> I think, like me, there's a vast majority of Sandinistas with no adjectives. . . . They don't feel represented either by the ramiristas [Sergio Ramírez's MRS] or by Daniel [Ortega]. For us, what's the alternative? Form another party? That would be ridiculous. . . . I've been sort of burned out. Right now I'm just watching things from afar. I'm not taking a fall for anyone. I look around, but there's no one to vote for. . . . I'm cynical!

The Sandinista Front, he argued, was "turning into a PRI [the Revolutionary Institutional Party of Mexico]. That's not a new analogy or anything, but it's going that way in the sense that power has become an objective in itself. . . . It's like *Jurassic Park*—the same dinosaurs running the show." But Alegría expressed little bitterness toward the new custodians of *Barricada*. Of Tomás Borge, Alegría said: "He's my friend, you know. The strange thing about Nicaragua is, I don't have any beef. What's done is done. . . . I don't bear a grudge against Tomás."[103]

Carlos Fernando Chamorro, for his part, was outspoken in comments to the media shortly after his dismissal,[104] but he soon reverted to his more typical equanimity. He moved on to found CINCO, which sought to systematize the study of the media, politics, and public opinion in Nicaragua. He published (together with

Guillermo Rothschuh) the first postrevolutionary study of national media, *Los medios y la política en Nicaragua* (1995). He founded a new weekly newspaper of political opinion, *Confidencial*.[105] And he became co-host of *Esta Semana* (This week), a current-affairs-oriented TV program, politely grilling guests from across the political spectrum—including the man who had orchestrated his dismissal from *Barricada,* Daniel Ortega. In an interview at his suburban home in 1996, Chamorro characterized his post-*Barricada* experience as a transitional one. He was engaged, he said, in "a process of reviewing my view of the world and of politics," and was in "no hurry" to complete the self-evaluation. Asked to reflect on fifteen years as *Barricada*'s director, Chamorro described the period in terms of personal, political, and professional evolution:

> Probably the most important part of my adult life I spent at *Barricada.* I grew up at *Barricada.* I have to say I'm happy I was able to survive *Barricada* and become much more the owner of myself in the last five or eight years. . . . *Barricada* also gave me a lot of friends, a lot of satisfaction, a lot of learning. Probably the most important thing is that I found my own place as a professional. I'm not longing anymore to be an economist or anything else. I know I'm a journalist. Again, that's thanks to surviving *Barricada.* I was able to move beyond my own understanding of ten years as a political cadre who was doing journalism; I became more a journalist than a political cadre. I think one of my skins has been left behind.[106]

But at the newspaper Chamorro once directed, the cadres had returned.

Chapter 4

Back to the Barricades

An Official Press Reborn

WHEN THE DUST settled at the new *Barricada* in November 1994, the paper's directorate—notably the core trio of Tomás Borge, Julio López, and William Grigsby—faced a challenge that was by nearly any measure unenviable.

In an immediate sense, the task of producing publishable copy would have to be accomplished despite a severe deficit in professional skills and capabilities. The defenestración and its aftermath had prompted the departure of most experienced staff and the arrival of dozens of new workers whose political loyalty was unquestioned but whose journalistic experience was often minimal or nonexistent. Even at the level of the paper's directorate, only William Grigsby could claim much in the way of hands-on media experience. Administrative and managerial expertise was also hard to come by. A year and a half after the October events, Grigsby frankly acknowledged the quandary: "Look, I think that in 1995 we lost professional quality. Because practically the entire personnel left." He argued optimistically that "now [1996] we are competing in terms of journalistic quality with anyone you can name." Nonetheless, *Barricada* still had "a long way to go."[1]

Just producing the paper was a daunting enough task; there was also the question of who would buy it. The well-publicized struggle at the paper had greatly compromised *Barricada*'s standing in the eyes of established readers—those who had shored up the declining, but perhaps sustainable, circulation levels of the early 1990s. Almost immediately after the defenestración, *Barricada*'s circulation went into free fall. Roberto Fonseca reported in December 1996 that the number of *Barricada* subscribers declined from 4,000 in October 1994 to 2,500 in May 1996, while overall circulation fell from 15,000 to 7,000 in the same period.[2] By January 1998, when for the first time in its history *Barricada* failed to appear on newsstands, some estimates put the circulation as low as 5,000.[3] Advertising revenue was also hard to find, even before the government of Arnoldo Alemán took power in 1996 and launched an advertising boycott of *Barricada* and other independent media.

Tomás Borge, the paper's new director, oscillated between predictions that *Barricada*'s circulation would stage a recovery and claims that even if it didn't, the paper could still fulfill its designated role in the Sandinista movement. A Reuters dispatch published in *El Nuevo Diario* shortly after the defenestración quoted Borge as "predict[ing] that *Barricada*'s circulation would increase and that, together with the party's radio stations and TV channel, [the paper] would lead the Sandinista Front to victory in the 1996 elections by bolstering its base of support among the poor."[4] On another occasion, though, Borge allowed that *Barricada* was "not exactly a commercial undertaking" (*un proyecto comercial*); "its primary objectives," he said, were "oriented toward service."[5]

Of course, it was not as though the new custodians of *Barricada* had inherited a project that was flourishing on a material level. It was tempting to link the difficulties of the ortodoxo-controlled *Barricada* to its semiautonomous predecessor, and in 1996 William Grigsby did so with a vengeance:

We practically had to take on [*subir*] a newspaper in dire straits economically, with a debt of two million dollars, and with a market that didn't receive the newspaper with the same acceptance as before, with a circulation that had sharply declined since the middle of 1993. We took on a newspaper that was frankly in bad condition, that had been in a backward state [*atrasado*] for fifteen years. We didn't have sufficient investment or financial capacity to rectify the situation right away. And a grave problem of personnel [existed] as well—[affecting] capacity in every area of the newspaper.[6]

"This isn't only a journalistic challenge," said Grigsby, "but also a challenge in terms of resources—whether we can obtain sufficient paper, sufficient *lamina* [blank photographic plates]. It's not just a professional challenge but a material and administrative one." *Barricada* additionally was forced to depend on support from the poorer sectors of society—the paper's natural constituency—who had to be persuaded to devote a fair chunk of their discretionary income to the newspaper. "The truth is that the people are dying of hunger," Grigsby said. "A pound of rice costs C$2.75 and a newspaper costs C$3.00."

Could *Barricada* find sufficient popular support to offset the decline in circulation and advertising? For all his optimism about the professional side of the operation, Grigsby doubted it. A more pressing concern, he indicated, was to preserve *Barricada*'s appeal to "the middle sectors," which didn't confront the same economic dilemma as the very poor. "Our market positioning directs us toward the lower middle class," Grigsby said. That meant the paper had to move beyond its pro-FSLN mobilizing imperative and cater to "many requirements with regard to show business, culture, and 'light' information."[7] But how would such apolitical (some would say reactionary) content be viewed by those who saw the *defenestración* as an opportunity for *Barricada* to return to the ultramobilized glory days of the revolutionary decade? All these questions lingered as the new *dirección* reached out to Sandinista militants and the wider Nicaraguan society. Nearly all would be answered to the decisive detriment of the new project.

"A Relative Objectivity Such As Decency Demands": Mobilizing and Professional Imperatives, 1994–98

> This newspaper is the property of the Sandinista Front. We recognize the Sandinista Front, and we jointly [*coyunturale*] apply its principles, its program, and its political line. But we have a personality with a space sufficiently broad to make not a newspaper of political propaganda, but a newspaper of political information.
>
> —William Grigsby

The editorial team that took over at *Barricada* after the defenestración saw and presented its mission as one of liberation.[8] "Under the pretext" of an autonomy project, Tomás Borge said in the autoentrevista credited to Juan Ramón Huerta, *Barricada* had become "aligned with a fraction of the FSLN." It had "abandon[ed] national interests in order to place itself at the service of a minority group, in which the old director of *Barricada* was registered." Did that mean *Barricada* would now return to being the official organ of the FSLN? Borge sidestepped the question. But he rejected the idea that reharmonizing *Barricada* with the dominant current of the front would lead to the paper's becoming merely "a party bulletin or pamphlet." Instead, *Barricada* would be "a professional newspaper, very broad, flexible, giving space to all [sectors of] national thinking." Symbolic of this ambition was the decision to preserve the masthead of the autonomy era: *Barricada* would continue to work *por los intereses nacionales,* "in the national interest"; Sandino's Stetson and the Nicaraguan flag would continue to be separated.[9] Nonetheless, said Borge, *Barricada* would "express—fundamentally—the Sandinista way of seeing the political and social contradictions of this country." He added: "We are going to make a newspaper that carries the banner of the most worthy popular causes; we are going to demonstrate that you can have a revolutionary newspaper that is, at the same time, professional. It's not a contradiction that the newspaper should be revolutionary and at the same time attractive. . . . Revolutionary indifference is detestable; revolutionary ardor and passion is the most noble face a journalist can present."

The new environment, though it posed its share of constraints, was also open to a more innovative and creative blending of mobilizing and professional considerations, in Borge's view. "The idea is not only to provide continuity," Borge confirmed, "but to widen the options that *Barricada* offers to readers."[10]

Juan Ramón Huerta, the ortodoxo staffer who had moved from black-sheep status to senior editor, also professed to find no contradiction between the paper's new mobilizing line and the professional standards entrenched under Carlos Fernando Chamorro: "We're trying to make a change in the political aspect of the newspaper—not in the professional aspect, because their project [i.e., before the defenestración] was very good in this respect. It's the same model we're trying to apply here. It hasn't changed, this concept of professional journalism. . . . The contradiction was strictly political."

Huerta added that, in his view, "Sandinista readers have the right to read about things other than party matters." And the constituency was a diverse one, extending beyond the militant core to "producers, economists, businesspeople." Accordingly, *Barricada* was "seeking a balance" between mobilizing and professional imperatives: "Logically, we should be able to sell our political proposal. But . . . if we start trying to sell our political proposal [to excess?], our readership will be reduced much further. We are clearly conscious of that phenomenon." Echoing Sergio de Castro's evaluation of early 1991, Huerta stressed that *Barricada* could not "abuse" readers' interests; "the people are tired of so much politics."[11]

Was a genuine balance of the imperatives still possible after the institutional restructuring of October–November 1994? In chapter 1, I argued that the bedrock of *Barricada*'s evolving autonomy and professionalism was the "firewalls"—some in place for many years by the time the autonomy project was officially launched—that had insulated the newspaper from personal and political interference by the party leadership. To recap briefly, these included:

• the banishing of political cadres from the newsroom early in the life of the paper (the first professional "uprising" against mobilizing dictates);

• the appointment of a single National Directorate member to mediate between the leadership and *Barricada,* which substantially reduced the directorate's micro-involvement in editorial policy;

• the construction of a New Editorial Profile in 1990 that downplayed mobilizing considerations and emphasized professional ones, including the cultivation of a much wider range of sources and outside commentary in the paper's coverage and a strict separation of editorials, news coverage, and personal opinion;

• the creation of an editorial council in 1990 dominated by establishment FSLN figures, a step removed from the fray of daily politics; and finally,

• the successful lobbying of the National Directorate to permit *Barricada*'s relaunching as a de-officialized publication working "in the national interest."

Barricada's new guard, as we have seen, was hardly so blind to the challenges it faced as to seek to "defenestrate" all these dimensions of the autonomy project along with Carlos Fernando Chamorro. Indeed, it was vital to preserve at least the appearance of institutional distance in *Barricada*'s dealings with the FSLN leadership. The task, though, was rendered more difficult by the fact that this leadership, in the form of Tomás Borge, now controlled the commanding heights of the newspaper's operations. Borge, accordingly, took pains to emphasize that he had no interest in interfering with daily editorial operations. In 1996 chief editor William Grigsby claimed the promise had been kept: "We [within *Barricada*] have control over the management of the paper; we determine what will be published and the prominence it will be given. That allows us to strike a balance, to avoid descending to the level of propaganda or pamphleteering. That depends on *us,* not on the leadership of the front."

Grigsby cast Borge's role in very much the same terms Chamorro had used to describe the role of the directorate representatives Carlos Núñez and Bayardo Arce during the 1980s and early 1990s. The fact that a member of the National Directorate was president of the editorial council, said Grigsby, did not present "a problem for professional journalism. To the contrary: it's the guarantee we have that there will not be attempts to manage us from the outside. I think we're lucky, in the sense that the two leaders of the front who best understand the problems of journalism are Bayardo Arce and Tomás Borge. . . . Tomás has been sufficiently flexible and open to all these [professional] concerns."[12]

How far did the rhetoric mesh with the reality? At the level of day-to-day functioning, several transformations were apparent. Perhaps the most striking was the recomposition of the editorial council and its almost immediate ossifying as a meaningful decision-making body at the paper. Neither William Grigsby nor Tomás Borge even bothered to mention the council in conversation, let alone to assign it a formative role in constructing a mobilizing or professional strategy for the paper. Watching now from the sidelines, Carlos Fernando Chamorro saw the shunting aside of the council as the best evidence of the new directors' unwillingness to diffuse party influence and control over *Barricada*'s project. The last attempt to sway the National Directorate before the defenestración, the "Ajustes" document of October 1994, envisaged an even greater role for the council; but this in retrospect was "all idealistic," Chamorro said. "For them, [the issue] was something totally different. It was simply a matter of, 'Why are we not controlling a newspaper that we own, like any other *patrón* [boss]?'" The council (consisting of Borge, Gloria Cardenal, Alba Palacios, and the Reverend Miguel Angel Casco) continued to appear on the masthead—but on 23 December 1996 it vanished, without comment or explanation, and did not reappear.

The erosion of the council's role also meant the marginalizing of Bayardo Arce as a mediating force. Arce continued to float at the periphery of the paper's operations as an advisor to the editorial council. But the council "doesn't work," Chamorro said bluntly in mid-1996: "I mean, he [Arce] told me the other day that the last time they had a meeting was four months ago."[13] William Grigsby defended Arce's continuing role at *Barricada*, though specifics were lacking. The paper, Grigsby said, had "frequent communication [with Arce] in order to consult him concerning operations we're undertaking in the marketplace—say, our relations with other media, or our political contacts with other forces. He has always been valuable to us."[14] Still, there was little indication that Arce exerted—or by this point even sought—influence over *Barricada*'s strategic course.

What power had once resided in the hands of Carlos Fernando Chamorro and the editorial council now devolved in certain (apparently decisive)[15] part to Tomás Borge. But the comandante's day-to-day involvement in the paper, at least through to the terminal crisis of late 1997, seemed surprisingly limited. Borge may have viewed *Barricada* as his personal toy, as his detractors alleged.[16] But he apparently sought little of the practical involvement that Carlos Fernando Chamorro had maintained.[17] He was often absent from the paper for extended stretches, pursuing his business involvements and political contacts throughout Central America and in Mexico. William Grigsby contended that Borge had "many responsibilities" at the newspaper, "supervis[ing] daily decisions" and maintaining "control over the daily operations" of *Barricada*. There was frankly little evidence of this during my four weeks of fieldwork at the paper in 1996; and Grigsby also stated that the political leadership of *Barricada* was exercised not by Borge, but by subdirector Julio López. Borge and López had regular conversations in which "decisions are made," said Grigsby, but without any "style of imposition" on Borge's part.[18]

It was Julio López whom many regarded as the brains behind the new *Barricada*. López had a direct line to the National Directorate not only through his relationship with Borge, but through his wife,

Mónica Baltodano, drafted to the directorate at the May 1994 party congress. Many observers had expected López himself to become a directorate member, given his prominence in the internal debate of the early 1990s. He was passed over, however; the nod may have gone to his wife instead, in part to help redress the gender imbalance among the FSLN leadership. The two were peas in a pod in any case, ideologically speaking; but now López, like Borge in the wake of the 1994 congress, lacked a pod to call his own. In October 1994, *Barricada* beckoned to both. According to Juan Ramón Huerta, López's role at the paper was "very important, because it is the guarantee that there will be cohesion between the interests of the party vis-à-vis [*frente a*] the population, and the interests of *Barricada* vis-à-vis the population. He is the main engine, the main catalyst of this cohesion. Before, there was no such cohesion. The forces of the party were on one side, the forces of the paper on the other."[19]

An evaluation of the degree of democratic decision making prevailing at the new *Barricada,* outside the governing triumvirate of Borge, López, and Grigsby, leads the analyst into rather subjective terrain. But the person who was perhaps the closest thing to a detached observer of the new experiment—Alfonso Malespín (see below)—found the new atmosphere at the paper both more highly mobilized and more rigidly hierarchical:

> I believe there was a more democratic daily life before [the defenestración]. We had daily [editorial] meetings before, and we discussed the things we were doing and how we were publishing them. We also criticized not only the director, but the editorial council—how they were running the newspaper. Now that doesn't happen, because there's a direct link between the party and the director, and he [Borge] randomly meets with Julio and William, so they have the line. William works mainly with the staff that are not involved in the political side of the newspaper; Julio meets the three members of the political staff, and they kind of have the picture first thing in the morning, which is basically the same as [pro-Sandinista] Radio Ya's and Radio Primerísima's.[20]

The firewalls constructed between editorials, news coverage, and personally signed opinion pieces also seemed in danger of disappearing at the new incarnation of *Barricada*. Nowhere was this more evident than in the ongoing dispute with the renovationist wing of Sandinismo. The defenestración at *Barricada* marked the climax, but not the end, of the battle; the new *Barricada*'s "dispatches from the front" were decidedly one-sided in tone and content. On 21 November 1994, barely three weeks after the defenestración, the entire editorial page of the newspaper was given over to an interview with Daniel Ortega, in large part devoted to the comandante's spin on the FSLN's internal divisions. A mocking column by Berenice Maranhao on 23 November referred to MRS leader Sergio Ramírez as "a case for Freud." Particularly interesting was the opinion page of 4 December. It featured no fewer than six articles on the subject of currents within the FSLN. Five denounced the actions of Ramírez and the other renovationists as "fractionalism," "scandalous," "a violation of FSLN statutes," "behavior irreconcilable with the Sandinista Front," and "playing the game of the right." The nondescript comments of a single MRS representative, José León Talavera, were tucked away at the bottom of the page. Three days later, a major unsigned article appeared on the opinion page, titled simply, "Ramírez Lies." Orlando Núñez provided a more sympathetic treatment of the MRS on 10 December, perhaps in the context of a renewed drive for unity by the ortodoxo-controlled Sandinista Assembly and National Directorate. But the basic tenor for coverage of the front's internal divisions had been set, and it would vary little over the formative period of the new *Barricada* in 1994–95. When Sergio Ramírez finally resigned from the FSLN in January 1995, for example, *Barricada* led off its coverage with Tomás Borge's *reaction* to the news, with a photo of *Borge* alongside. On *Barricada*'s opinion-editorial page the resignation was denounced as a "political travesty."[21]

Borge declared the internal problems of the FSLN resolved with

Ramírez's departure.[22] That did not stop *Barricada* from taking regular potshots at renovationist statements and activities thereafter. In August 1995, for example, the paper reported Sergio Ramírez's claim that Daniel Ortega, Mónica Baltodano, and Bayardo Arce were part-owners of a Nicaraguan bank. The headline read: "Sergio Ramírez: Gossip and Liar."[23] In December, when Ramírez accused Sandinista leaders of manipulating student strikes in Managua, *Barricada*'s headline was similarly provocative: "They Offend Students and Vilify the FSLN: *Ramiristas Wash Their Hands* [of responsibility]." Ramírez's charges, the article proclaimed, constituted an "insult to the decision-making powers of the university students and professors" and "a vile calumny against the leaders of the FSLN."[24]

These last, shrill contributions were not editorials, nor did they appear on the op-ed page; only one even carried a reporter's byline. As such, they were typical of *Barricada*'s new blurring of mobilizing and professional imperatives. As late as mid-1996, editor in chief William Grigsby defended the pugnacious coverage. "Ramirismo is at war with us," he declared. "And they fight dirty, using their communications media [*El Nuevo Diario,* presumably] to denigrate and attack the Sandinista Front." Grigsby acknowledged that *Barricada* had responded by adding a certain "tint" to coverage of the MRS and other renovationist forces. "We have made a decision that we will not give any space to Ramirismo as long as they are at war with the Sandinista Front." He denied that the ortodoxos were waging an offensive of their own: "We are in a war against Somocismo, not against them [the renovationists]."[25] How all this squared with Tomás Borge's pledge to "giv[e] space to all [sectors of] national thinking" was unclear.

Avowedly anti-Sandinista figures and forces were also treated with open contempt after October 1994. It is impossible, for example, to imagine an article appearing in the autonomy-era *Barricada* like the one published on 2 July 1995 under the headline, "The Fury and the

Hatred of *La Prensa.*" This was *Barricada*'s response to "immoral speculation" over Daniel Ortega's alleged involvement in a kidnapping plan—allegations that had been given heavy play in the pages of *Barricada*'s longtime nemesis. The *Barricada* of the early 1990s had taken pains to refer to its political and professional adversaries in respectful terms. Now *La Prensa* was referred to as a "filthy," "servile" publication.[26]

The erosion of professional firewalls was evident too in the paper's coverage of Violeta Chamorro's UNO government. Juan Ramón Huerta claimed in conversation that "we are very respectful in our treatment of the different parties";[27] but the analyst could hardly fail to be struck by the increasingly aggressive and personalized tone of the paper's reporting of regime policies and actions. When police fired on protestors in downtown Managua in May 1995, *Barricada* ran banner headlines reading, "Chamorro Represses" (17 May) and "Violeta Guilty" (18 May). When police and student demonstrators clashed in December of the same year, leaving one student killed and thirty-five students (as well as several police) injured, *Barricada* again ran the news on its front page, with the headline: "Chamorro Repeats [Somoza's] Massacre of 1959"—a reference to one of the earliest outbreaks of student protest against the dictatorship. This rhetoric would have seemed out of place even as an op-ed contribution to the semiautonomous *Barricada*. "FSLN Denounces Maneuvers of the New Traitors" was another representative headline of this period.[28]

The July 1995 story reporting *La Prensa*'s accusations against Daniel Ortega went on to heap plaudits on the Sandinista comandante, calling him "a leader whose name already belongs to the history of Nicaragua and Latin America." Ortega, *Barricada* wrote, "has no need to kidnap anyone in order to gain support that he has [already] acquired through his tenacity, valor, and unswerving loyalty to the interests of his people."[29] Such worshipful coverage of FSLN leaders was also typical, and stood as the obverse of the odium now heaped upon the front's political opponents—whether conservative or pro-revolutionary. In November 1995, as Ortega celebrated his birthday, *Barricada* wrote that "the people" celebrated along with him: "Hundreds of Sandinistas showed up yesterday morning at the offices of Radio Ya to celebrate the birthday of Cdte. Daniel Ortega and to back the decision of the FSLN National Directorate to nominate him as the [party's] presidential precandidate for next year's elections."[30] Half of the astrology page of the same edition was turned over to Ortega's horoscope, with entries like, "To understand him, it is necessary to know and love him." The feature articles, again, were not tagged as editorial or official statements of any kind.

Related and equally illuminating evidence of post-1994 transformation was found on the editorial page—or rather, *not* found there. The paucity of formal editorial commentary was a striking feature of *Barricada*'s new project. At least through the close of my fieldwork in mid-1996, the new *Barricada* had rarely featured editorials; before the defenestración, they had been ubiquitous. The final old-style editorial seems to have appeared on 5 November 1994, as the old guard was moving or being shifted out. Thereafter, nearly all op-ed articles were signed opinion pieces. Occasionally front-page editorials, tagged as such, would appear with headlines like "Everyone with Open Ears to the Call of the FSLN," which promised little in the way of serious or sustained analysis.[31] Carlos Fernando Chamorro offered a somewhat perplexed comment on the phenomenon: "You read *Barricada* between October 1994 and now, a year and a half. Probably in those eighteen months they have published thirty editorials, no more. Why? Because they don't have any capability or capacity to write? Or because they don't feel confident enough? There's something very weird."[32]

An alternative explanation might lie in the fact that the paper's reporting was now so imbued with editorializing that there was little point in formally separating the two. This suggested the dismantling of another firewall between mobilizing and professional imperatives.

And it was matched by the notable reluctance of the new dirección to draft an editorial profile to replace the seminal document that underpinned *Barricada*'s autonomy project. (One was in the works as of late 1997, but was aborted by events, as we will see.) Perhaps the closest the paper came after the coup to clarifying "our role as a Sandinista medium of communication, and the terms of debate in our editorial pages" was a pronouncement of 16 August 1995, seeking to reconcile the idea of a privileged Sandinista space with the proclaimed need to remain open to all social sectors:

> *First.* We aspire, with our editorial space, to foment free discussion of ideas and to create public-opinion leaders [*forjadores*]. . . . Our *Opinions* page is open to all Nicaraguans who wish to express their points of view on themes of interest, be they political, economic, cultural, scientific, social, or of any other nature.
>
> *Second.* Our editorial space, we hope, will be a privileged space to express a Sandinista focus, in the broadest sense of the word, and this [newspaper's] directorate will seek to ensure . . . that this page will in a special way be a space in which militants of the Sandinista Front may express themselves.
>
> *Third.* Our *Opinions* page does not discriminate on political or ideological grounds. We do not fear the healthy debate of ideas; on the contrary, we stimulate and encourage it. The only restrictions in the opinions page are those imposed by space and by the respectful attitudes [and] civilized norms [integral to] the healthy debate of ideas.
>
> *Fourth. Barricada* clearly distances itself from intolerant or disrespectful positions. . . . We feel that personal offense and the oft-misunderstood settling of scores [*pasada de cuentas*] are not, and cannot be, the terms of debate; nor are they an appropriate procedure for resolving political contradictions.[33]

As a statement of overarching editorial policy, this was pretty thin gruel. Viewed together with the other developments, it prompted suspicions that what was at stake was not just a transformation in the tone of editorial commentary, but a downgrading of editorial and professional considerations per se.

Periodismo Amarillo

If the new *Barricada* risked alienating readers with its return to the more polemical tone of old and its often slapdash professional skills, could the deficit be offset by appealing to the lowest common denominator of human interest? Did periodismo amarillo—yellow journalism—figure prominently in the new project, as it had in the attempts during the autonomy era to cultivate a lighter, less politicized tone? If so, how pervasive a presence was it in the pages of the post-1994 *Barricada,* compared with its predecessor?

Anyone who expected *Barricada*'s new directorate to repudiate periodismo amarillo in favor of a more ideologically pure (and puritan) product was in for a surprise. Yellow themes and strategies seem to have played an even more substantial role in the thinking of the new dirección than they had between 1990 and 1994. The influence of William Grigsby may be visible here. The balance of political and apolitical coverage appears more or less to have been his to determine; and Grigsby was, after all, a former staff reporter with *El Nuevo Diario,* the most yellow (and popular)[34] of the Nicaraguan dailies. In a 1996 interview, Grigsby acknowledged that periodismo amarillo "sometimes" appeared in *Barricada,* but added: "I don't think we've reached the level of *El Nuevo Diario* in terms of our headlines and information. We don't have the *morbid* side of *El Nuevo Diario*'s sensationalistic approach [*nota roja*]."[35] Juan Ramón Huerta also claimed that although the new *Barricada* was "yellow, *very* yellow at times," it was "different . . . from *El Nuevo Diario*. We don't engage in speculation or ridicule. We are very respectful of people's dignity and honour. We're more discreet; we talk about [these matters], but in a manner that is less sensationalistic."[36]

In an attempt to compare the prominence of periodismo amarillo in pre- and postdefenestración versions of *Barricada,* I surveyed front-page images of sex and violence—the amarillista staples. Six months (March to August) of *Barricada* front pages were sampled from both 1994 and 1995. Sexually suggestive and violent imagery was tallied, with the former defined as photographs or other representations of fashion models, women in bathing suits or other skimpy attire, women in suggestive poses, and beauty pageant contestants. (No such images of men alone were detected in either sample period.) Simple representations of conventionally attractive women were not counted. Violent imagery, meanwhile, was defined as including photographs or other representations of corpses or visibly wounded victims of violence. Certain images of more abstract violence, such as photographs of police clashing with demonstrators, were not tabulated unless they met the separate requirement of visible injury. Where gray areas arose, the survey erred on the side of inclusion—but consistently, I hope. Ambiguous cases—especially where sensationalism crosses over into hard news, and vice versa—are mentioned in the footnotes.

As with most mainstream media environments, the degree of explicitness of the violent imagery far exceeded that of the sexual imagery, which was comparatively tame in both pre- and postdefenestración versions of *Barricada.* Analysis suggested the front-page prominence given to sexually suggestive imagery remained roughly equal for both incarnations of *Barricada.* Seventeen examples were detected in both the 1994 *Barricada* and its successor. In the area of violent imagery, however, the tallies differed dramatically. The survey counted just ten front-page images of violence for *Barricada* in six months under Carlos Fernando Chamorro, but a striking forty-two in 1995. The count suggests a significantly greater resort to at least one of the amarillista staples in the period following the defenestración.[37] A separate tally—of the paper's constantly declining circulation— suggests that this was not enough to bridge the gap between readers' informational (and sensational) desires and the new *Barricada*'s ability to satisfy them.

Barricada's New Comandante:
An Interview with Tomás Borge

> In this country, there are two characteristics. Everybody wants to be president, and everybody wants to have a newspaper.
>
> —Francisco "Paco" Gómez

One noticed the transformation in the director's surroundings first. Tomás Borge did not occupy the same office that Carlos Fernando Chamorro had during his tenure at *Barricada*. He was tucked away down a secondary hall, in an inner sanctum guarded by a very personable assistant, whose main task seemed to be explaining to callers and casual drop-ins why Comandante Borge was not in the office or (just as likely, it seemed) not in the country. Borge traveled often and for extended periods: to Mexico to liaise with his contacts in the PRI (one of his recent publications was a highly sympathetic study of Carlos Salinas's modernization mission in Mexico); or perhaps to Cuba, to catch up with his longtime friend and revolutionary comrade Fidel Castro.

Borge's travel itinerary mirrored his somewhat rootless existence since the Sandinista election defeat, touched on in chapter 3. The oracular, intellectual side of Borge had seemed unappeased since he vacated the Ministry of the Interior, particularly after the Special Congress vetoed the position of FSLN president which Borge's status as founder and éminence grise would have entitled him to fill. Like Julio López, then, who had suffered a similar setback at the directorate level, Borge may have welcomed the appointment to *Barricada* as a chance to play a vanguard role in party policy and ideology—in Borge's case, influence of the type he had enjoyed in the 1980s, when he was second only to Daniel Ortega in the Sandinista power structure.

Borge was absent from *Barricada* for most of my four weeks of fieldwork in 1996. He swept through the hallways only once while I was present—long enough for me to petition him for an interview, not long enough to actually secure one. It was not until my final evening in Nicaragua, as I was clearing my research materials from the *Barricada Internacional* office, that the summons came for a conversation with the comandante.[38] Entering the inner sanctum was like entering a shrine: the walls were blanketed with framed photographs of Borge with the internationally famous, including Fidel Castro, Pope John Paul II, and Gabriel García Márquez. Against this backdrop was Borge's desk, and behind it, Borge himself. Small in stature, still vigorous despite the years and Somoza's tortures, the comandante rose to greet me. I delivered my questions. Borge answered them rapid-fire. Half an hour later, he was breezing out to his next appointment.

This was the paradox of Borge's role at *Barricada*. If the newspaper was his trophy, he seemed rarely around to polish it. Indeed, Borge himself depicted his role as on the one hand strategic and on the other symbolic. "I am the strategic leader of the enterprise [Editorial El Amanecer] and of the newspaper," he told me, and "it's me who makes the decisions." But practical direction of the operation devolved to his two immediate subordinates: Julio López and William Grigsby. López, according to Borge, served as the "day-to-day director, the immediate authority on the newspaper." As editor in chief, meanwhile, Grigsby was guardian of the "professional" side of the operation.

The symbolic dimension of Borge's presence lay, obviously, in his status as founding member of the FSLN and senior member of the Sandinista National Directorate. In the wake of the defenestración, there was "a much closer relationship" between *Barricada* and the front, said Borge, "since I am one of the most important leaders of the Sandinista Front. I was president of the Special Congress, I am vice secretary of the party, and I will be running as a candidate for the national parliament [in the 1996 elections]. Therefore, the relationship between the newspaper and the party is much closer."

"In spite of that," Borge contended, "the newspaper has autonomy. It doesn't obey orders from anyone, not even from the directorate of the party. That doesn't mean that we are deaf to the suggestions of the National Directorate. But in the final instance, we as newspeople make our own decisions. This isn't a bulletin of the Sandinista Front."

At several other points in Borge's testimony, though, the paper's close integration into the overarching FSLN propaganda strategy seemed plain. *Barricada*'s function in the 1996 election campaign would be to serve as "a newspaper of propaganda for our candidates," although "at the same time, the newspaper has to serve as an instrument of national unity and reconciliation." *Barricada* would work closely with other Sandinista broadcast media: "Within the framework of the electoral campaign as a whole, we will make a common front, with a common plan of action." The concept of objectivity that had underpinned *Barricada*'s autonomy project was likewise significantly reworked in Borge's formulation. "I've opposed practices like, for example, writing headlines that reflect the personal opinions of the writer. But objectivity is relative. We are partisans in political activity. We are professionals, but in the service of a particular cause. One way or another, that will be reflected in our pages."

In a sense, Borge argued, *Barricada*'s objectivity had actually increased since 1994. The reason, he said—echoing the long-standing ortodoxo allegations—was that the newspaper was no longer an intimate ally of the government in power. Now, said Borge, "we are very critical of the government." As a result, and despite *Barricada*'s attempts "to be objective" in its political coverage, "the government has taken reprisals against us." (The alleged campaigns of regime discrimination against *Barricada* Borge would cite again and again in the year and a half that followed, as *Barricada* drifted toward the precipice.) The formerly cozy relationship with the UNO government had guaranteed the Chamorro-era version of the paper a steady flow of regime largesse. "Remember that the [former] director of the newspaper was the son of the president of the republic," Borge said, not bothering to dress his personal critique of Carlos Fernando Chamorro in the guise of insinuation, as was the more common ortodoxo practice.[39] "This facilitated [getting] ads, and in return the paper would serve as the spokesperson for the government. Now the situation has changed in both respects. We are no longer the spokesperson for the government, nor do we receive material benefits from them. On the contrary, we've been repressed in many ways by the government's policy of denying us advertising. They've threatened to take the enterprise away from us because of the debts we still have to the state." Other Nicaraguan media, Borge asserted, were spared these "political reprisals."

Government disfavour, though, was only one source of the economic crisis *Barricada* now confronted, according to Borge. Prices of key inputs had continued to rise steeply. "We had very serious problems with paper, which became very expensive, coinciding with the wider economic crisis in the country." It was hard to deny, too, the fact that readers had abandoned *Barricada* en masse, at least initially. "Many people stopped buying the paper, and the circulation declined" along with advertising revenue. The combined pressures had led Borge and other senior personnel to "make very serious personal sacrifices" in an attempt to keep the paper afloat. "For example, I don't earn a single cent. I started off earning a very modest salary, but I had to give it up, because the newspaper couldn't even support my salary as director. So I renounced that salary as a contribution to redressing the financial situation. There'll come a time when I resume my honorarium, because there have been many months now during which I haven't claimed a cent. Other members of the [newspaper's] directorate have also sacrificed their salary for the sake of the newspaper, in order to honour the salaries owed to reporters and other workers at the newspaper."

Nonetheless, Borge declared himself satisfied that the new *Barricada,* after a rough start, had begun to stabilize. "When we assumed responsibility over the paper, we found out that there hadn't only been political and ideological deviations, but an acute deficiency, even corruption, in the administrative management of the enterprise. We took over an enterprise that was extremely precarious in financial terms—indebted up to its eyeballs, with serious administrative problems and grave symptoms of internal corruption. So we've had to undertake the task not only of correcting the political compass of the newspaper, but also of cleaning up the enterprise in the economic sense."

Borge professed himself satisfied with *Barricada*'s blending of "serious news with light news," and its coverage of "literary issues and issues beyond politics." Did he perceive any discord between the paper's mobilizing role on behalf of the FSLN, and the sensationalist, amarillista content that also featured in its content? Borge acknowledged that periodismo amarillo could be found in *Barricada*'s pages. The paper, he said frankly, "has been working to increase its circulation, and the only way of selling more copies in this country, unfortunately, is by relating horrendous crimes, tales of broken heads, rapes, the other heinous things that take place in daily life." Intriguingly, Borge acknowledged that his sporadic presence at the paper meant that excesses had sometimes occurred in this sphere: "Every time I drop my guard, the newspaper puts out things I don't agree with—especially when I'm not in the country. That's the natural tendency of newspaper people in this country, to be amarillista." In retrospect, the comment may be seen as an oblique reference to an emerging conflict between Borge and his subordinates—especially William Grigsby, the strongest advocate and most experienced practitioner of the amarillista "line."

Like Grigsby, though, Borge took pains to contrast *Barricada*'s sensationalism with that of its crosstown rivals—not only *El Nuevo Diario,* but also *La Prensa.* In addition to being *Barricada*'s "political and ideological" rival, "the vehicle of the renovationists," *El*

Nuevo Diario was much more "extreme" in its sensationalism. *La Prensa,* meanwhile, "the vehicle of the extreme right," was also amarillista, but its yellowness was "political in character": "Every time they hunt down some scandalous news about the Sandinista Front, they publish it without further research. This has led to very serious distortions against us."

Whatever challenges *Barricada* now confronted under his direction, Borge said, the defenestración of October 1994 had been inevitable. The paper and its sponsor had been on a direct collision course. "It was totally inconceivable that the newspaper which was the moral property of the Sandinista Front, which was founded and inspired by the Sandinista Front, which arose from the front's own efforts, could print in its pages attitudes that were contrary to the Sandinista Front. It was essential that the director of the newspaper be someone who would identify with the owner [*dueño*]. That's why we installed a new director." The 1996 version of *Barricada,* he said, was "much more open than the version that existed in the past. [The pre-1994 *Barricada*] *claimed* to be a very open newspaper, but was in reality very closed—or rather, it was open to anything that constituted a subtle or even an open attack against the Sandinista Front and its directorate."

The FSLN's militant base had been cheered by the decision to restore party control over *Barricada,* Borge reported. That same base now offered promising avenues of growth and outreach. "I think that now probably half the readers are militants of the Sandinista Front. A circulation as broad as the one we have—which is still less than *El Nuevo Diario* or *La Prensa*—can only be explained by the [support shown by] Sandinista militants, who are many tens of thousands strong. The political constituency of FSLN consists mostly of poor people, but in spite of that, many people buy the newspaper." Overall, said the comandante—with a hint of the machismo for which he was renowned[40]—*Barricada* was "much better liked" than it had been a year or a year-and-a-half earlier. "It's a newspaper which combines seriousness with a certain zest. *Barricada* is like a girl who walks down the street in a mini-skirt and attracts the glances of passersby. It's like a lady with a nice body and expressive eyes."

Two Who Stayed: Juan Ramón Huerta and Alfonso Malespín

In any study of an institution in transition, the testimony of individuals who bridge definable eras in the institution's functioning is particularly valuable. Only they can provide an intimate comparative perspective on which features have endured and which have been transformed, perhaps irrevocably. It is worth, then, devoting a section of our analysis to the fortunes and opinions of two of the editorial staff who stayed on as *Barricada* moved into its new epoch: Juan Ramón Huerta and Alfonso Malespín.

As noted, Huerta was one of a tiny handful of Managua-based editorial staffers—three, to be precise—for whom the defenestración came not a moment too soon. Together with Carlos García and Pablo Emilio Barreto, he constituted a nucleus of disaffected ortodoxos at the paper. In the immediate wake of the defenestración, departing staff members roundly assailed him, notably for putting his name to the autoentrevista with Tomás Borge (see chapter 3). But no one was surprised that Huerta, García, and Barreto stayed on to assist with the new *Barricada*—nor that they came to constitute the core of the paper's post-1994 "political staff."

At the time of the defenestración, Huerta had worked at *Barricada* for more than a dozen years. He joined in 1982, after spending several years as a radio journalist in Jinotega province and (like many at the postdefenestración version of *Barricada*) serving a stint under Comandante Borge at the Ministry of the Interior. *Barricada* was his first experience with print journalism. He was promptly dispatched to cover the catastrophic 1982 hurricane that laid waste to Corinto and other settlements along Nicaragua's Pacific coast. As with many of his contemporaries in the revolutionary media, Huerta learned as he worked, reporting by day, attending classes in journalism and other subjects at the University of Central America (UCA) by night.

As the war with the contras became a conflagration, Huerta found himself assigned more and more regularly to northern Nicaragua, where bands of rebels filtered down through the mountain passes from their bases in Honduras. Over time, together with his other journalistic compañeros, Huerta was transformed into something Nicaraguan journalism had never known: a corresponsal de guerra (war correspondent). Despite their mobilizing essence, the corresponsales, as noted in chapter 1, also provided *Barricada* with one of its first and most significant sources of professional pride and institutional identity. Young journalists and revolutionaries like Huerta found themselves under fire, living and sometimes fighting alongside the regular forces of the Ejército Popular Sandinista (Sandinista People's Army; EPS). "We never would have imagined that we would be writing stories about combat," Huerta recalled in 1996. "About huge operations with seven or eight battalions, seven or eight hundred soldiers each. And I lived like a soldier; I followed the same rules the soldiers did. I didn't go around with a sign around my neck saying I was a journalist."[41]

In such circumstances, ordinary notions of objectivity were clearly out of the question. Furthermore, Huerta said, "I didn't have the experience or skills that I have today. I was a very passionate journalist. I'd been a militant of the front, and whenever I thought about a particular thing, I'd go about it in a very subjective way." This "journalism of propaganda" made sense at the time. "I don't regret this stage. It was the type of journalism the revolution needed. He now claimed, though, to "have a greater separation [*distanciamiento*] from my subject." At the height of the war, Huerta received a scholarship to study in Germany and the Soviet Union.

He was thus unable to contribute to the war reportage published in book form (under the title *Corresponsales de guerra*) in 1984. "I really regret missing that chance to contribute to the writing of history," he said wistfully.

As the war wound down, Huerta, back in Nicaragua, pursued a diverse journalistic agenda, reporting successively on the end of the war and the beginning of reconciliation, the Sandinista election defeat, and the renewed clashes of 1990–91 between recontras and recompas. Always he based himself near the story, in Matagalpa or Jinotega provinces, rather than commuting from Managua. "I wanted to be closer to the phenomena," he said. In the end, he was given the editorship of *Municipios* (formerly *Regiones*), part of *Barricada*'s attempt to expand its municipal and regional coverage. "The country was becoming more institutionalized," Huerta said, and "from the very beginning the newspaper contributed to this process." The municipalities and departments were viewed as "the most concrete expression . . . [of] the democracy of the future," as well as a blind spot in the paper's past coverage.

When *Barricada* implemented its New Editorial Profile in 1991, Huerta claimed he initially backed the changes: "I was one of those who supported the project of deofficialization." It was, after all, Huerta—together with Guillermo Cortés—who had authored the seminal 1988 study "Critical Journalism in the Daily *Barricada*" as part of his studies at the University of Central America. In that work (discussed in chapter 1), Cortés and Huerta bluntly criticized *Barricada*'s dependence on official sources and its stultifying reporting style. Accordingly, Huerta said, he was all for *Barricada* "balanc[ing] its agenda and transcend[ing] the official agenda. Look, here a political-party newspaper doesn't have any reason to exist. A newspaper has to be competitive."

But for Huerta, the front still needed and deserved a privileged space in *Barricada*'s pages. The New Editorial Profile was supposed to guarantee that space. But the paper's fulfilment of its militant obligation—and perhaps its definition of precisely what constituted the Sandinista Front or Sandinista opinion—began to be aggressively questioned by early ortodoxos like Rosario Murillo and Mónica Baltodano. Huerta said he felt sympathy for their arguments. If right-wing newspapers could express the political line of their owners and affiliated parties, paying little heed to alternative opinion, why should *Barricada* not emphasize the words and actions of those sectors frozen out of other media?

Thus, while his relations with *Barricada*'s directorate remained "good from a professional point of view," it became increasingly clear to Huerta that "a difference of political attitude" existed. He found he "could not be a hypocrite"—the term he applied to those who worked for a Sandinista institution while espousing views that tarnished the front and undermined the continuing viability of the revolution. Some *Barricada* journalists, he felt, were "criticizing the Sandinista Front with such hatred that they might have been criticizing an enemy. That was the source of my contradiction with them. Constructive criticism, yes—but after a while the newspaper became more anti-Sandinista than *La Prensa* or *La Tribuna!*"

The basic fault line at the paper, for Huerta, ran between "militant journalists and more 'professional,' 'objective' journalists." The project of the latter, then dominant current he described as "a utopian proposal. Journalists always have a political attitude toward life and social phenomena. Anyone who says he doesn't is a hypocrite and a liar. Me, I believe in revolutionary change. And so my mentality, my attitude must be constructed along the same lines: [to reflect] solidarity with the majority of the people. I can't extricate myself from this in order to become an impartial journalist." On the other side of the divide, he saw "journalists with an attitude that was very loyal to the dueños [owners], to the patrones [bosses]—an attitude that was right-wing in the sense that it wasn't in keeping [*consecuente*] with the popular cause."

Huerta said that "on various occasions" during the early 1990s, his reporting was interfered with on grounds that he considered political (see chapter 3). It is worth noting that the charges pertain to the prominence given his stories and accompanying photos; Huerta did not claim his articles had been censored or pulled. Nonetheless, it seemed clear evidence of a growing, and intolerable, contradiction between the front's political line and *Barricada*'s editorial policies. In this light, although it represented a "violent change" in *Barricada*'s operations, the defenestración was in the natural course of events. "It was necessary to make a change in the political aspect of the newspaper—not in the professional aspect, because their project in this respect was very good." Huerta felt the attention that the coup commanded nationally and internationally was excessive: "Every newspaper in the world has the right to change its director when it is convenient."

The new *Barricada* was confronted with the "titanic challenge" of building a new project around staff who often lacked "the most basic knowledge of news gathering." Nonetheless, in Huerta's estimation, the fears of those who expected *Barricada* to return to the ultramobilized journalism of the revolutionary decade had proved groundless:

> There was a real lack of confidence on the part of people who thought we were going to remake the paper along the lines of the 1980s. But we have demonstrated the contrary, and now many people are returning to us. . . . It's not that we're perfect—we've committed many errors at every stage. But the transition we've made is to a newspaper that can be more believed in. I feel a lot of pride when an official in an embassy buys *Barricada* because he believes it and not to find out what was the most recent murder that took place. *Barricada* has become a newspaper that provides guidelines and parameters for businesspeople and the political parties. We're very respectful in our treatment of the different parties, and that's increased our credibility; they have greater confidence in us.

The paper's new relationship with FSLN leaders was closer,

Huerta conceded, but this did not imply constant interference in *Barricada*'s operations. "We have relative independence as far as the daily contents of the newspaper are concerned. No member of the National Directorate participates [in this process]. The director [Borge] is a member of the National Directorate, but he doesn't come here as a member of the directorate; he comes as the director of *Barricada*. This is his responsibility." Under the new arrangement, relations between party and paper were better, according to Huerta. "There is more cooperation, but not imposition. . . . Before, there was no cohesion. The forces of the party were on one side, the forces of the paper on the other. Now we have a single force [*una sola fuerza*]."

In these straitened but, for Huerta, optimistic circumstances, *Barricada* was looking ahead to the challenge of mobilizing the Sandinista Front's militants for the 1996 electoral campaign. It would do so, however, in a manner "completely different" from its last such attempt, in 1989–90. *Barricada* would adhere closely "to the interests of the Sandinista Front," but in a more discreet manner than in the past. "The electoral program needs to be presented in a way that is more sensitive to the needs of the people," Huerta asserted. "We're not going to make propaganda. We have a sense of greater responsibility."

The major challenge in the new era, for Huerta, was to integrate mobilizing and professional imperatives—to harmonize the journalist with the militant. "The Sandinista Front needs journalists who believe in creativity and criticism, and who contribute through their work to generating ideas for change. Who promote solidarity, a sense of social responsibility, security, and respect for institutions and, fundamentally—something that's very important—[economic] production. Journalists who also speak of social ills, not in an amarillista way, but in a constructive way." This, he felt, was a viable model for revolutionary journalism in postrevolutionary Nicaragua:

The Sandinista Front has changed in the face of national politics in this country. It is still the largest and best-organized party in the country. The fact that it is participating in an election campaign signifies that it is increasingly becoming a party of elections. But it is a party that has not abandoned [the idea of] deepening the changes and achievements that the revolution initiated in 1979. What has happened is that these achievements, these profound changes, must [now] reckon with both internal and external forces and must coexist with neoliberal politics. But that doesn't signify that we have renounced the revolution. The revolution doesn't only consist of seeking radical change without taking into account objective circumstances.

Huerta's own "objective circumstances" would become more favorable still in the aftermath of the interview—briefly, anyway. In 1996 the growing conflict between Tomás Borge on the one hand, and Julio López and William Grigsby on the other, led to the resignation of the latter two figures from the paper (see below). In February 1997, Juan Ramón Huerta would be drafted to serve as editor in chief—in time to preside over *Barricada*'s death throes.

ALFONSO MALESPÍN HAD the distinction of being the only editorial staffer at *Barricada* to emerge from the rubble of the defenestración without alienating any of the bitterly opposed factions in the dispute. This in itself is a remarkable feat. It can be explained by Malespín's unique status at *Barricada*—his "privileged position," as William Grigsby put it.[42] Since his arrival at the newspaper in the early days of the autonomy experiment, Malespín had been "a case apart," in Sofía Montenegro's words. While the three other editorial staffers who stayed on after the defenestración were, Montenegro said, "militantly involved with the position of the orthodox [current], and . . . pro-Daniel [Ortega] from head to toe," Malespín "was more distant. . . . He was one of the youngsters, more aloof to all these things. He took a more individualistic position."[43]

In a 1996 interview, Malespín described how he was brought on board in 1990 when *Barricada* began to look for "journalists who could write articles without the influence of the political part of the Sandinista Front." Malespín, who was working with Managua's Institute of Culture at the time, had never been an FSLN militant. He was thus well positioned to write the more detached and objective political reportage that *Barricada* now sought. As ortodoxo opposition to *Barricada*'s political reporting deepened, Malespín was drafted to supplement the corps of political reporters.[44] It was he who would provide the most extensive coverage of the 1994 upheaval at *Barricada,* in the newspaper's own pages.

Malespín spoke glowingly about most aspects of the autonomy experiment. "The only line" his superiors gave him, he said, "was if it's news, go ahead and write it." The increased emphasis on training and professional exchanges allowed him to travel widely—to Germany, Colombia, the United States. From 1991 to 1994, he said, "I believe *Barricada* . . . was the most successful institution the Sandinistas had. It had become one of the most reliable newspapers in the country; it was a newspaper that was read mostly by the leaders of the country—the politicians, the diplomats, the government, middle-class professionals and technicians, college students." The only problem, in his view, was that it lacked the kind of news that Sandinista leaders and militants wished to read; it refused "to make news happen around the Sandinista agenda." Daniel Ortega and other ortodoxos wanted instead "a newspaper that was clearly identified with the political line of the party."[45]

The clashing priorities brought Malespín into regular conflict with those among his Sandinista sources who rejected *Barricada*'s new, more dispassionate tone. "I had serious difficulties covering the Sandinistas. They were kind of angry. It was really hard to find them so they would express their point of view. But at the same time, they were saying all the time that they were not taken into consideration by the newspaper!" The coolness from ortodoxo quarters may have led *Barricada* to emphasize the activities of both renovationist and regime forces. But the engagement was always a critical engagement, Malespín contended. He rejected the notion that the paper had become a tool of Sergio Ramírez's Movimiento de Renovación Sandinista: "It wasn't that they [*Barricada*'s directorate] were involved with the MRS. The thing was, they had made the decision here to make a professional newspaper. The decision was, OK, we are a Sandinista newspaper, but we have two sides. We're not going to write news that would privilege this side or the other. The official leaders of the party thought that decision was a big mistake. They thought *Barricada* should be writing the political news from their standpoint."

He likewise dismissed charges that *Barricada* under Carlos Fernando Chamorro had been too cozy with the regime that Chamorro's mother headed:

> If the Sandinistas were the opposition to the government, it was logical, from our perspective, to be an opposition newspaper. And in order to do that, we had to write a *lot* about the government. What did we publish? We uncovered corruption, theft, wrongdoing, all the things [i.e., abuses] that were happening with the privatization process.... Mainly our news was about how the government was creating more unemployment; creating a new class in which the interests of the state and private enterprises were mixed; giving away almost free some very, very expensive enterprises around the country. . . . There wasn't any other newspaper that was publishing news about government corruption at the time.

Malespín did not gloss over the mismanagement and corruption that had influenced the administrative side of the newspaper in the early 1990s; his comments on this score have already been cited (chapter 2). But the eventual decision to cancel the autonomy experiment, in Malespín's opinion, was made for entirely different—and explicitly political—reasons. "Long before [October 1994], there was a group of Sandinista leaders that had decided to change the newspaper completely, to make changes in the news line, the editorial line, the director, and part of the staff."

When the ax fell, Malespín nonetheless chose to remain at *Barricada*. "I thought that it was better to stay, for several reasons. One was that if we stayed, we would have a better chance to . . . [ensure] that the newspaper would not become so inclined toward a Sandinista political position." He acknowledged the obvious: that "almost all the members of the staff thought otherwise."

A year and a half after the *defenestración*, Malespín was still ensconced at *Barricada,* but his role at the newspaper had undergone a significant shift. As already noted, the new *dirección* moved him from the political beat to the "lighter," less political pages, *De todo un poco,* and to the post–Sofía Montenegro incarnation of *Gente.* The move reflected "a combination of both" Malespín's own wishes and the preferences of *Barricada*'s directorate to refashion the paper's political coverage from the ground up:[46] "I told them that I couldn't write news as they wanted me to, because it was clear, right from the start, that that wasn't the way I'd learned. They felt the same way. So I was transferred to *De todo un poco* and *Gente.* They were clear that as long as I kept a distance from any political interpretation of an issue, I could develop the agenda I wanted to in *Gente* and *De todo un poco.*"

Even in this politically peripheral position, Malespín encountered occasional "difficulties" with the exponents of a more militant stance in the paper's coverage, "especially when we interview people who are not Sandinistas, or people who are identified with the right-wing parties. They believe there are plenty of people out there to interview and write about [who are sympathetic to the Sandinistas]. When we've discussed this issue, I've told them, OK, we look at things from different perspectives. You see it from the political side; I see it from a journalistic or generic point of view." His own perspective, Malespín said, led him to a contrary belief: that "you don't have to convince the people who are already convinced. You have to convince the people who are *not* convinced. In order to do that, I believe you have to publish the most professional, the most balanced, the most honest newspaper you can."

Despite the political suspicions and aspersions sometimes directed his way, Malespín believed his opinions and arguments carried a certain weight with the new dirección of the paper. *Gente* as a tabloid-sized supplement folded only a few months after the defenestración and shifted to a couple of broadsheet pages within the newspaper proper. But it remained one of *Barricada*'s few commercially successful ventures, boosting sales significantly on the day it appeared, as it always had. Some of this popularity rubbed off on Malespín, *Gente*'s new caretaker. As well, at an institution where members displayed a high degree of political like-mindedness, Malespín appeared to enjoy something of the status of the devil's advocate. William Grigsby and Julio López, he said, "ask me a lot" for comments and constructive suggestions. "Because they know I'm the critic!" Were his views well attended to? "Well, they listen at times. But not all the time."

Malespín remained hopeful that what many perceived to be the greatest weakness of the new *Barricada*—its excessively partisan tenor—could be overcome. But he thought it was unlikely to happen before the 1996 elections. For that vote, he said, *Barricada*'s directors "wanted a newspaper like in 1989." Thereafter, he speculated that the overriding fact of the "financial crisis" at *Barricada*, together with the "rejection the newspaper has suffered" in the form of declining readership and national influence, might "move the directors to publish a more balanced newspaper. They haven't gotten to that point yet. But they are trying."

Decline and Fall

It wasn't working. *Barricada* between October 1994 and January 1998 lurched from crisis to crisis. The paper was never able to establish a clear or consistent institutional identity, at least in the opinion of Juan Ramón Huerta. Interviewed in 1998, *Barricada*'s last editor recalled the postdefenestración period as a time of confusion and interpersonal conflict at *Barricada:*

> The truth is that when Carlos Fernando left, they [his successors] had no clear idea what kind of newspaper they wanted. Even by the time *Barricada* was finished, there had never been a clear idea what kind of newspaper they wanted. They had a basic conceptual problem. In the era of Grigsby and Julio López, one day *Barricada* would appear yellow [amarillista], the next overly politicized, the next more professional, all depending on the editor who closed that day's edition. There was no coherence in their policy. If William Grigsby said it was necessary to attack someone and not provide that person with any opportunity to respond, that was that [*pues así iba*], and we had to mount a charge [*enderezar la batería*] against that person or institution or sector of society. . . . It was a determined use of the newspaper for propaganda purposes [*en términos de la propaganda*] and in the service of special interests [*intereses muy particulares*].

Tomás Borge, meanwhile, Huerta described as a vestigial presence:

> Borge was to a certain extent decorative. He was constantly out of the country—in the Dominican Republic, in Panama, in Mexico. He only came to the newspaper to change its editorial profile. . . . He wasn't a director who would sit down and discuss it with you if he had an idea for a change. He'd come and ask for the editor on duty, not seeking him out in the editorial [offices] but calling him to his own office—a policy completely at odds with the horizontal character that the directorate of a newspaper should have. He'd call [the editor] to his office and say, "Hombre, what are you running today?" He [Borge] would tell him: "I've brought this and that bit of news [to publish]." He'd say, "I don't want you to run with that," or "I want you to run on the front page a speech I gave in the Dominican Republic fifteen days ago." Things like that.[47]

A pervasive, morale-sapping backdrop to the "identity crisis"[48] was the hemorrhage of readers that had begun with the defenestración. If this had stabilized briefly around the the time of my 1996 fieldwork (something that is by no means certain), it resumed its downward slide shortly afterward. Advertisers too deserted *Barricada* in droves, many of them "because the policy of Grigsby and López was to mount a charge against the bourgeoisie, and it was they who gave us the ads," in Juan Ramón Huerta's view. As readers abandoned the paper, so too did staffers, alienated by the poor and sometimes tardy salaries and by the lack of direction at the FSLN's flagship. "Many journalists left," said Huerta. "Today, they're excellent professionals in other communications media. *Barricada* was forming new and excellent journalists as student trainees, paid C$2,000 [about $200] a month; but when students felt the need to improve their situation and demanded a salary increase, they'd be told no. And that journalist whom we had formed, whom we had developed to a high standard, left. And we'd set about forming new ones."[49]

The full dimensions of the crisis, though, did not become apparent until after the national elections of October 1996. *Barricada*—or rather Editorial El Amanecer, the publishing operation that subsidized the paper—had counted heavily on winning a contract with the Supreme Electoral Council to print the ballots for the voting. The contract was worth about $1.5 million. To maximize its competitive advantage, El Amanecer invested heavily in new machinery and equipment and put forward the lowest bid.[50] According to Alfonso Malespín, Rosa Marina Zelaya, the president of the electoral council, "had assured Tomás Borge that *Barricada* would get the contract."[51] In the end, though, it went to *La Prensa,* leaving *Barricada* bereft.[52]

There was one further hope: that the FSLN would rebound from the electoral disaster of 1990 to recapture national power in 1996. Had it done so, it is likely that the resources available to *Barricada*—in the form of state-sector advertising and publishing contracts—would have increased. The paper certainly did what it could to promote the FSLN's candidates, above all Daniel Ortega. "Nothing restrains the Sandinista fervor of the people," read a typical headline during the campaign.[53] A week before the elections, *Barricada* confidently, if prematurely, proclaimed: "Daniel . . . ¡Presidente!" Ortega, the paper reported, was "virtually" certain to be "the future president of Nicaragua, and will possibly win in the first round."[54] *Barricada* also heaped derision on Arnoldo Alemán's Liberal Alliance, referring to its candidates standardly as Somocistas and Arnoldistas.[55] According to Juan Ramón Huerta, the paper was used outright as a "propaganda instrument," and "also for a dirty-tricks campaign [*para campaña sucia*]" against the FSLN's opponents.[56]

The rhetoric did not subside with the vote of 20 October 1996. After a brief interregnum in which the results were proclaimed to be "uncertain" (21 October), the paper declared a "Colossal Fraud!" (23 October), linking alleged abuses in the process to the tradition of electoral manipulation under the Somoza dictatorship.[57] When the Supreme Electoral Council issued its official results, which gave Alemán a victory over the FSLN by 51 percent to 41, *Barricada*'s front page fumed: "May God Forgive Them! Results Illegitimate—The Struggle Continues."[58] Likewise, as the new National Assembly was sworn in and Alemán officially declared the victor, *Barricada* proclaimed: "Fraud Consummated—Poor Nicaragua!"[59] "Out of Shame" (*por vergüenza*), read the headline of an editorial of 25 November, the Supreme Electoral Council "Should Resign."[60]

The defeat of 1996 immediately spawned a far-reaching internal crisis at *Barricada*. A further wave of staff cuts had long been impending, but according to Alfonso Malespín it had been deemed politically undesirable in the run-up to the presidential elections. Now it was unavoidable; and Malespín, along with ninety-one other staffers, found himself cast out of the paper in early December. A few days later, an article at the bottom of the back page announced the surprising resignations of editor in chief William Grigsby and sub-director Julio López. López's letter of resignation referred to "the reasons I expressed" to Tomás Borge, but these were not cited.[61] According to former *Barricada* staffer Roberto Fonseca, writing in

Confidencial, the departures were linked to a debate over *Barricada*'s future direction.[62] The configuration of the debate remains unclear, but according to Alfonso Malespín, Grigsby and López both "thought it was time to . . . take a step back and try to retake the road the newspaper was traveling until 1994." Borge, meanwhile, felt, "What we need is a *Barricada* that looks like the one we have right now, with some changes in content." A clash of personalities also figured in the drama, according to Malespín. Grigsby and López felt "that in order for *Barricada* to survive, it was necessary that Borge step aside. They considered him a big part of the problem. . . . He has a very poor image with the government and [the private-enterprise group] COSEP, and they thought that as long as Tomás remained in *Barricada,* the paper would have more and more problems getting advertisements."

Whether as a result of Borge's leadership or not, *Barricada* indeed encountered even more severe difficulties in securing advertising as 1997 dawned. Part of the problem was the decision by the new Alemán administration to centralize state-sector advertising in the hands of five agencies, including one (Comunicaciones) run by one of Alemán's relatives. The February 1997 decision was denounced by most Nicaraguan media, who feared a return to the Black Code of the Somoza dictatorship, when state-sector ads—constituting twenty to thirty percent of total advertising revenue in Nicaragua[63]— were used for politically partisan purposes. Persistent rumors circulated at the same time that a presidential advisor had issued orders both to governmental ministries and to sympathetic private businesses, "indicating to them which media should not receive advertising."[64] Throughout 1997, *Barricada* and its director would cite the government's campaign as the principal source of the "profound financial crisis" in which the paper found itself.[65] Tomás Borge accused President Alemán of having "decided on his own to liquidate this enterprise, not only by denying us state advertising, but also by pressuring private enterprise to deny us advertisements."

Advertisers, he claimed, were now "fear[ful of] being seen as sympathizers of the Sandinista Front."[66]

There was clearly more at work, though, than the "sadistic reprisals" of the government.[67] Nicaragua's economic and political elite had found reasons to support *Barricada* between 1990 and 1994—whether because they wished to back the paper's attempts to bring about concertación and reconciliation, or because they appreciated *Barricada*'s new professionalism, or even because they considered Carlos Fernando Chamorro a fellow aristocrat. But there was precious little reason for them to do so after October 1994. If the FSLN had decreed the end of *Barricada*'s autonomy experiment and the outward-looking stance toward other social sectors that defined it, why would those sectors be enthusiastic about supporting a more militant and inflammatory project with their subscriptions or advertising córdobas?

It was hard to avoid the conclusion that the crisis afflicting *Barricada* was at heart one of legitimacy. This was evidenced by the fact that it was not only "the most obsequious sectors of private enterprise" who shied away from advertising in *Barricada*.[68] A plaintive, at times almost hysterical editorial commentary of 23 December 1997 also faulted "progressive sectors, or even worse [those] identified with the Sandinista Front" for their "execrable, illegitimate, and immoral attitude" toward *Barricada,* which the editorial's author (Borge?) found "absolutely incomprehensible." "Public opinion identifies as Sandinista hundreds of enterprises and public personalities," the editorial raged. "Where are the advertisements of these hundreds of firms and public personalities that control them, directly or indirectly?" The answer, apparently, was, "In the other communications media."[69]

Meanwhile, the ordinary Sandinista militants whom Borge had confidently expected to purchase *Barricada* after the defenestración instead stayed away in droves. The fact that "the militants militantly don't buy it," in Sofía Montenegro's pithy mid-1996 assessment, was borne out by the further erosion in subscriptions and overall circulation by late 1997. *Barricada* seems to have survived that long only because of extensive personal subsidies from Tomás Borge himself. The comandante is estimated to have poured between half a million and one million dollars into the publication between 1994 and 1997.[70] In early December 1997, Borge took the additional step of seeking a mortgage from a private bank for his property in the Managua neighborhood of Bello Horizonte. He was turned down;[71] instead, he surrendered a mansion on the lakeshore of Xiloá, outside Managua, valued at $540,489, and two vehicles with a value of about $80,000, to help offset *Barricada*'s debt to the Nicaraguan Institute of Social Security (INSS).[72] This still left the paper owing $400,000 to the INSS, however, and no closer to solvency. An internal financial statement of November 1997 showed a loss of more than $30,000 for the month of September alone, with nearly as much owed to employees in the form of unpaid wages.

There was thus an air of desperation surrounding Borge's attempts to restructure *Barricada*'s operations and secure new sources of funding and investment. The December 1996 defenestración of ninety-two staff members was followed, in July 1997, by a "dramatic circular letter" directed to "militants and sympathizers of the FSLN, urging them to contribute economic resources" and claiming that *Barricada* was "on the verge of disappearing" (Borge's phrase).[73] Various schemes were floated to seek outside investors in the Dominican Republic; prominent Sandinistas, including Humberto Ortega, were also courted.[74] In September 1997 a former *Barricada* insider—Xavier Reyes, who had left the paper a year before the defenestración—was persuaded to return as an advisor. He was subsequently joined by Francisco "Paco" Gómez, a Spanish journalist who had been hired away from *El País* to work at the Managua daily *La Tribuna*. Fired from *La Tribuna*—allegedly as the result of pressure exerted on the paper's directorate by the Alemán government—Gómez received a phone call from *Barricada* general manager Soroya Montoya, who asked him to speak in person with Tomás Borge. Borge, said Gómez in 1998, "told me during the interview that he loved my point of view, that he needed something like that in the newspaper":

> He told me, "Look, now I am alone. I feel that the other members of the party, even Daniel, don't want to know anything about the newspaper. They tried to close it." That's what Tomás and Soraya told me: that the party tried to close the newspaper in June 1997, because the accounts were in such a disastrous state. He told me he knew that the newspaper was a very bad product. He really insulted all the staff that were working for him. This was his constant point—that these were mediocre people; that he needed a new team, with new ideas. . . . He told me, "I want you to design a new newspaper. We don't have any romantic attachment to *Barricada*. . . . You can start from scratch."[75]

Hesitant at first, Gómez signed on after Xavier Reyes accepted a similar offer: the participation of Reyes, he said, made the venture seem somewhat less pyrrhic. It was then he learned just how dramatic a housecleaning Borge apparently envisaged. According to his account, *Borge was in fact deep in negotiations with the Alemán administration to sell the* Barricada *property, valued at about $2 million, to the government;* fire most remaining staff; use the proceeds of the property sale to pay off the paper's debts; close *Barricada*—the quid pro quo allegedly demanded by Alemán—and reopen under a new name. "The arrangement was: OK, we [the government] will buy the property and give you two million dollars—one million now and one million later. Then you close *Barricada* and sign an agreement stating that the name *Barricada* will never be used again. . . . The negotiations were very, very close to success. I remember that in November, the command of Tomás and Soraya was: 'We have to stay open until January [1998]. In January, we're going to close this deal. But if we close before then, we'll lose the money.'"

Gómez said that Borge "called me all the time, at seven in the morning, ten at night. Before every meeting with the government, he called me and told me what point the negotiations were at. What did I think? What did I suggest he should do?" In the end, said Gómez, the deal was scuttled when *Barricada*'s workers struck in December (see below). "Obviously, the strike ended the negotiations, because the government saw that *Barricada* would close by itself, and in a matter of days."[76]

Independent of the advice he could offer on behind-the-scenes financial negotiations, however, Gómez, together with Reyes, was charged with preparing a diagnosis of *Barricada*'s problems and a "new profile" to guide the newspaper—or its successor project. This initiative too was torpedoed by the labor strife of mid-December—at which point both Gómez and Reyes departed the paper. But the draft document they prepared, "A Brief Description of the Situation," offers a vivid depiction of the catastrophic state of affairs at *Barricada* during its bleak final months. "The current situation at *Barricada*," wrote Gómez and Reyes, "can be characterized in one word: disarray." At the heart of the problem the authors perceived "the lack of a clear structure in the journalistic hierarchy, the absence of a true journalistic director, excessive political influence over the daily information [published], the lack of motivation of the workers, the lack of quality in some of the members of the editorial team, and the economic problems of the enterprise."

Gómez and Reyes described "a lack of authority and the absence of a rational system of work," with an editor in chief—Juan Ramón Huerta—who had "serious problems in directing the editorial department."[77] Borge, though unable to "lead and orient the day-to-day work" of the newspaper, was unwilling to "renounce his role," preferring instead to "intervene sporadically in the decisions of the editorial department, in the selection of the contents and their position on the page." This paradoxical (*sí pero no*) arrangement served only to vitiate the editorial structure "and create tensions," while Borge's "direct involvement with the FSLN provoked a tendency

toward self-censorship among editorial staff. They are always wondering what Tomás Borge will think, before they consider what is in
the best interest of readers." In a replay of the early days of *Barricada*'s life, moreover, Gómez and Reyes reported that "members of
the FSLN address themselves directly to our editorial staff in order
to give them directions or to suggest [subjects for] coverage"; while
the fact that editor in chief Huerta and various of his subordinates
were also "active party members" meant that "on many occasions,
political influence was not external but internal."

In a 1998 interview Gómez described the almost total absence of
morale he found at *Barricada*—in part a holdover from the defenestración that was fully three years old by the time he arrived. "It was
very sad. The editorial nucleus—Juan Ramón Huerta, Carlos
García, these people—felt like traitors" for having stayed on after the
dismissal of Chamorro and the departure of most other editorial
staff. "I remember the first day, we talked all day about that! I was saying, 'Hey, man, why are we talking about 1994? We're in 1997 and we
have to think about the future.' But no, they were always saying:
'. . . I'm still here because I'm loyal to the front, loyal to the revolution.' I told them, 'Man, the revolution is gone. I'm sorry. I liked the
revolution. But the front doesn't want to know anything about this
newspaper, or about you.'" In their "Brief Description," Gómez and
Reyes likewise pointed to "a certain feeling of guilt or inferiority"
among veteran staff, one that had "spread to the new reporters" at
the paper, spawning a pervasive "lack of self-esteem and professional pride." One result was constant backbiting among different divisions of the operation: "An enterprise must work as a team, pushing
in the same direction. It would be difficult for this to happen at the
present [version of] *Barricada.* The different departments are riven
with suspicion and distrust. The editorial department considers the
administration to be the enemy and accuses them of bad policymaking . . . in sales and marketing. . . . The administration distrusts the
editorial department because the product that reaches the street is

not good and because [editorial staff] have been incapable of making the changes necessary to solve the problem."

Was there a way out? In a follow-up draft document, "Notes toward a Profile," Gómez and Reyes suggested incorporating "the positive experiences of the past" by creating "an independent . . . and pluralistic newspaper."[78] Their prescriptions bore a striking resemblance to the vision advanced in the New Editorial Profile of 1990:

> While reaffirming its leftist vocation, [*Barricada*] must not be seen as the official organ of any political party. The paper [should] declare itself a defender of the rule of law [*del Estado de Derecho*] . . . help to strengthen democratic institutions, and denounce whatever abuses they commit. . . . The newspaper [should] reject all types of pressure from political parties, economic groups, religious or ideological [interests], and people who seek to influence the editorial line to benefit themselves. At the same time, its pages should be open to all ideological, political, religious, and social tendencies, with the exception of those who break the law, promote the use of force to obtain their ends, or seek to systematically discredit [others].

Gómez and Reyes proposed that *Barricada* dedicate itself to a model of "social journalism" drawing its inspiration from conceptions of "public journalism" prevalent in the United States. At the heart of the project would be an intimate involvement with Nicaraguan "social movements," through the activation of "various permanent forums of discussion" centered around children, women, and other groups, each of which would provide representatives to liaise with *Barricada*. The result would be a "more human" and "dynamic" journalism, infused as well with the energies of new workers on the paper's staff: Gómez and Reyes envisaged building a new editorial team around a nucleus of capable and experienced personnel, but with the wholesale dismissal of others, and the addition of recent journalism graduates who would learn from the veterans and continue their professional studies at the newspaper itself.

The events of December 1997 and January 1998 did not quash

discussion of such a revamped project entirely, as we will see. They did, however, lead to the departure of Gómez and Reyes from *Barricada,* and—rapidly—to the end of the daily *Barricada* itself.

Chapter 5

The Death of Barricada

WHATEVER OTHER THREATS had confronted *Barricada* in October 1994, the institution at least did not have to fear rebellion within its own ranks. Even the decimated and disgruntled blue-collar staff of El Amanecer's Plant B did not actively demonstrate support for the defenestración of Carlos Fernando Chamorro by striking or otherwise demonstrating en bloc. The threat came instead from outside the immediate parameters of the institution; the defenestración was perceived by the vast majority of *Barricada* staff, by the public at large, and by myself as an intervention by a distinct and opposed political force.

In the last weeks of 1997 and into 1998, the prospect of outside intervention—at least by Sandinistas—was minimal. The relationship between *Barricada* and the FSLN leadership was formally a mutually supportive one. That support, though, was confined mostly to the level of rhetoric. The FSLN was in no position to subsidize *Barricada*—except by rather desperate and individual means, as with Borge's personal dispensing of largesse and the decision by him and other senior staff to renounce their salaries so that reporters and

221

blue-collar personnel could be paid. The two other channels of possible sustenance—consumer purchases and advertising revenue—were nonstarters for the reasons already outlined. And now, fatally, rebellion arose among staffers themselves.

The first inklings of revolt came on 12 September 1997, when *Barricada* editorial staff declared their refusal to write another word for the paper until back wages for August and the first half of September were paid. "To avoid a scandal," the administration issued a one-time payment of C$300 to each staff member; Borge pleaded with workers for two months' breathing space, the time to be spent seeking foreign investors for the enterprise.[1] The truce in fact lasted three months, though staffers spent the interregnum making repeated appeals to Daniel Ortega to intervene in the dispute. The last of these, in late October, had something of the character of an ultimatum: "We, the workers of the *Barricada* daily, urgently request a meeting for next Monday, 27 October, at ten o'clock, in the Andrés Valle room of the newspaper, or in any other place you indicate. The objective of our [proposed] meeting with you is to explain in person [de viva voz] the economic crisis that has rendered us incapable of sustaining the enterprise, and to analyze, in a definitive manner, the alternative solutions. . . . We respectfully request your most prompt and positive response."[2]

"I don't respond to threats," was Ortega's alleged answer. "Speak to Tomás."[3]

Finally, on 20 December 1997 two *Barricada* staffers, Xavier Rayo Valle and Pedro Vindell, launched a hunger strike demanding $80,500 in back wages and other benefits. By this point, *Barricada* was a month late in paying its Managua-based staff; for correspondents in the regions, wages were arriving as much as three months late. Health benefits—the contractual right of *Barricada* workers to receive treatment at Managua's Cruz Azul Clinic—had been suspended, along with transportation subsidies for night shift workers. Food subsidies for the children of *Barricada* staff were also cut.

Vilma Núñez, a longtime Sandinista who was now president of the

Nicaraguan Center for Human Rights (CENIDH),[4] was brought in to mediate the dispute. On 22 December an agreement was reached, ending the hunger strike after sixty hours. Borge promised to pay all back wages—now reckoned at C$1 million (about $100,000)—by 31 January 1998. *Barricada*, on its front page, proclaimed the agreement "a triumph of maturity."[5]

One last burst of guarded optimism was mustered. An opinion piece of 30 December declared that 1998 would be "the year of *Barricada*," despite the "profound financial crisis" afflicting the paper.[6] But the first weeks of the new year passed without a savior appearing on the horizon and (if the account of Paco Gómez is given credence) with a breakdown in the secret negotiations to sell the *Barricada* property to the Alemán government and refound the paper under a new name. On 26 January two *Barricada* staffers—Carlos García and Freddy García—made a final direct appeal to Daniel Ortega. They called the situation at the party newspaper "a time bomb":

> In business terms [*empresarialmente*] the situation is grave. *Barricada*, since December, has been distributed only in the capital. The distributors, for lack of wages, have refused to maintain the full reach of distribution. The delivery people have also failed to [get the newspaper to] subscribers. The lack of paper is evident and prevents us from publishing more than twelve pages. We likewise have no possibility of printing the paper in full color. . . . To further aggravate the situation, the final benefit inherited from the revolution, the cafeteria, closed.[7] The same goes for the medical dispensary and other benefits, such as the payment of bonuses [e.g., the "thirteenth-month" bonus common in Nicaraguan enterprises], the INSS [social security benefits], and innumerable other social benefits.[8]

There was no last-minute intervention from Ortega. But the end, when it came, arrived with shocking suddenness. At 7 P.M. on Friday, 30 January 1998—a day before the deadline for payment of back wages to staff—Tomás Borge called staff representatives to his office for a forty-five-minute meeting in which he announced the temporary closure of *Barricada*, effective immediately. By the time the meeting broke up, representatives from other Nicaraguan media were already arriving at the *Barricada* complex; Borge addressed them irritably and left.[9]

Staffers predictably responded with "first panic, then fury" to Borge's announcement. They nonetheless set about preparing a four-page edition of *Barricada* for publication the following day, with a front-page headline to read: "Aquí estamos: *Barricada* se debe al pueblo" (Here we are: *Barricada* should be with the people). According to *El Nuevo Diario*, the text for the edition was prepared and laid out and an agreement was reached with El Amanecer general manager Soraya Montoya to supply paper for printing. But "when we tried to print that night," editor in chief Juan Ramón Huerta told END, "Montoya had already left, leaving the paper wrapped up with instructions that [El Amanecer] shouldn't pay any attention to us." Huerta called it "the final betrayal."[10]

It was not, however, the final act in the *Barricada* drama. Editorial staff arrived at the *Barricada* offices as usual on Saturday, 31 January.[11] Said Huerta, "We're coming to work because the MITRAB [Ministry of Labor] still hasn't notified us of any suspension, and we don't want to be accused of abandoning our jobs."[12] The workers found support from an unlikely source: the minister of labor in the Alemán government, Wilfredo Navarro. On 2 February, Navarro declared the closure of *Barricada* illegal under Article 13 of the Labor Code, which required the ministry's authorization for any such action.[13] According to Juan Ramón Huerta, the response from the Sandinista rank and file was also strong: "Our people were with us. They brought us bread, coffee, money." Media workers across the Nicaraguan spectrum also expressed their solidarity. "But the owners, by contrast, remained completely indifferent—as though they had never struggled for the interests of the workers," said Huerta. "This was one of the greatest contradictions. It created in me, and in many other compañeros, a real feeling of dejection and a critical attitude—not toward Sandinismo, but toward the party leadership. When a labor problem arose in a private enterprise [*Barricada*], the Sandinista leadership were the first to abandon the struggle of the worker." Tomás Borge and Daniel Ortega were behaving like "patrones," bosses—"the most noxious figure to the working classes."[14]

The same day, a workers' delegation petitioned Managua's First Civil Court to grant an injunction against Editorial El Amanecer and *Barricada*'s director for violating the terms of the 22 December agreement mediated by Vilma Núñez.[15] As it transpired, the strategy was unnecessary. On 3 February, the Nicaraguan Institute of Social Security (INSS) acted, placing a three-month embargo on the operations of El Amanecer. The enterprise allegedly owed some C$11 million—more than $1 million—to the INSS, debts that extended as far back as 1993.[16]

While the hunger strike dragged on, an extraordinary initiative was launched by the self-constituted directorate of the "new *Barricada*." It targeted many of the leading lights of the era of semiautonomy (1991–94). Among them were Roberto Fonseca, Sergio de Castro, Daniel Alegría—and Sofía Montenegro, who described receiving a telephone call from Orlando Núñez:

> I was quite surprised. I said, "Orlando, what are you calling me for?" He said, "Well, you know the crisis that is going on with *Barricada*?" I said, "Well, yes." Then he came out with this *incredible*—from my point of view—proposal. He told me that they had had a meeting the night before, until very early in the morning, with the people of the past *redacción* [editorial team] and entrepreneurs of the front, who were willing to put up $500,000 to start a new newspaper. . . . They thought that most of the people who had left the first [semiautonomous] *Barricada* should come back and be hired again. Orlando was calling me to tell me that they had thought of me, and the proposition was, one, that I should reopen *Gente* [the former supplement directed by Montenegro]. They told me I could do whatever I wanted with it. And I could be a member of the new editorial board. . . . He told me that they had spoken about this with Daniel Ortega, and he had accepted.

They had spoken to the journalists, and they had agreed not to put up a fight if we came back again as their bosses and editors.

Montenegro said she was stunned by the proposal: "I couldn't believe my fucking ears! . . . I said, 'In the first place, how *dare* you approach me? The front haven't even paid me what they owe me from the last time [I worked at *Barricada*]. Now that you don't have *any* credibility, you want people like myself to put our names and faces [to the project] . . . in the name of *what?*'" The offer, Montenegro said, "provoked a turmoil within me. You know, I'd been distancing myself [from the events of 1994], but this shit was reviving all my old anger. I told [Núñez], 'Yes, there's the possibility for a new paper. But not with you.'"[17]

What was going on behind the scenes in February 1998 was a concerted attempt to revive *Barricada*, or a quasi-*Barricada*, as a means of reasserting Sandinismo as a print-media force. In mid-February, a window of opportunity appeared, with an agreement between *Barricada* staff and the FSLN leadership to sell the newspaper's plant and property, and use the money to pay the $80,000 claimed by staff. All rights to the name *Barricada*, meanwhile, were turned over to an anonymous society, Renacer (Rebirth), headed by Orlando Núñez, now a National Directorate member and director of the organization CIPRES. From a material and marketing viewpoint, the plan for a *Nueva Barricada* involved two share issues aimed at raising $40,000 in start-up capital, half of it from those directly involved in the project (from back wages owed), the other half from a broad cross-section of pro-Sandinista business and opinion. International support was solicited; a Dutch activist pledged a computer, and a friend of Juan Ramón Huerta's in Estelí, $3,000.[18] Four thousand copies would be published, at sixteen pages, initially in Managua only.[19] Among the names mooted for the new project were *Nueva Barricada* (the name used generically here to refer to the project), *Siglo Veintiuno*, *El Guardián*, and *El Jardín* [The garden]—the last of which, pointed out *Confidencial*, seemed "more appropriate for a beer hall."[20]

Editorially, the project proposed by Paco Gómez and Xavier Reyes the previous December was to serve as the foundation for a newspaper that would be "a totally independent enterprise," one that "exclude[d] all members of the Sandinista directorate" from the running of the newspaper.[21] The paper would also be institutionally separated from Editorial El Amanecer, which would become the personal property of Tomás Borge—compensation for the money he had invested in *Barricada* over the previous years. In return, Borge would assume all the debts that El Amanecer still owed to the government (e.g., in social-security payments) and to suppliers of raw materials.[22]

A draft editorial profile emphasized the new project's professional dimension, envisaging *Nueva Barricada* as "a newspaper for the twenty-first century," "independent," "pluralist," with a "left" editorial definition but providing "service to the interests of all Nicaraguans."[23] Juan Ramón Huerta described the project as an attempt to recapture the sense of "professional pride" that had animated *Barricada* journalists in the 1980s and during the autonomy project: "We wanted to take the best of Carlos Fernando's project, because it was a very good project professionally," even though contaminated by "a political bias." The new *Barricada*, by contrast, would adhere to standards of "strict professionalism."[24]

But if the prospects at first seemed promising, at least for a successful launch, optimism dissipated when the worst scandal in FSLN history descended upon the front's leader and perennial presidential candidate, Daniel Ortega. On 2 March 1998, Juan Ramón Huerta, *Barricada*'s final editor and a key member of the "provisional committee of [the new] *Barricada*," received a summons from Zoilamérica, stepdaughter of Ortega and his longtime partner, Rosario Murillo. "I'd had friendly relations with her for a long time. She invited me to a meeting where [she said she] would be making a family decision. I arrived, and imagine my surprise! The family decision was to divest herself of the name Ortega and to denounce Daniel Ortega for raping her from the age of eleven!"

Huerta was the final interview subject of a research project that had occupied the better part of the decade. He had been out of town for most of the summer 1998 research stint in Managua, but I tracked him down the day it ended. Trudging along the road to Huerta's small but tidy home in the journalists' "colony" that is a feature of many Latin American cities, I was confronted by an apparition. Looming up through the windshield of an oncoming Pathfinder were the broad pugilist features of Adolfo Calero, point person for the contra rebels in their dealings with the Reagan administration during the 1980s. Calero regarded me coolly from the passenger seat of the Jeep as it sped past. Clearly, much had changed since my first visit to Nicaragua—in 1986, at the height of the contra war, when Calero was public enemy number one and persona maxima non grata.

Much had changed in Juan Ramón Huerta's life as well. He described the transformations over sweet black coffee at his kitchen table, detailing *Barricada*'s final months, the efforts to start the new project, and his final rupture with the Sandinista leadership. Huerta said he had been impressed by the support Daniel Ortega had rendered *Barricada* throughout its death throes, despite his unwillingness to respond to last-minute appeals from staff. Now he was stunned to find Ortega behaving in a "diametrically opposite" fashion when it came to his stepdaughter's allegations. "In the *Barricada* case, Daniel Ortega showed his face and came out in our defense," said Huerta. "It was as a result of his efforts that they ended up paying us [back wages]—he personally involved himself in the case. We could speak frankly with him about everything." After the death of *Barricada*, as well, Ortega was receptive to "the necessity of making a new newspaper" and to the proposed editorial profile. But Ortega was keeping mum on the subject of Zoilamérica's accusations and refusing to surrender his parliamentary immunity from prosecution.

The accusations, which Huerta fully believed,[25] left him in an "impossible" ethical and personal position. After two decades of dedicated militancy, he suddenly felt "a moral, historical, and human obligation to be critical" of the FSLN and its leaders. But by taking Zoilamérica's side,[26] Huerta immediately and irrevocably alienated himself from his coplanners on the *Nueva Barricada* project. On the very day—2 March—that Zoilamérica issued her denunciations, the Renacer enterprise had been founded to oversee the launch of the *Nueva Barricada*. But when Huerta backed Zoilamérica, his coworkers "called me up and told me I was being very hard on the leadership of the front, that I was entering into opposition to Sandinismo, and [that I was] therefore a contaminating element—dangerous, a threat to the new project. I told them that if that was the way they felt, I didn't want to be accused of causing problems in the new *Barricada*. Owing to their lack of confidence, and to avoid contradictions with my compañeros, I wrote a letter of resignation."

Whether or not Huerta's departure and the post-Zoilamérica disarray within the front were the decisive factors, the "provisional committee" of the new *Barricada* would never meet again. "They said they would be on the streets in May," said Huerta. "In May there was no sign of them. Then came the [FSLN] congress. I remember a friend who told me something [at that time] that worried me greatly. He said: 'Let's wait and see. It all depends on what happens in the congress whether *Barricada* is published or not.'" For Huerta, the passing comment indicated that the new *Barricada* would not be a truly "journalistic project"—a more autonomous publication along the lines of the 1991–94 version—but rather "an instrument of the thoughts and interests of whoever was elected in the congress ... a partisan project." Now it was July, and still there was no new Sandinista daily. "Unfortunately, although it pains me to say it, the people have forgotten about *Barricada*," Huerta lamented.

He was in any case largely a spectator, still struggling to absorb the personal and political implications of his break with the front. The lifelong militant could no longer hope for employment in the Sandinista media or related institutions. That had its advantages, perhaps: Huerta pronounced himself glad to be "a free agent," liberated from the constraints of political partisanship. To keep bread on the table, he had worked with the Nicaraguan Union of Journalists (UPN), and traveled around the country to sound out the possibilities of municipal-level publishing in the regions. He was contemplating writing a more reflective account of the Zoilamérica scandal. "I don't feel disillusioned," Huerta emphasized. "On the contrary, now I feel free to say things that previously I considered it my responsibility not to say. I'm always thinking of the future. If Sandinismo is ever to return to power here, it will have to become more transparent and self-critical, to recognize its errors. I will never leave Sandinismo, but I will struggle within its bosom to denounce things that need to be denounced."

Huerta seemed, nonetheless, a little shell-shocked as he surveyed the eventful last couple of years. They had seen him rise to the editor's chair of *Barricada*, only to find the paper careening toward its final crisis. He had played a leading role in the abortive attempts to found a new Sandinista daily. Now, suddenly, he was at odds with the entire organized front, a leading advocate for Zoilamérica, and a trenchant critic of the most powerful Sandinista in the country.

The transformation resulted from a twin betrayal, in Huerta's view. The first violation of trust came with the canceling of the *Barricada* project, which he saw FSLN founding father Tomás Borge as having engineered. Now there were the explosive allegations of sexual abuse leveled against Daniel Ortega.[27] Huerta could hardly credit that "the leadership in which I had believed so much, in which I had such confidence, had left me feeling so uncomfortable from the personal point of view—to say nothing of [my reaction] as a militant of a revolutionary party. I couldn't control my distress. I realized at that moment that either the Sandinista leadership would change or the party would disappear."

He was not optimistic. "The Sandinista Front has become the type of party it always criticized—a traditional party, election oriented, wheeling and dealing [*de componenda*], making pacts. "*Las luces de un partido revolucionario aquí se han apagado*," Huerta said pensively. "The lights of a revolutionary party have gone out here."

Conclusion: Barricada *in Comparative Perspective*

The *Barricada* story illustrates a number of the means by which media workers, especially those in "soft" authoritarian societies, seek to balance mobilizing with professional imperatives, and in particular to open greater space for the latter. This closing discussion draws upon comparative research into other media systems (notably Russia, Jordan, and South Africa)[28] to generalize about the types of strategies employed, and the overriding factors and variables that may act to constrain professional functioning.

Nicaragua must first of all be seen as an exemplar of underdeveloped media systems. The ramifications of low levels of development for professional functioning are numerous. First of all, underdevelopment correlates with high levels of poverty and illiteracy, which strongly militates against the written press as compared with its broadcast media counterparts.[29] Newspapers are comparatively expensive media products, meaning that even in a revolutionary society like 1980s Nicaragua, *Barricada*'s readership was disproportionately tilted toward middle- and upper-class elements (still more so after 1990). Distribution difficulties, dependence on material imports, and a paucity of advertising revenue are all marked features of this type of media system. All acted at various points to limit *Barricada*'s reach and potential impact. Regime subsidies during the 1980s offset these difficulties to a certain extent, but when they were progressively withdrawn, beginning in the later 1980s, the impact on *Barricada* was immediate and in many ways devastating. This was still more true after the defenestración of 1994 and the election of a right-wing government in 1996 that appeared to dedicate itself to maximizing the material travails of opposition media outlets.

The strategies employed by *Barricada*'s staff were often typical of those employed by media workers internationally to preserve a degree of institutional independence and advance a conception of professional journalism, even if this sometimes ran counter to mobilizers' interests and stated preferences. *Taking advantage of splits in sponsors' ranks* is one time-honored strategy. With the Sandinista Front divided and dislocated after its election defeat in 1990, *Barricada* found the ideal moment to forge a more autonomous agenda that allowed greater breathing space for the professional ambitions its staff had long harbored. "Right now, the front is going through a very hard time," said staffer Guillermo Cortés in 1991. "It[s leadership] has lost authority, credibility, legitimacy. It's difficult for them to lead even their own organizations. Even if they wanted to have greater control over *Barricada*, the situation itself prevents it. Well, we're taking advantage of that."[30] But when the ortodoxo contingent established hegemony and imposed "unity" within Sandinista ranks, the professional space opened to *Barricada* was doomed, and finally—in October 1994—closed.

Exploiting a soft authoritarianism was an important avenue open to *Barricada* during the revolutionary decade of the 1980s. The Sandinista regime, as we have seen, was a comparatively tolerant and open one, providing a space for opposition media unusual not just for left-revolutionary regimes in this century, but even compared with liberal-democratic societies in conditions of war or national emergency. The effect on the FSLN's official organ was multifaceted. The paper was able to develop its own sense of professional identity—and then to lobby the leadership of the front, successfully, for greater institutional room to express that identity. These negotiations presaged the more dramatic transformations of January 1991; they would hardly have been countenanced in, for example, Castro's Cuba, the left-revolutionary society that was closest to Nicaragua in both the geographic and the political sense. Unknown elsewhere, too, was the existence of a broad range of opposition media throughout the Sandinista years in power. The reflex relationship between *Barricada* and *La Prensa* was a powerful spur to *Barricada*'s professional imperative; staffers spoke of a sense of disorientation in *both* mobilizing and professional senses when *La Prensa* was banned.

Barricada also employed a variant of the *piggybacking* strategy common in authoritarian media systems, in this case by exploiting its privileged relationship with the ruling regime. Usually piggybacking strategies are manifested in the relationship between the regime (or factions thereof) and the media organ's director or editor in chief. The degree of professional space granted to newspapers under authoritarianism often correlates directly with the trust established between senior figures at both the regime and the institutional level. Favored editors and directors may use their greater leeway to bolster the professional imperative and institutional autonomy of their paper—even when this irritates or alienates other important regime players. Much of the success of *Barricada*'s autonomy project in the early 1990s can be ascribed to the proximity of its director, Carlos Fernando Chamorro, to the inner circles of Sandinista power. (Chamorro, as noted, headed the FSLN's Department of Agitation and Propaganda for a time in the mid-1980s.) Partly as a result, *Barricada* was never exposed to the kind of prior censorship visited upon the other Nicaraguan dailies in the 1980s (even the pro-Sandinista *El Nuevo Diario*); the chief censor during this period, Nelba Blandón, referred in an interview to "a relationship of trust" existing between the front and its official organ under Chamorro's direction.[31] As well, it is unlikely that *Barricada*'s FSLN sponsor would have been willing to grant the far-reaching independence that it did in December 1990 to a paper headed by a more mercurial, less sympathetic figure than Chamorro. The trend carried over to the post-defenestración era: whatever stability *Barricada* enjoyed was derived in large part from the guiding role played by Tomás Borge, a sitting member of the FSLN National Directorate and one of the leading figures in the history of the Nicaraguan revolution.

Barricada's post-1990 trajectory also points to some regular and predictable, though not ubiquitous, features of the media in times of political transition. The first point to note here is that such epochs almost—though not quite—inevitably prove enormously turbulent for the media (and other) institutions forced to navigate them. The onset phase of transitions standardly features an explosion of new media outlets; indeed, this is one of the most reliable indicators that liberalization and transition processes are underway. Established media thus tend to confront a range of new competitors, many of which may benefit from a lack of association with the ancien régime. In the Nicaraguan case, the onset phase began well before the fall of the Sandinista government, confronting *Barricada* with renewed competition from its erstwhile rival *La Prensa* as well as a new daily that targeted much the same middle- and upper-class constituency as *Barricada*, namely *La Tribuna*. Likewise, however, the flowering of new media outlets is almost always followed by a rapid winnowing, as economic pressures combine with (and help to spawn) a decline in public interest compared with the heady early days of liberalization. Nicaragua's calamitous economic state in the 1990s was in many ways typical of the economic crisis that generally haunts political transitions in the Third World, where the majority of such transitions have taken place. We have seen that the period between 1990 and the defenestración of 1994 represented a constant struggle for survival for the newspaper—a struggle that, under the post-1994 management, proved impossible to wage with success. We also saw that a number of the most significant professional decisions taken at the paper between 1990—indeed, 1987—and 1994 reflected a desire to reach out to new constituencies and develop new journalistic projects and content. While a mobilizing imperative clearly underlay some of this outreach and exploration, material requirements—the need to find new readers and advertisers—were profoundly influential.

Newspapers and other media outlets also tend to be one of the most *sought after prizes* in the transitional era. The Nicaraguan media landscape is not as complex or developed as that of other transitional societies I have studied, notably Russia and South Africa. There were correspondingly fewer actors and forces contending for power (including media power) during the transition, and so Nicaragua did not witness the scenario so common to postcommunist Russia, with various political figures, parastatal corporations, media magnates (both domestic and foreign), and mafiosi all struggling for a piece of the media pie. Nonetheless, it is clear that for the Sandinista Front, preservation of control over the party's media flagship was deemed essential to the party's political viability in the transitional period. As noted above, the onset of the transition threw the Sandinista Front into near calamitous internal upheaval, creating splits in sponsors' ranks and granting *Barricada* crucial breathing space to advance the professional project that most of its staff had long cherished. This opportunity was magnified by the disappearance of most restrictions on media functioning, both in the last years of the revolutionary government and under Violeta Chamorro's transitional regime. But when power within the front, still *Barricada*'s sponsor, coalesced around the ortodoxo contingent led by Daniel Ortega, *Barricada*'s days as a semi-independent institution were numbered. The determination of the ortodoxos to reestablish control over a "wayward" organ obviously reflected *Barricada*'s perceived political significance in the transitional era, which had eroded or destroyed the party's parastatal hold over other key Nicaraguan institutions.

It may be that political liberalization and transition also tend to make publics less tolerant of excessive partisanship in journalistic work, in part by increasing the influence and appeal of the hegemonic Western model of the relationship between mass media and society. Close adherence to a mobilizer's ideological line may bring rewards in the form of stable sponsorship (though in the end even this was denied to *Barricada*), a familiar editorial style and agenda (though after 1994 *Barricada* journalists had to cope with the caprice of Tomás Borge), and perhaps the political satisfaction that accrues to militant journalists from their service to a cause. But the fact that even Sandinista militants abandoned *Barricada* in its final years suggested that the partisan journalism of the postdefenestración era was unappealing even to partisans. The model was hard to abandon for those, like the ortodoxo FSLN, with a "permanent conception of the press as an extension of the party apparatus," as Carlos Fernando Chamorro put it in 1998.[32] But the 1991 comments of Nicaraguan communications theorist Guillermo Rothschuh seem prescient in retrospect. "It's been proven in Nicaragua that this kind of journalism provokes a certain if not total rejection by the readership, a certain distance and cautiousness," Rothschuh told me. "Because people understand that what comes first isn't defense of the interests of society as a whole, but of a particular party or governing regime."[33] Seven years later, and possibly wiser, Juan Ramón Huerta considered "the Nicaraguan reader today" to be "more demanding. You have to provide him or her with a coherent product—not at the behest of the owner [*por la voluntad del dueño*], or because you personally believe it to be true."[34]

Lastly, the *Barricada* saga is a reminder that political transitions—both at the national and institutional level—can never be considered immune to rollback and retrenchment. Though there has been no return to the dictatorial atmosphere of the Somoza dynasty, the new freedom extended to *Barricada* after 1990 proved extremely vulnerable to pressure from elements within the FSLN that adhered to the older (revolutionary and prerevolutionary) model of journalism as an expression of mobilizers' interests and priorities. In this regard, it is perhaps fitting that *Barricada*'s longtime director, Carlos Fernando Chamorro, should have the final word. In mid-1998, I asked Chamorro how he would generalize from *Barricada*'s experiences. "One angle would be to say that transitions do not always produce the results you're looking for," Chamorro responded, after pondering the question for a while. "You can have different outcomes—advance or regression. There's no way to predict that transitions in the press will always lead to modernization, or pluralism, or whatever it is you're looking for."

Chamorro nonetheless thought that *Barricada* had helped pave the way for the emergence of a truly national and independent journalism in postrevolutionary Nicaragua—one that would renounce partisanship while "not giving up on promoting the transformation of society, and people's participation in decision making. Is that a political role?" Chamorro asked rhetorically. "Yes, I think the role of the press is political in that sense. I see a very close connection between the press and democracy, and a very political role for the press. Not a *partisan* role—but not neutral, either."[35]

Postscript

In May 2000, with midterm elections approaching in Nicaragua, the Sandinista Front resuscitated *Barricada* as a party weekly, overseen by Tomás Borge. According to the *Los Angeles Times*, "The newspaper is being printed at cost. Sandinistas holding elected office are being charged an unspecified fee to cover those costs because the newspaper has no advertising yet. Distribution relies on party activists who buy 100 copies at 30 cents each and resell them to friends at cost. The volunteer editor and a managing editor paid by the party supervise three staff writers and a photographer." There were no plans to return to

Figure 5.1. The first edition of *Barricada*, 25 July 1979 *(from a facsimile circulated for publicity purposes in the 1980s).*

Figure 5.2. The final *Barricada*, never published: mock-up for the front page of 31 January 1998. *Supplied by Juan Ramón Huerta, who signed it: "a souvenir from the last editor of* Barricada."

daily publication. In Borge's words, "A daily newspaper is a costly, complicated undertaking. We do not have the economic conditions for that."[36] But even weekly publication soon proved impossible. The revived *Barricada* expired in August 2000, after about a dozen issues.

On 5 November 2001, Sandinista presidential candidate Daniel Ortega conceded defeat in national elections for the third consecutive time. The FSLN succeeded in gaining a greater proportion of the popular vote than in 1996, but still fell far short of the total amassed by Enrique Bolaños, the Liberal Party candidate. The election defeat threw the Sandinistas into a new crisis, with rumors that Ortega would step down as party leader. At the time of writing (late November 2001), there was no indication that a revived Sandinista print-media presence was remotely in the offing.

Notes

All translations from printed sources are my own, unless otherwise stated. Interviews were conducted in both Spanish and English, as indicated in the bibliography.

Introduction

1. Alegría interview, 10 May 1996.

2. The programs were the twenty-one-year-old *Sucesos* on Radio Sandino, directed by José Estaban Quezada; *Perfiles* on Radio Stereo Ya, directed by the Mexican-Nicaraguan Karen Santamaria; and *Noticias,* also on Radio Ya. See Alvaro Cruz Rojas, "Periodistas marcharán hoy para protestar censura sandinista," *La Tribuna,* 28 October 1994.

3. Edgard Solórzano, "Carlos Fernando: 'Regresión Total,'" *El Semanario,* 27 October–3 November 1994.

4. Chamorro recalled arguing before staff that "the FSLN was perpetrating a political intervention in the paper with no authority. Because my appointment came from the board of directors of *Barricada* . . . and therefore it was [the board], and nobody else, that could call for my resignation. . . . We fought to the last detail to make evident that *Barricada* was an autonomous institution and not a party extension." Two days later, Chamorro received a formal notice of dismissal from the vice president of the board. Chamorro, pers. comm., 25 September 1998.

5. Tim Johnson, "Sandinista Left Stifles Moderates," *Miami Herald,* international edition, 28 October 1994.

6. Alegría interview, 10 May 1996; Sergio Cruz, "Periodistas lamentan destitución de Carlos Fernando Chamorro," *Barricada,* 26 October 1994. For a sampling of the international coverage in English at the time, see "Nicaragua's Sandinistas Fire Newspaper Editor," Reuters dispatch, 25 October 1994; Johnson, "Sandinista Left Stifles Moderates"; and John Otis, "Sandinistas Weeding Out the 'Best and Brightest,'" *Washington Times,* 26 October 1994.

7. Guillermo Cortés Dominguez, "El funeral" (*Siglo Veintiuno* column), *El Semanario,* 10–16 November 1994.

8. Carlos Fernando Chamorro, "Lo que se juega en *Barricada*," *Barricada*, 25 October 1994.

9. Johnson, "Sandinista Left Stifles Moderates."

10. The terms deployed throughout this book for the two main "currents" of *Sandinismo* in the 1990s are *ortodoxos* and *renovationists*. The *ortodoxo* label conveys something of the doctrinaire character of the current that dubbed itself the Democratic Left after January 1994. That doctrinaire tenor will, I believe, be evident at numerous points throughout this book. For now, suffice it say that when one saw articles in *Barricada* in the early 1990s with headlines like "The Sandinista Party: Revolutionary Instrument of the People" or "A Popular and Revolutionary Party," one could be fairly sure they were written by prominent members of the ortodoxo strand, rather than by renovationists or *Barricada* journalists themselves. (The two examples cited were authored by Mónica Baltodano and Julio López and were published in *Barricada* on 25 January and 30 January 1994.) The term *renovationists*, meanwhile, seems best to encompass the broad dissident current within the front. Most commonly associated with Sergio Ramírez's Movimiento de Renovación Sandinista (MRS), it also included many Sandinistas—including key *Barricada* staffers—who were in no way formally affiliated with Ramírez or the MRS. It might be argued that the term *renovationists* lacks the slightly pejorative overtones of *ortodoxos;* I leave it to the reader to decide whether the merits of the nomenclature outweigh its disadvantages.

11. According to Carlos Fernando Chamorro, Ortega had requested the decision be postponed. "The interesting thing is that the other members of the National Directorate considered it urgent to make the decision before the July [1991] congress, and they did not wait for Ortega to make the decision." Chamorro, pers. comm., 25 September 1998.

12. Chamorro interview, 16 May 1996.

13. Tomás Borge, "Saldremos victoriosos," *Barricada*, 25 July 1995.

14. See "Sección: Entrecomunicadores," *Medios y mensajes* (Managua), April 1996.

15. "Tomás asume *Barricada*," *Barricada*, 31 November 1994.

16. López interview, 8 May 1996.

17. For a summary, see Adam Jones, "Beyond the Barricades: The Sandinista Press and Political Transition in Nicaragua, 1979–1991," *New Political Science*, no. 23 (Fall 1992): 63–90.

18. See Adam Jones, *The Press in Transition: A Comparative Study of Nicaragua, South Africa, Jordan, and Russia* (Hamburg: Deutsches Übersee-Institut, 2001).

Chapter 1

1. Christopher Dickey, *With the Contras: A Reporter in the Wilds of Nicaragua,* rev. ed. (New York: Touchstone, 1987), 19–28, 40–43, 55–57. Franklin Montenegro was also known by his *nombre de guerra,* Sagitario. After his capture he was imprisoned, then shot "while trying to escape."

2. Montenegro interview, 8 March 1991. Onofre Guevara, a venerable figure in the above-ground Socialist Party press before 1979, joined *Barricada* in 1980 and went on to become one of the core members of the editorial team: "I remember that when Carlos Fernando [Chamorro] introduced me to the group, I had the mistaken idea that everybody else had loads of experience [in journalism]. I said that my aim was to learn all I could from them. I remember one person started to laugh. I thought she was making fun of me. Later I asked her why she'd laughed, and she said, 'Because we didn't have anything to teach you!'" Guevara interview, 2 April 1991.

3. *La Prensa* had been destroyed by aerial bombing in one of the final vengeful spasms of the Somoza dictatorship.

4. Montenegro interview, 15 March 1991. Several other staffers confirmed the "very communist-oriented" salary arrangements in the newspaper's earliest incarnation (Chamorro interview, 28 February 1991). According to Montenegro, "In 1980, they began to pay us—not a salary, but what in the Front has always been called an 'aid' [*ayuda*], a symbolic amount on which you have to live." Montenegro interview, 15 March 1991.

5. Chamorro interview, 28 February 1991.

6. The directors were Carlos Carrión during the first week of publication; Julio López (who returned to *Barricada* in October 1994, as part of the ortodoxo takeover of the paper); and Luís Chiri Guzmán (from September 1979 to May 1980). "Their relations[hip] with the staff . . . was the typical one of the political commissar." Carlos Fernando Chamorro, pers. comm., 25 September 1998.

7. The Department of Agitation and Propaganda was one of seven "Auxiliary Departments" constituting the National Directorate staff, a bureaucratic body of about six hundred party functionaries. For more information on the structure of Sandinista party organization, see Dennis Gilbert, *Sandinistas: The Party and the Revolution* (Cambridge, Mass.: Basil Blackwell, 1988), 48–52.

8. George Black, *Triumph of the People: The Sandinista Revolution in Nicaragua* (London: Zed Press, 1981), 108. Pedro Joaquín's image today adorns the Nicaraguan fifty-córdoba banknote—certainly one of the rare instances worldwide in which a professional journalist has been memorialized in this manner.

9. The anti-Sandinista *La Prensa* was owned by Violeta Chamorro and directed by Pedro Joaquín Chamorro Jr., with Jaime Chamorro serving as business manager; Xavier Chamorro, brother of Pedro Joaquín Sr., was editor of *El Nuevo Diario*. The arrangement attracted considerable international attention during the 1980s. See, for example, Alan Riding, "Newspaper Family Typifies Nicaragua's Divisions," *New York Times*, 24 May 1980; Jonathan Evan Maslow, "The Junta and the Press: A Family Affair," *Columbia Journalism Review* 19 (March/April 1981): 46–52; Lawrence Wright, "War of Words: Nicaragua's Newspaper Family Tears Itself Apart over Its Revolutionary Legacy," *Mother Jones*, June 1983; and "A House Divided," *Time*, 17 October 1983. The only faintly comparable case I have heard of is Colombia in the early 1990s, where, "incredibly, all the major television news programs"—five in all—were "run by the children of former presidents." See Jenny Pearce, "The People's War," *NACLA Report on the Americas* 23, 6 (April 1990): 17.

10. Chamorro interview, 28 February 1991.

11. On this subject, see the comments of Carlos Fernando Chamorro: "[The concept of vanguardism] is typically Leninist. But there was also some confusing notion of Gramscian hegemony that we aspired to. At least these were some of the discussions that a few of us had at the Department of Propaganda and Political Education [DEPEP, renamed the Department of Agitation and Propaganda (DAP) in 1984]. The idea was that we had to win the ideological battle, *in a context of political pluralism*. This implied building strong ideological institutions and influencing all dimensions of culture and ideology, as a way to compensate for the material limitations of

the political and transformational project. But in the end, it proved much more Leninist than Gramscian." Chamorro, pers. comm., 25 September 1998; emphasis mine. Sofía Montenegro also discussed the Gramscian influences in a 1991 interview: "From my point of view, by practice and almost by intuition, this [the Sandinista Revolution] is the most Gramscian of revolutions. . . . We always thought of the media the way Gramsci saw it, as an 'organic intellectual' [force]. The interpretation is that the media, and also the journalist, should play the role of critical consciousness of the revolution. The media should educate the people and [should] use culture in the educational process. Gramsci didn't provide a full theory on this. He had only the *Prison Notebooks*—just ideas, very much masked because of the repression Gramsci himself was subjected to. . . . But I guess, in a way, of all the theoreticians of the left, he's the one who thought most about the problem of ideology, of communication. He was from my point of view more dialectical and less authoritarian about how ideas should be worked with. Not by imposing them, but by developing a consensus. That's the main idea of Gramsci that has worked itself into the spirit of the Sandinistas, whether they're conscious of it or not. Many of them have acted in this manner without being conscious of it, without ever having read Gramsci." Montenegro interview, 15 March 1991. For more on Gramsci's contribution to communications theory (and its unfortunately fragmentary character), see John Downing, *Internationalizing Media Theory: Transition, Power, Culture* (London: Sage Publications, 1996), 199–204.

12. For an account of the genesis of a revolutionary press in Nicaragua, see "The Sandinista Press, 1961–79," in Adam Jones, "Beyond the Barricades: The Sandinista Press in Transition, 1979–1991" (Master's thesis, McGill University, 1992), 21–23. According to Carlos Fernando Chamorro, in the prerevolutionary period "the task of the underground press was very important. It was always under the surveillance of very high cadres." The publications "played, I guess, their role in promoting some basic elements of internal cohesion within the FSLN's structures." Chamorro interviews, 28 February, 28 April 1991.

13. Chamorro interview, 18 April 1991. Lenin uses the phrase "an instrument of socialist construction" in "The Immediate Tasks of the Soviet Government" (1918). See V. I. Lenin, *Selected Works: One-Volume Edition* (New York: International Publishers, 1971), 418.

14. In 1981, Chamorro told the *Columbia Journalism Review* that "the duty of the revolutionary press is to help build. We were left after the civil war with a desperate situation—tremendous unemployment, the destruction of our productive resources, and particularly the ignorance of the people about their own culture. . . . The function of journalism now is to assist in the reconstruction of Nicaragua by orientation and teaching—not merely by the presentation of isolated information that might otherwise be called objective truth." Quoted in Maslow, "Junta and the Press," 52.

15. Montenegro interview, 8 March 1991.

16. Quoted in Phil Ryan, *The Fall and Rise of the Market in Sandinista Nicaragua* (Montreal: McGill-Queen's University Press, 1996), 120.

17. *Barricada,* 25 August 1979.

18. Lenin's strategic revision of Marx—the idea that historical stages like capitalism could be skipped on the path to communism—centered on the role of a relatively small, highly motivated revolutionary strike force to seize control of the state and the instruments of production. The vanguard could then turn this apparatus to its own purposes, gradually disseminating a revolutionary message of such force that the public would be drawn en masse to the revolutionary project. Revolutionary media were meant, and in fact proved, to be essential propaganda tools in this long process. Their main role, though, came to be that of instruments in a sophisticated apparatus of coercion. The majority population of the various republics, it transpired, had to be dragged rather than drawn into the embrace of the Soviet state.

19. Gilbert, *Sandinistas,* 31.

20. "Perfil editorial de *Barricada,*" cited in Guillermo Cortés Domínguez and Juan Ramón Huerta Chavarría, "Critical Journalism in the Daily *Barricada,*" monograph prepared for the Degree in Journalism at the University of Central America (UCA), Managua, submitted 30 June 1988, 4–5. A nearly identical version of the profile can be found in "Profiles of the Communications Media," an internal document of the Department of Agitation and Propaganda prepared under Carlos Fernando Chamorro's aegis in the first trimester of 1985 (privately supplied).

21. *Inherently* parastatal, since the vanguardist strategy is based on seizure of the state apparatus, its merging with existing or newly created revolutionary institutions, and its deliberate use to entrench revolutionary power.

22. Chamorro quoted in "One Year of Revolutionary Information," *Barricada*, 26 July 1980.

23. Then *Barricada* staffer Guillermo Cortés used the "main dish" phrase in an interview on 8 April 1991.

24. Montenegro interview, 16 March 1991. A small-scale content analysis examined *Barricada*'s front pages for June 1984, at the height of the contra war. The front pages of twenty-seven editions were surveyed. Of these, eighteen of the above-the-fold headlines were directly related to the war effort. In two further cases, secondary stories—above the fold and alongside the main story—also concerned the war. A 1988 monograph by *Barricada* staffers Guillermo Cortés and Juan Ramón Huerta "found that 64 percent of the total area of *Barricada* front pages between 18 and 24 March 1986 consisted of stories concerning the military aggression against Nicaragua." See Jones, "Beyond the Barricades" (thesis), 42.

25. Reyes interview, 13 April 1991.

26. Chamorro interview, 17 April 1991.

27. Cortés interview, 15 April 1991.

28. See Jones, *Press in Transition*. In chapter 1 of that work (pp. 23-24) I explore the mobilizing imperative: "The mobilizing imperative that dominates a given press system or newspaper institution, and the identity of the sponsor and primary mobilizer, is easily enough isolated by asking a few basic questions. Who owns the institution? Who pays the staff, and covers the cost of inputs? If it is not the state or regime directly, what is the relationship between the sponsor and the state or regime? If we expand the analysis beyond simple survival, the broader mobilizing imperative can likewise readily be ascertained. What constituency does the newspaper target? What is the stated agenda of the institution, as this is expressed in editorial page 'leaders'? (Where, in other words, do 'leaders' lead, and whom do they seek to lead?) Which taboo areas are respected—that is to say, what social, economic, and political options tend to be *foreclosed,* rendered 'unthinkable,' in the paper's reportage and editorial commentary? What, at its heart, qualifies as 'news'? Which social sectors and class interests tend to be selected out for special attention, treated more favourably and attentively, as measured (for example) by the kind of supplements the paper publishes? Given the limitations of the social sciences, it is best to consider all these questions in tandem. Any of them alone, however, may serve as a fairly reliable lead

to the source and character of the wider mobilizing imperative, in both its material and editorial manifestations.

"The guardians of the mobilizing imperative seem best located, across media systems, in the nexus of owners, managers, and senior editors. These together control the 'strategic heights' of any newspaper's operations"; emphasis in original.

29. A turning point appears to have been reached in 1982, with the building of a stable journalistic and administrative staff; a move from the cramped quarters of *Novedades* to larger and better-equipped facilities; the implementation of stable salary arrangements; and the establishment of a distribution network and stable supplies of ink and newsprint, enabling an increase in circulation.

30. Chamorro interview, 28 February 1991. For the published journalism from this era, see *Corresponsales de guerra: Testimonio de cien días de sangre, fuego, y victoria* (Managua: Editorial El Amanecer, 1984).

31. Jones, "Beyond the Barricades" (thesis).

32. See Mark Everingham, *Revolution and the Multiclass Coalition in Nicaragua* (Pittsburgh: University of Pittsburgh Press, 1996).

33. Phil Ryan offers a concise summary of the events: "An outspoken opponent of the Somoza regime, *La Prensa* had represented since the FSLN's victory an uneasy mixture of pro- and anti-government journalists. In April [1980], however, the paper's owners, the Chamorro family, opted to transform *La Prensa* into a unified opposition newspaper, and replaced editor Xavier Chamorro with his nephew Pedro Joaquín Chamorro Jr. The staff, which opposed the action by an estimated three to one majority, closed the paper in protest, accusing the Chamorro family of wanting to turn *La Prensa* into 'the spokesman of minority, privileged and anti-popular sectors.' The paper reopened a month later, after the family agreed to give Xavier the capital necessary to open a competing paper, *El Nuevo Diario*, to which the majority of *La Prensa*'s former staff transferred." Ryan, *Fall and Rise*, 120.

34. See John Spicer Nichols, *"La Prensa:* The CIA Connection," *Columbia Journalism Review* 27 (July–August 1988): 34–35.

35. Francisco Goldman, "Sad Tales of *La Libertad de Prensa,*" *Harper's,* August 1988, 56.

36. It is also worth noting that Nicaragua lies at the heart of one of the

most heavily penetrated broadcasting environments in the world. In 1985, at the midway point in the revolutionary decade, Nicaraguans could access broadcasts from an estimated "76 foreign AM and FM radio stations," compared with just 15 stations under the umbrella of the Sandinista-supervised CORADEP network. Howard H. Frederick, "The Radio War against Nicaragua," in Armand Mattelart, ed., *Communicating in Popular Nicaragua* (New York: International General, 1986), 73–75.

37. Noam Chomsky, "The Decline of the Democratic Ideal," in *Deterring Democracy* (London: Verso, 1991), 325–26.

38. To my knowledge, the only study in English of media policy during the entire revolutionary decade is my own: "Sandinista Media Policy and Legislation, 1979–90," appendix to "Beyond the Barricades" (thesis). Particularly interesting is the Sandinista relationship with the Maoist newspaper *El Pueblo,* the only paper whose plant was actually seized. *El Pueblo* was closed two days after the revolutionary victory, for a month, as a result of its criticisms of the new governing junta and its opposition to the disbanding of the *milpas* (popular militias) that had sprung up during the insurrection. "The paper, its plant confiscated, did not publish again during the Sandinista years in power, though a monthly paper belonging to the [Maoist party] . . . appeared between 1980 and 1986 under censorship. *El Pueblo* resumed publishing in March 1990 following the Sandinista election defeat" (app., p. ix).

39. In the mid-1980s, an American reporter, Michael Massing, witnessed the anomalous sight of "a truck backed into *La Prensa*'s loading dock, disgorging 300-kilogram rolls of newsprint marked 'Made in the USSR.' The trucks arrived throughout the day, delivering 700 tons in all—enough to keep the paper going for three or four months. Thus," Massing noted tongue-in-cheek, "did Soviet generosity help keep the flame of press freedom alive in Nicaragua." Massing, "Nicaragua's Free-Fire Journalism," *Columbia Journalism Review* 27 (July-August 1988): 33. Professional (not to mention family) bonds also linked the staff and directorates of the three politically opposed Managua dailies. Business managers, for example, would meet to discuss matters of common interest and hammer out practical agreements—to conduct joint tours of Costa Rican newsrooms, or to deny space to advertisers who refused to settle debts owed to another paper. See Jones, "Beyond the Barricades" (article), 87 n. 26.

40. Murillo interview, Managua, 24 April 1991; emphasis hers. Carlos Fernando Chamorro concurred: "The Sandinista Revolution never established any kind of limitations on [U.S. cultural values]—on music, movie stars, these types of things. . . . I mean, when I was a teenager, 13, 14, 15 years old, obviously I loved [the rock group] Santana, and I loved to see the movie of Woodstock." Chamorro interview, 28 April 1991. The author remembers a 1986 parade of Sandinista children in León's central square, in which anti-imperialist slogans were lustily chanted while John Mellencamp's song "R.O.C.K. in the U.S.A." played through loudspeakers.

41. "The New Nicaragua Demands a New Journalism," *Barricada,* 13 August 1979.

42. Montenegro interview, 8 March 1991; emphasis hers.

43. Alegría interview, 25 February 1991.

44. Chamorro interview, 19 March 1991.

45. Reyes interview, 13 April 1991; Chamorro interview, 28 February 1991. Sofía Montenegro also spoke of "the tradition, the habit of reading *La Prensa* had established, and the sort of visual familiarity people had with the most popular newspaper—its big headlines, its design and layout." Montenegro interview, 8 March 1991.

46. Chamorro interview, 28 February 1991.

47. This and preceding quotes from Chamorro interviews, 28 February and 28 April 1991; emphasis his.

48. Ibid.

49. Reyes interview, 13 April 1991; emphasis mine.

50. Montenegro interview, 15 March 1991. Carlos Fernando Chamorro concurred: "In general it was dull, yes. . . . I guess we were all stimulated when *La Prensa* reappeared in October 1987." Chamorro interview, 3 April 1991.

51. Chamorro interview, 3 April 1991.

52. Reyes interview, 13 April 1991.

53. Chamorro interview, 28 February 1991.

54. Ryan, *Fall and Rise,* 119–20.

55. Like most statistics in Nicaragua, *Barricada*'s circulation is difficult to verify independently. A peak circulation of 130,000 in 1985 was claimed by Carlos Fernando Chamorro in a 1991 interview (28 February). The fifth-anniversary edition of *Barricada* cited a figure of 120,000 for special print

runs, and a regular circulation of 110,000—"a quantity . . . unheard of in the history of Nicaraguan journalism." Chamorro was quoted as saying the circulation figures pointed to the "beginning of the overthrow of bourgeois press hegemony in Nicaragua" ("Five Years of Revolutionary Truth," 25 July 1984). Joan Coxsedge lists *Barricada*'s circulation as 110,000 in 1984. Coxsedge, *Thank God for the Revolution: A Journey through Central America* (Sydney: Pluto Press, 1986), 121. The usually reliable Nicaraguan magazine, *envío*, gave a circulation figure of 105,000 for early 1986 (up from 90,000 in late 1985 and 75,000 in 1983). This is close to the figure claimed by Chamorro. See "*La Prensa:* Post-Mortem on a Suicide," *envío*, August 1986, 32.

56. Correspondingly, according to Carlos Fernando Chamorro, when the Sandinistas introduced "stabilization" measures in 1987 that included a lifting of subsidies, "circulation declined steeply. Because when the subsidies were suspended, the people had to pay for food and other things, and they no longer bought newspapers as they had in the past." Chamorro interview, 28 February 1991.

57. Said Guillermo Cortés, one of *Barricada*'s war correspondents, "Listen, this isn't propaganda. *Barricada* was like *food* [for the troops]. It was company, contact with the outside world." An incidental result was that *Barricada*'s war correspondents enjoyed a privileged status among both officers and regular troops of the Popular Sandinista Army. According to Cortés: "Of course we received orders, and were subject to the military structure. We couldn't move about freely. But we were treated practically like officers of a battalion. We didn't have to do guard duty. We had access to the commanding officer's kitchen. Nobody could give you a tough order—even the officers' orders were given in a different tone of voice. . . . If you got tired, [the soldiers] carried your knapsack. They took care of you. Because for them it meant a lot that a journalist would accompany them, that we weren't just war correspondents who arrived as spectators." Cortés interview, 9 April 1991; emphasis his.

58. Chamorro interview, 28 February 1991.

59. Chamorro interview, 19 March 1991.

60. "A Publishing Operation That Educates the Nation," in *Barricada*'s eighth-anniversary edition, 24 July 1987.

61. Chamorro interview, 28 February 1991.

62. As in Cuba, the regime's attempts to evade the U.S. economic embargo led it to establish a variety of front organizations in other countries. After the election defeat of 1990, many of these appear to have become the private property of Sandinista leaders, along with entrepreneurs like Herty Lewites.

63. Arce's comments were paraphrased in Shirley Christian, "Ortega's Leadership Criticized by Sandinistas," *New York Times*, 24 March 1992.

64. Blandón interview, 15 April 1991; the claim was confirmed by several *Barricada* staffers, not for attribution. Ex post facto measures taken against *Barricada* usually amounted to little more than chiding, though individual staffers (e.g., Sofía Montenegro) could receive greater sanction, as discussed below.

65. Evidence for this rather bald assertion I glean from the extensive interview record, especially from the 1991 research; the public declarations by *Barricada* staff criticizing pressure from Daniel Ortega and others in the early 1990s; and from the near unanimity of the staff's response to the defenestración.

66. Reyes interview, 13 April 1991.

67. Ibid.

68. Chamorro interview, 19 March 1991; emphasis his. Onofre Guevara recalled that the "political aspect" of dealings with individual directorate members necessitated an equal apportioning of space and attention, down to the most minor details: "Carlos Fernando was careful to balance the activities and representation of every member of the directorate, even down to the size of the photos and the space the article took up." Guevara interview, 2 April 1991.

69. Montenegro interview, 15 March 1991.

70. Reyes interview, 13 April 1991.

71. Cortés interview, 9 April 1991.

72. Montenegro interview, 15 March 1991; emphasis hers.

73. Chamorro interview, 12 April 1991. Sofía Montenegro offered another revealing account of interaction between the Sandinista and state-socialist styles. On certain occasions during the 1980s, she said, "we in Nicaragua came to know these [state-socialist] systems a little better, not only by traveling there and witnessing how people acted on their own turf, but by watching how they performed when they lived *here*. For example, you'd

meet with some East German doctors here, and invite them to your house, to go drinking, to go to the beach. And they'd always be a little awkward, saying, 'Well, . . .' Then we found out they had to get *permission* from their party in order to mingle with Nicaraguans. We said, *'What?'* That sort of thing couldn't enter anybody's head here." Montenegro also stated that had she grown to political maturity in one of the state-socialist countries, "I would have been a dissident. I can say that unflinchingly, without any doubt." Montenegro interview, 6 May 1991; emphasis hers. Her fractious relationship with the front throughout the 1980s lends credibility to the claim.

74. Montenegro interview, 8 March 1991. Attesting to the moderate approach of Sandinista leaders to internal party discipline, Montenegro found her punishment "not too bad. I didn't have to apologize for my behavior, and I was given the chance to explain why I'd done it. . . . Nonetheless, it was a formal sanction for me."

75. Montenegro interview, 8 March 1991; emphasis in original. The article in question appeared on 30 January 1987, under the title, "Convención Bautista discute qué hacer con su hospital." The fateful final paragraph read: *"Aunque de hecho, todos los allí presentes dijeron que no quieren ver a Ortega, porque 'les cae mal'"* (Even though, in fact, all those present said they did not wish to see Ortega, because "they didn't like him"). The paper published an apology on 31 January, describing the passage as resulting from "an involuntary human and technical error." On 3 February a brief front-page announcement appeared, stating that "from today, . . . compañeros Xavier Reyes, subdirector, and Marcio Vargas, chief of information, have ceased to exercise their functions at this newspaper and will be reassigned to other revolutionary media outlets, where they will assume other responsibilities." Vargas was subsequently sent to work for Agencia Nueva Nicaragua, and served as its correspondent in Mexico. Reyes was shifted to Radio Sandino and later to the Sandinista TV channel. Both Reyes and Vargas returned to *Barricada* after the 1990 elections, with Reyes becoming a member of the paper's editorial council. "Nobody in the front objected to my decision to bring them back," recalled Carlos Fernando Chamorro. "At that moment, I was absolutely free to put together my own staff. For *Barricada*'s staff, it felt like a vindication." Both Reyes and Vargas left *Barricada* in 1993, before the defenestración, "probably perceiving it in advance," according to Chamorro. Pers.

comm., 25 September 1998. Reyes, in a slightly bizarre development, was brought back as a consultant in the final months of *Barricada*'s life, as discussed in chapter 4.

Ironically, given the events of October 1994, it was also the 1987 crisis at *Barricada* that led to Chamorro's return as director of the paper. With Reyes and Vargas gone, Chamorro was shifted from the DAP to his old post until a replacement director could be found for *Barricada*. It was a shift he had not anticipated making, but which he considered lucky in terms of his subsequent career in the media. One month back in his old post led to another and then another, until, said Chamorro, the front's leadership decided it would be easier to find a replacement for him as chief of the DAP than as director of *Barricada*. Chamorro interview, 22 July 1998. In this conversation Chamorro also confirmed the details of Sofía Montenegro's account of the crisis.

76. See Jones, appendix to "Beyond the Barricades" (thesis); the quoted passage is Sánchez's own evaluation of *La Semana Cómica*, in an interview: "My Caricatures Are Belligerent, Fiery," *Pensamiento Propio*, no. 42 (May 1987): 27.

77. Sánchez's death came mere months after the Sandinista election defeat of 1990; many FSLN supporters felt it as a further twisting of the knife.

78. See James C. Scott, *The Moral Economy of the Peasant: Rebellion and Subsistence in Southeast Asia* (New Haven: Yale University Press, 1976).

79. Montenegro interview, 8 March 1991.

80. Interview with Alexei Pankin, Moscow, 20 May 1997.

81. For a broader comparative treatment of the moral economy of journalism, see Jones, *Press in Transition*, ch. 1.

82. A good account of the conflict on the Atlantic Coast is Stephen Kinzer, *Blood of Brothers: Life and War in Nicaragua* (New York: Putnam, 1991), ch. 16.

83. Selser interview, 9 May 1991.

84. Cortés interview, 9 April 1991.

85. Montenegro interview, 15 March 1991.

86. Eduardo Estrada, "El recelo nos autocensura," *Pensamiento Propio*, no. 34 (July 1986).

87. "Nuevo perfil editorial de *Barricada*," internal document, December 1990.

88. Cortés and Huerta, "Critical Journalism," 183, 191.

89. Maslow, "Junta and the Press," 46. Salman Rushdie, on a visit to Nicaragua in July 1986, bluntly described *Barricada* as "the worst newspaper I've seen in a long while." Rushdie, *The Jaguar Smile: A Nicaraguan Journey* (New York: Vintage, 1987), 34.

Chapter 2

1. The policy—both political and editorial—against negotiations with the contras was "very strong . . . a permanent component of Sandinista propaganda," according to Guillermo Cortés. "Tomás Borge said the stars would fall from the sky and the seabeds would dry up before they would negotiate with the contras. And [suddenly] they negotiated! . . . It was heartbreaking, hard to understand." For a revolutionary journalist, said Cortés, it was "impossible to make such an automatic turnabout. There had to be a policy of assimilation" to the FSLN's new line. Though Cortés eventually reconciled himself to the new policy, he said many other Sandinistas had "feelings of bitterness" about the decision to open negotiations—especially since it failed to bring the anticipated reward at the ballot box in 1990. Cortés interview, 9 April 1991.

2. "Text of Nicaraguan Agreement on a Cease-Fire," *New York Times*, 25 March 1988.

3. Ryan, *Fall and Rise,* 219.

4. Quoted in Ryan, *Fall and Rise,* 219–20. Carlos Fernando Chamorro recalled writing the editorial in a personal communication, 25 April 2001.

5. Reyes interview, 13 April 1997.

6. Chamorro interview, 17 April 1991.

7. Guevara interview, 2 April 1991.

8. Montenegro interview, 15 March 1991; emphasis hers.

9. Chamorro interview, 17 April 1991; emphasis his. The term *periódico del sistema* and the *Excélsior* example would also be mentioned in the New Editorial Profile of 1990—but as models rendered obsolete by events: "On the assumption of an electoral victory of the FSLN, before February 25 [1990] it was thought that *Barricada* should evolve to convert itself into a publication of the 'system': a kind of Mexican *Excélsior* in Nicaraguan society that would permit the governing FSLN to count on a periodical [that

was] formally liberated from official party bonds, in a manner that would allow it to project itself more broadly as a journalistic institution dedicated to strengthening the national consensus and democracy." For more information on *Excélsior*, see Robert N. Pierce, *Keeping the Flame: Media and Government in Latin America* (New York: Hastings House, 1979), ch. 5; and William A. Orme Jr., ed., *A Culture of Collusion: An Inside Look at the Mexican Press* (Coral Gables, Fla.: North-South Center Press, University of Miami/Committee to Protect Journalists; distributed by Lynne Rienner, Boulder, 1997), the best recent overview (in English) of Mexican media.

10. To the 9 April 1991 interview quoted above, Cortés added, presciently: "I don't know if, when the Sandinista Front recovers from the electoral defeat and repairs itself organizationally, when it feels stronger and more solid with its new statutes and program, it will want to exercise greater control [over *Barricada*]."

11. Chamorro interview, 17 April 1991. Of all the Sandinista supporters whom I interviewed or spoke with informally, only one—Rosario Murillo—claimed to have anticipated the FSLN's election defeat. Murillo said she had been "very skeptical about us winning the elections. . . . I thought about it [the possibility of defeat] every day." Murillo interview, 24 April 1991. According to Sofía Montenegro, another Sandinista media figure, Róger Sánchez (see chapter 1), also "was almost sure we would lose. . . . He never dared to *print* his prediction [in *La Semana Cómica*], because we were already in the middle of the election, he'd chosen his side, and he didn't want to bad-mouth it." Montenegro interview, 6 May 1991; emphasis hers.

12. Montenegro interview, 10 March 1991. Carlos Fernando Chamorro considers the claim that only *Barricada* and the National Directorate functioned in the immediate aftermath of the election defeat to be "a little exaggerated," since it "excludes and minimizes the role of a very important actor, the army and security forces." Chamorro, pers. comm., 25 April 2001.

13. More than a year after the defeat, Montenegro contended Sandinistas were still experiencing trauma akin to the loss of a loved one: "What we're seeing . . . among Sandinistas is a process of mourning. . . . What is valid for an individual who has suffered a personal loss is valid for the [Sandinista] movement as a whole. . . . We're not dealing with someone's death as such, not even the death of the party, but it's a sense of loss that psychologically has the same effects. And this big loss has been compounded by all kinds of

other losses: of salary, of employment, of social benefits. . . . Some people are for the first time having to confront their death and their rebirth, and a lot of them are dropping to the floor under the burden. They have lost, some of them, their reason for living." Montenegro interview, 10 March 1991.

14. Ibid.

15. In the weeks prior to the Chamorro government's accession, the FSLN and state leaders coordinated a hurried campaign of resource distribution, designed to provide for the future of a party and movement that had never seriously considered the prospect of losing power. Under Laws 85 and 86, passed before the official transition, the Sandinistas turned over to militants and supporters title to some twenty thousand homes, fifty thousand urban plots, and nine thousand landholdings comprising well over a million acres of land. The indecorous speed with which laws were passed and property turned over testifies to the FSLN leadership's extreme preoccupation with laying a material foundation for the front's survival—and the ad hoc nature of preparations made for just such an eventuality.

16. For fine, accessible overviews of Nicaraguan politics, economy, and society during the Violeta Chamorro era, see David Close, *Nicaragua: The Chamorro Years* (Boulder: Lynne Rienner, 1998); and Thomas W. Walker, ed., *Nicaragua without Illusions: Regime Transition and Structural Adjustment in the 1990s* (Wilmington, Del.: Scholarly Resources, 1997). See also Ilja A. Luciak, *The Sandinista Legacy: Lessons from a Political Economy in Transition* (Pensacola: University Press of Florida, 1995).

17. Chamorro interview, 18 April 1991.

18. It is tempting to see here the influence of the periódico del sistema model first advanced in 1987–88.

19. Chamorro interview, 16 May 1996.

20. *Barricada*, "Nuevo perfil editorial de *Barricada*."

21. Ibid.

22. Ibid.

23. *Barricada*, "Reglamento del consejo editorial de *Barricada*," unpublished internal document, undated (1990).

24. "*Barricada* en el debate sandinista," editorial, *Barricada*, 4 February 1994.

25. Michael Schudson, *Discovering the News: A Social History of American Newspapers* (New York: Basic Books, 1978), 26.

26. William Ruehlmann, *Stalking the Feature Story* (New York: Vintage, 1979), xi–xii.

27. Carlos Fernando Chamorro, pers. comm., 25 September 1998. On social responsibility theory, see John V. Nerone, ed., *Last Rights: Revisiting Four Theories of the Press* (Urbana: University of Illinois Press, 1995), ch. 3. The authors point out the impact of the social-responsibility model on North American newspapers in a way that helps to highlight some of the parallels with *Barricada*'s autonomy experiment: "In general, major newspapers and magazines became more audience oriented. News was more interpretive; consumer, business, and lifestyle news competed with political news for space in newspapers and magazines. . . . Newspaper managers not only allowed publication of a variety of letters to the editor and opinion or commentary columns but also instituted daily corrections to set straight published, factual errors. . . . By the last decade of the twentieth century, few newspapers or magazines arrogantly devoted their energies to hyping political parties or candidates favored by wealthy media owners and, instead, turned to reader surveys to learn more about what the community or nation wanted to read. . . . newspapers and magazines were far more stringent in seeking news and editorial balance than they had been fifty years earlier" (p. 83).

28. *Barricada*, "Principios y normas éticas de *Barricada*," unpublished internal document, April 1991.

29. All quotes are from *Barricada*, "Nuevo perfil editorial de *Barricada*."

30. Chamorro interview, 28 April 1991.

31. Cortés interview, 15 April 1991.

32. Ibid.

33. Montenegro interview, 10 March 1991; emphasis hers.

34. Chamorro interview, 16 May 1996; emphasis his. Although it is beyond the bounds of the present work, it is worth noting that *El Nuevo Diario* went through its own process of modernization and professionalization in the 1990s. Its political sympathies in the intraparty debate were solidly with Sergio Ramírez's Movimiento de Renovación Sandinista (MRS—see chapter 3). In 1996, though, the paper distanced itself from Ramírez, as it had earlier distanced itself from the ortodoxos. There were several other interesting experiments in Nicaraguan journalism during the

late 1980s and into the 1990s. One was *La Crónica*, a politically independent weekly begun with Dutch funding in 1988, which succumbed to infighting and closed in 1991. *La Crónica*'s founders decried the "low intellectual and political level" of the nation's press, and the paper presented itself as a "different, democratic voice in favor of social progress," according to one of its editors, Edwin Yilescas. See Stephen Kinzer, "In Nicaragua's Press, a Softer Voice," *New York Times*, 25 November 1988; and "Chronicle of Missing Funds," *Barricada Internacional*, 2 June 1990. *La Tribuna*, sponsored by the wealthy Nicaraguan businessman and presidential hopeful Haroldo Montealegre, survives at the time of writing despite being the lowest-circulation Managua daily. In spite of its politicized origins, it also defined itself against the mission of the traditional party-affiliated press, prompting *Barricada* to develop a marketing strategy designed to meet the new competitor's challenge. For a good overview of the political and professional orientation of a number of small-circulation publications that sprang up in the wake of the Sandinista election defeat, see Guillermo Fernández, "A Modest Publications Boom," *Barricada Internacional*, 22 September 1990.

35. Kreimann interview, 4 April 1991; emphasis his.

36. Castro interview, 22 April 1991.

37. "Enquesta 'Gran Promoción Madre' *Barricada*—Radio Ya," internal document, 1990.

38. *Barricada*, 1 April 1991.

39. Chamorro interview, 28 April 1991; emphasis his.

40. Chamorro interview, 3 April 1991.

41. Series beginning with Sylvia Torres, "Mi padre me violó," *Barricada*, 6 June 1994; Pablo Emilio Barreto, "SIDA: 'Bomba de tiempo,'" *Barricada*, 21 July 1994; series beginning with Arquímedes González, "'Conseguía coca por sexo,'" *Barricada*, 22 September 1994; Carlos García Castillo, "Desempleo explosivo," *Barricada*, 23 July 1994; Roberto Larios, "San Jacinto–Tizate a punto de paralizarse," *Barricada*, 13 August 1994. An amarillista tint is evident in some of the headlines, though the tenor of the articles in question is more straightforward than sensacionalistic.

42. Beginning with Dorothy Whitaker, "Nostalgia por San Andrés," *Barricada*, 13 September 1994.

43. Oliver Bodán, "Forenses: no somos *muerteros*," *Barricada*, 3 July 1994.

44. Noel Irías, "Travestis conquistan Managua nocturna," *Barricada*, 7 July 1994.

45. "Informatica: Una nueva sección semanal," *Barricada*, 9 July 1994.

46. See the *Barricada* reportage beginning with Sergio Cruz, "Nicas exponen pellejo en busca de un sueño," *Barricada*, 16 January 1994.

47. Malespín interview, 17 May 1996.

48. Carlos Fernando Chamorro B., "*Barricada* hacia el periodismo del 2000," *Barricada*, 25 July 1994. In "Más lectura para su tiempo libre" (*Barricada*, 11 July 1993), Chamorro proclaimed the Sunday edition "the beginning of a new tradition in national journalism": "Our intention is to offer more varied reading for all the family, on a day when everyone has more free time for reading."

49. "*Barricada* es noticia," *Barricada*, 27 December 1993.

50. Chamorro interview, 28 April 1991.

51. For a case study of the decline in the influence of mass organizations, see Pierre La Ramée and Erica Polakoff, "Transformation of the CDS and the Breakdown of Grassroots Democracy in Nicaragua," *New Political Science* 18/19 (Fall/Winter 1990): 103–23.

52. Chamorro interview, 28 April 1991; emphasis his.

53. Montenegro interview, 3 April 1991.

54. Chamorro interview, 28 April 1991; Montenegro interview, 3 April 1991.

55. Montenegro interview, 3 April 1991.

56. "Enquesta 'Gran Promoción Madre' *Barricada*—Radio Ya."

57. Montenegro interview, 11 April 1991.

58. Alegría interview, 10 May 1996.

59. For the text (and a reprinted copy) of the letter, see *Barricada*, 11 November 1994. Montenegro described the tussle this way: "You must remember that on the editorial board [*consejo editorial*] of *Barricada*, I was the only woman. [Montenegro's status as an observer at council meetings was semiofficialized over the course of the autonomy experiment, as the *Barricada* masthead reproduced in chapter 3 suggests.] There was the opinionated attitude of [directorate representative] Bayardo Arce, who said that my thing was too fucking feminist. In one way or another [those views] found an echo in Roberto Fonseca and Sergio de Castro. . . . When I began to defend the project with the passion that is quite characteristic of me, they

began to laugh, and I got angry. And I said, 'Well, this I do not discuss; here is the shit [i.e., *Gente*]; you do with it what you want.' And of course they didn't accept my resignation. . . . For me this was a normal discussion of the consejo editorial. . . . The motivation [of those who aired the letter after the defenestración] was, one, to prove I had 'contradictions' with the staff and with Carlos, which for me are normal on any staff; and to prove that I resigned long before, and therefore [in November 1994] nobody was firing me. If I am the one that resigns, I am not entitled to an indemnity [payment]." Montenegro recalled that certain changes were eventually implemented in the *Gente* project, with her agreement: "The pressures on *Barricada* were so much that I said, I will put my differences on the back burner and think of the global project, not just of my little parcel that was *Gente*." Montenegro interview, 22 May 1996.

60. Juan Ramón Huerta, "Los retos inmediatos de *Barricada*," *Barricada*, 2 November 1994; Borge, "Saldremos victoriosos."

61. Cuadra interview, 26 April 1991.

62. "The Qualitative Evaluation of the Daily *Barricada*" ("Evaluación cualitatativa del diario *Barricada*," internal document of the *Barricada* editorial council, April 1992) cited a circulation of 30,000 for *Barricada*, compared with 34,000 for *La Prensa* and 40,000 for *El Nuevo Diario*.

63. Chamorro interview, 16 May 1996.

64. "We lost $210,000 from one day to the next, overnight." Kreimann interview, 4 April 1991.

65. Chamorro interview, 16 May 1996.

66. Ibid.

67. Kreimann interview, 4 April 1991. The broad range of the estimate, Kreimann said, could be explained by the parastatal character of *Barricada* under the Sandinista regime. "It's a technical thing. Let me give you an example. You're the Ministry of Education, and you're going to sign a $2.5 million contract with me to print so many books. That requires one ton of paper, let's say. But you [via FSLN arrangements with East Bloc countries] are going to *give* me the ton of paper, which let's say is worth a million dollars. So I assume a debt to you in the amount of $1 million. And then you [via the interparty arrangements] give me the ink and metal plates to print the books, so I assume a further debt. So in the end, you sign a contract for $2.5 million, but only pay $500,000" (emphasis his). *Barricada*'s income

from the publishing of state textbooks and other materials was probably affected by similarly nimble accounting tricks, but there is no doubt it was indispensable to the paper's economic functioning, especially in the latter half of the 1980s.

68. Chamorro interview, 16 May 1996.
69. Kreimann interview, 4 April 1991.
70. Chamorro interview, 16 May 1996.
71. Ibid.
72. Kreimann interview, 4 April 1991; emphasis mine.
73. All quotes from the New Editorial Profile.
74. "Nuevo gerente en *Barricada*," *Barricada*, 22 April 1994. Kreimann's last day on the masthead was 21 April 1994. His space was filled the next day by Ronaldo Gómez, who, in Alfonso Malespín's estimation, "couldn't do anything" to reform the paper's administration in the few months that remained before the defenestración. Malespín interview, 17 May 1996.
75. Malespín interview, 17 May 1996.
76. Grigsby interview, 15 May 1996.
77. Chamorro interview, 16 May 1996.
78. "Corruption existed in the former administration of *Barricada*," Borge told *La Prensa*, "[but] corruption for which Carlos Fernando Chamorro was not responsible; we certainly had problems with Carlos Fernando, but these were of a political character." A caution: the quote is translated from a posted version of the article on the <soc.culture.nicaragua> Usenet newsgroup, 12 February 1998; no date for the article's publication in *La Prensa* was cited, and the issue was not on the shelves of the Biblioteca Nacional (the library was in the middle of a major move at the time of my research in the summer of 1998).
79. Chamorro interview, 16 May 1996.
80. Grigsby interview, 15 May 1996.
81. Malespín interview, 17 May 1996. Carlos Fernando Chamorro's own estimate is "between $1.5 and $2 million." Chamorro, pers. comm., 25 April 2001.
82. Montenegro interview, 22 May 1996.
83. Alegría interview, 10 May 1996; emphasis his. Only days after the defenestración, Chamorro publicly refuted charges that *Barricada* had

been on its last legs before his dismissal: "The company has economic problems, as does every journalistic company in Nicaragua. These economic problems have been confronted head-on, and there is a medium-range recovery plan in place that consists of different stages. . . . To me it's a shame that this intervention [the defenestración] is generating a climate of uncertainty that makes it more difficult to put into practice the economic recovery plan that is now underway." Chamorro quoted in Solórzano, "Carlos Fernando."

84. "Evaluación cualitativa del diario *Barricada.*"

85. Grigsby interview, 15 May 1996.

86. Ortega quoted in Carlos Fernando Chamorro B., "La religión de una secta," *El Nuevo Diario*, 30 November 1994. The quote was drawn from a press conference Ortega gave in Cuba, as reported by the Mexican news agency Notimex, which reprinted the story in Nicaragua. Chamorro, pers. comm., 25 September 1998.

87. Respondents in Matagalpa, interviewed in Juan Carlos Sarmiento, "Continuar el profesionalismo perdido," *Barricada*, 2 November 1994.

88. This quote, which seems rather a classic straw man, is found in Elena Ramos, "Commitment, Dialogue, and Unity," *Barricada Internacional*, December 1994, 10; originally from *El País*, as noted; emphasis mine. Chamorro denounced Ortega's comments in his postdefenestración piece for *El Nuevo Diario*, "La religión de una secta."

89. Chamorro interview, 23 May 1996. The Qualitative Evaluation of 1992 also claimed that *Barricada* had "constantly striven to conduct investigations around governmental corruption, restoration [of properties] to Somocistas, the blurring of distinctions between state and private business, the conflicts of interest, . . . etc."

90. Malespín interview, 17 May 1996; emphasis his.

91. Noel Irías, "*Mordidas* en lo fino," *Barricada*, 13 June 1994.

92. Series beginning with Roberto Larios, "*Meca* del contrabando," *Barricada*, 4 July 1994.

93. Roberto Larios and Dolores Rugama, "Banades: 'Un precedente,'" *Barricada*, 19 August 1994.

94. Daniel F. Alegría, "*Barricada* descubre a Tony Ibarra en Detroit," *Barricada*, 15 October 1994.

95. "Adiós soberanía económica," *Barricada*, 9 April 1994.

96. "Protesta del transporte: Una advertencia," editorial, *Barricada*, 16 September 1993.

97. "Transporte: Más leña al fuego," editorial, *Barricada*, 17 September 1993.

98. "Cambiar política económica, en vez de reprimir," editorial, *Barricada*, 21 September 1993; "No más violencia, basta de muertes," editorial, *Barricada*, 22 September 1993; David Gutiérrez-López, "Balas, anarquía y muertos," *Barricada*, 22 September 1993; Aracely Martínez, "Una bala asesina mató a Saúl," *Barricada*, 23 September 1993.

99. Chamorro interview, 16 May 1996; emphasis his.

100. All of Chamorro's comments in this section are drawn from the interview conducted on 23 May 1996; I have not referenced the quoted excerpts separately.

101. "*Barricada* en el debate sandinista," editorial, *Barricada*, 4 February 1994.

102. The reference, of course, is to the children's game in which a papier-mâché figure is bashed with sticks to release the sweets or gifts inside.

103. Murillo interview, 24 April 1991.

104. Murillo's defense: "My father owned lots of properties that I could have inherited. I gave it all up for the revolution. I used to be a rich person. I have nothing now—only the house where we live, which doesn't belong to me personally. I live on what I earn from my work." Murillo interview, 24 April 1991. For his part, Ortega commented in a 1994 interview with *El País*: "It's not a crime to live in Las Colinas; the crime is staying put in Las Colinas. Unquestionably, my status is privileged. The question is, What do I use it for? It would be one thing to distance myself from the people and dedicate my time to getting rich; it is something else to use the means I have at hand to work for a revolutionary project." Ortega quoted in Elena Ramos, "'I'm Not Leaving the FSLN,'" *Barricada Internacional*, December 1994.

105. In a 1998 communication Chamorro clarified exactly why the piñata issue was so sensitive: "The real internal debate had to do with the fortunes of the new capitalists—people who had lent their names to cover the legal transfer of properties for the front, and who ended up privatizing them for themselves. The most conspicuous cases are Tomás Borge and Humberto Ortega, but they are not the only ones. Thus, to question the

piñata implied exposing the power of certain top individuals, and was equivalent to a breakdown or a party split." Pers. comm., 25 September 1998.

106. Carlos F. Chamorro B., "La salida del general Ortega," *Barricada*, 5 August 1993.

107. The day after Chamorro's article appeared, *Barricada* gave space to a response from Julio López, probably the leading intellectual of the DL current (and future subeditor of *Barricada*), entitled "To defend the EPS [Sandinista Popular Army]"; the article rejected "the idea of making concessions" to the right-wing by easing Ortega out. *Barricada* also printed on its front page statements by Tomás Borge that expressed strong opposition to "the dismissal of the Chief of the Army of Nicaragua and the dismantling of the Armed Forces of this country." See López, "Defender al EPS," *Barricada*, 6 August 1993; "Destitución del Jefe EPS es inadmisible," *Barricada*, 8 August 1993.

108. ETA stands for Euskadi Ta Askatasuna (Basque Fatherland and Liberty). Canadian readers will recall this as the raid that uncovered the false documents used by David Spencer and Christine Lamont, then jailed in Brazil on kidnapping charges. Until the discovery of the documents, Spencer and Lamont had denied any connection to El Salvador's left-wing guerrillas.

109. Chamorro interview, 16 May 1996; emphasis his.

110. All Chamorro quotes in this section are from the 16 May 1996 interview; emphasis his.

111. Montenegro interview, 10 March 1991.

112. Cortés interview, 15 April 1991; emphasis his.

113. Montenegro interview, 22 May 1996.

114. Ibid.; emphasis hers.

115. The text of the declaration was reprinted in *Barricada* on 13 July 1993.

116. Ortega quoted in Noel Irías, "FPI asaltan Radio Ya," *Barricada*, 25 April 1993.

117. Noel Irías, "FSLN y COSEP rechazan toda actividad armada," *Barricada*, 2 July 1994.

118. See the front-page report in *Barricada* on 22 September 1993. This ambivalence was not entirely new. While proclaiming himself publicly

against the use of violence in April, Ortega had denounced acts of sabotage and arson against FSLN targets allegedly organized by a right-wing Nicaraguan businessman, Fruto Chamorro. "We are not lovers of violence or war," Ortega stated, but "if the government cannot protect the life of a citizen, one must defend it however one can [*éste la defienda como pueda*]." Manuel Alvarez, "Ortega defiende la lucha armada," *Barricada*, 18 April 1994.

119. *El Semanario*, 10–16 November 1994. The trend continued through the 1996 national elections, when Tomás Borge announced that if "Somocismo" triumphed—in the form of Arnoldo Alemán's presidential candidacy—he would "sleep with a gun under my pillow once again" and consider "return[ing] to the mountains." Renewed clashes over the property issue in March 1997 prompted Daniel Ortega to deliver himself of a particularly incendiary proclamation: "The war over property has started here. Blood has started to flow." If the government did not act to reverse a wave of evictions, "it w[ould] be a declaration of total war." See David Koop, "Nicaragua Campaign Opens under Pall of Bloody Past," Reuters dispatch, 2 August 1996, <clari.world.americas.central>; and Koop, "Ortega Warns of Property War in Nicaragua," Reuters dispatch, 17 March 1997, <clari.world.americas.central>. In a July 1998 rally to commemorate the nineteenth anniversary of the Sandinista revolution, which I attended, Ortega delivered probably his most explicit postrevolutionary endorsement of the legitimacy of violent struggle. Referring again to the Alemán government's attempts to roll back property legislation, he proclaimed: "However much some might say that the option of armed struggle is a thing of the past [*que la opción armada está descartada*] and who use this to strip the people of their conquests, let them put such a notion from their minds, because the people and the Sandinista Front are ready to take up arms whenever it is necessary to defend popular conquests." Those who sought by force to strip workers and peasants of their property "are going to provoke an armed uprising in the country and a new revolution." He urged the government "not to oblige us to organize anew guerrilla squads and People's Commando [units] . . . in the cities and in the mountains"; "let them not think that we do not have the will [*la decisión*] to fight on this ground." Quoted in Xiomara Chamorro, "Daniel amenaza con retomar lucha armada," *El Nuevo Diario*, 20 July 1998.

120. "Unidad contra la violencia," editorial, *Barricada*, 21 August 1993.

After a car bomb attack rocked Estelí in August 1994, *Barricada* published "Our Condemnation of the Violence," pledging: "*Barricada* will never cease to reiterate that the method of irrational violence is not conducive to solving the grave social problems of the country, but rather aggravates them and delays any solution. . . . The police authorities must investigate and detain those responsible for all acts of irrational violence . . . because this is healthy for society and for all political sectors." "Nuestra condena a la violencia," editorial, *Barricada*, 10 August 1994. See also the editorial of 26 April 1993, similarly titled "Nuestra condena," and reiterating that "For reasons of principle, *Barricada* has always rejected all terrorist acts, whether they come from extremists of the right or left."

121. "El saldo de la tragedia," editorial, *Barricada*, 22 July 1993.

122. Excerpts from Murillo's open letter (published in *El Nuevo Diario* on 2 September 1990) appeared in English in *Barricada Internacional*, 22 September 1990—along with *Barricada*'s response, originally published as an editorial on 4 September. "The right to criticize is valid for everyone and *Barricada* cannot escape the opinions that may exist among Sandinistas on the role this paper plays vis-à-vis national public opinion. But the right to criticize cannot be confused with the distortion of reality and malicious accusations that lack merit and a constructive spirit. *Barricada* has never pretended to own the truth. We are not a cathedral, nor is the Sandinista Front a church ruled by dogma. On the contrary, we aspire to be a point of convergence in the process of political regrouping of Sandinista forces. . . . We believe that true pluralism must extensively cover the diversity of opinions that exist within Sandinismo in order to move, through the debate of ideas, toward a political consensus on which the unity of revolutionaries should be based."

123. In a 1991 interview, Murillo made it plain that she was especially rankled by *Barricada*'s decision to give prominence to the views of self-declared enemies of the FSLN. "How can you have [Managua Mayor, subsequently President] Arnoldo Alemán, who is hated by everyone, who is a fascist—how can you put him to speak there [in the pro-Sandinista press]? I don't understand that. It's like thinking the new political culture means having your enemy saying in your spaces whatever he wants to say, and having him say in his *own* spaces atrocities about you—along with whatever he wants to say about how wonderfully he's doing. In what country in the

world do you have that kind of opposition press?" Murillo interview, 24 April 1991; emphasis hers.

124. *Gente*, 14 October 1994. Sofía Montenegro's response, in the same issue, is worth quoting for its staunch defense of the professional imperative: "In *Barricada* we give space to a diversity of opinions, even if they do not correspond to our editorial position. . . . To depict the [U.S.] blockade as an inconvenience, a shame, as something that degrades and depresses Cubans, is to express solidarity with their burden. The excuse of 'martyrology' [*martirología*], and the deliberate omission of the [human] drama, may be all very well for a committee of solidarity, but not for a medium of information."

125. Sarmiento, "Continuar el profesionalismo."

126. "*Barricada:* Fiel a los intereses nacionales" (front-page interview with Borge), *Barricada*, 2 November 1994; emphasis added.

127. Alegría interview, 10 May 1996.

128. Chamorro interview, 23 May 1996.

129. For examples of ortodoxo-style commentary and interviews published in 1993 and 1994, see Mónica Baltodano, "Concertación y lucha popular," *Barricada*, 25 September 1993; "El partido sandinista: Instrumento revolucionario del pueblo," *Barricada*, 25 January 1994; an interview on the *Debate* page on 10 April 1994; Julio López, "Un partido popular y revolucionario," interview, *Barricada*, 30 January 1994, and López's response to Carlos Fernando Chamorro's op-ed piece calling on army chief Humberto Ortega to "make way for . . . a new chief," "Defender al EPS," *Barricada*, 6 August 1993. See, lastly, the two-part article by Daniel Ortega, "La democratización y la unidad del FSLN," *Barricada*, 23-24 August 1994.

130. The ortodoxo *Barricada* journalist Juan Ramón Huerta did contend in 1996 that material he had written about the front was "relegated to the inside pages or changed," though he didn't "remember specific examples": "For example, certain declarations of Daniel Ortega were not given space in the paper, when Daniel Ortega was saying things of importance to the nation, because Daniel was saying them. Or they would choose an unflattering photo to run alongside them." Huerta interview, 22 May 1996. According to Carlos Fernando Chamorro: "I was particularly careful to *choose* different opinions [for the op-ed page]. When there was something really strong on a certain issue, I would try to choose a balanced opinion.

But they [*Barricada*'s opponents] would always tell you that that was a trick, because one article was, I don't know, an inch longer than the other, or whatever stupid thing." Chamorro interview, 16 May 1996 (emphasis his).

131. "Evaluación cualitativa del diario *Barricada*."

132. Malespín interview, 17 May 1996.

133. "Un periodismo para una sociedad democrática," *Barricada*, 20 September 1994 (document dated 19 September); emphasis added.

134. Chamorro interview, 16 May 1996.

135. Alegría interview, 10 May 1996; emphasis his.

136. Chamorro interview, 16 May 1996.

137. For an English translation of excerpts from Tirado's article, see *Barricada Internacional*, August 1991, 17.

138. Chamorro interview, 23 May 1996.

139. Ibid. Sofía Montenegro likewise emphasized that it was the ability to distance itself from the propaganda requirements of the Sandinista Front that earned *Barricada* a new respect among nontraditional readers. The key, she said, was "the fact that we began to criticize the front, [while] also being the 'auditors' of the actions of the government, in a correct manner. This gained us credibility in the eyes of the government, the broad public, and decision makers." Moreover, Montenegro added, tongue-in-cheek: "The fact that Daniel Ortega was attacking us was a source of great credibility." Montenegro interview, 22 May 1996.

140. From J. R. Castillo y Asociados to Orlando Murillo, general manager, *La Tribuna*, 25 May 1994; privately supplied.

141. "Estudio: Lectores medios escritos en Nicaragua: el caso *Barricada*" (Managua: August 1994), privately supplied.

142. Chamorro interview, 23 May 1996.

143. As Kent Norsworthy notes, "The experiment that *Barricada* was engaged in prior to 1994 was in many ways without parallel in Latin America, where, for the most part, the press is closely tied to specific political or economic groups. *Barricada*'s 'autonomy' experiment, where strictly journalistic criteria were to prevail, stood out not just on the Nicaraguan scene, but when compared to dailies throughout much of Latin America. In this regard, *Barricada* was successfully blazing a trail that journalists committed to the independent, professional exercise of their craft could follow throughout the region." Pers. comm., February 2001.

Chapter 3

1. Adherents of this tendency placed a strategic emphasis on an uprising among the urban working classes. The future director of *Barricada*, Carlos Fernando Chamorro, was originally affiliated with this tendency, as were a disproportionate number of senior *Barricada* staffers. Sofía Montenegro recalled in 1991 that "There was . . . friction among different Sandinista tendencies" at *Barricada* in the very early days of its operation. "For some reason, most of the people who got involved in *Barricada* were from the Proletarian tendency, but friction remained. After a while, though, the tendency thing was erased. People saw clearly that unity was the answer. In the end, we were all Sandinistas." Montenegro interview, 8 March 1991.

2. As its name implied, the core group foresaw a protracted rural insurrection (such as Sandino had waged against the United States in the 1920s and 1930s) as the best method of undermining the Somoza dictatorship. Tomás Borge, the FSLN cofounder who would become *Barricada*'s director after 1994, was a leader of the GPP, though he spent most of the immediate prerevolutionary period in the dictatorship's jails.

3. For an overview of the factional split and eventual reunification, see Black, *Triumph of the People*, 91–97, 142–48. The influence of the factional division on the eventual composition of the National Directorate, and the gradual emergence of Daniel Ortega as first among equals, is examined in Gilbert, *Sandinistas*, 41–48.

4. The document was published as "Relanzar la lucha el 19 de julio," *Barricada*, 13 July 1993.

5. "Surge propuesta Sandinismo de las mayorías," *Barricada*, 11 February 1994.

6. Guillermo Fernández Ampié, "The FSLN's Most Serious Crisis," *Barricada Internacional*, September 1994, 4–5. William I. Robinson offers the following assessment: "The international press has characterized the FSLN crisis and the split as a fight between 'orthodox' hard-liners under Ortega's leadership and 'moderate' social-democrats led by Ramírez. In reality, the split is considerably more complex, reflecting the difficulty of finding answers to the questions facing all progressives in the South (and the North): What type of project is viable and realistic, especially for a small, peripheral nation, given global forces which are too powerful to con-

front head on, the impossibility of withdrawal from the international system, and well-known limits to social change in any one country?" It is worth noting that despite his even-handed presentation of the divisions, Robinson views "the Ortega 'Democratic Left' fraction" as having "gained control of party assets and [gone] on a virtual witch-hunt, purging opponents and expelling them from the party's organs and media outlets." Robinson, "Sandinistas Face the Future," *Crossroads*, [1995?].

7. Montenegro interview, 22 May 1996; emphasis hers. Coverage in *Barricada Internacional* at the time of the First Congress cited similar reasons for the reluctance to reconstitute the directorate: "Many believed that the ideal method for electing the DN's members was, indeed, by direct, individual and secret vote. However, the argument that this would imply risks to the organization's future, in the context of the current political situation, swayed the vote. Some believed it unfair the desire [*sic*] to 'get even' with certain leaders for their past behavior, because, insofar as the DN is a collective body, all decisions had been made jointly. Accordingly, the leaders should receive criticism collectively and not individually. Others said that some members of the leadership would be favored over others if they were put to individual vote. This would compromise the notion of joint leadership, created to strengthen [the] collective spirit." "The FSLN's Congress: Blow By Blow," *Barricada Internacional*, August 1991, 6.

8. Chamorro, pers. comm., 25 September 1998.

9. Alegría interview, 10 May 1996.

10. Guillermo Rothschuh Villanueva, "*Barricada*: ¿Un test para el sandinismo?" *Barricada*, 3 November 1993.

11. In a rare study of postrevolutionary Nicaraguan media, Guillermo Rothschuh Villanueva and Carlos Fernando Chamorro B. state, "Television has become the dominant medium of entertainment and cultural influence in Nicaragua," and is gaining "increasing importance as a medium of orientation and debate for public opinion." A survey carried out for the book found that 83.5 percent of respondents stated that they watched television daily and 73.4 percent listened to the radio; but while 62.8 percent claimed to read publications of various stripes, only 27.8 percent bought newspapers daily, compared with 22 percent "now and again." For informational needs, television was the preferred medium of 45.1 percent of respondents, compared with 42.8 percent for radio and just 11.4 percent for newspapers. A

1992 survey (cited on p. 82) measured public confidence in the different media: the resultant breakdown was 41.4 percent for television, 28.3 percent for radio, and 17.7 percent for newspapers. The most common reason given (90.1 percent of respondents) for preferring television was that the public "can see what's happening." Rothschuh and Chamorro B., *Los medios y la política en Nicaragua* (Managua: CINCO/Friedrich Ebert Stiftung, 1995), 45, 80–81. For a good general overview of media transformations in the 1990s, see Kent W. Norsworthy, "The Mass Media," in Walker, ed., *Nicaragua without Illusions*, 281–95.

12. Montenegro interview, 22 May 1996.

13. The play on words "Frente Danielista de Liberación Nacional" was current in Managua in mid-1998 and was mentioned to me in passing by Juan Ramón Huerta (interview, 28 July 1998).

14. Even Ortega's behavior in the 1990s displays strong signs of moderation and realpolitik. A good recent example was the front's decision to draft a landowner and leader of the virulently anti-Sandinista business organization COSEP as the FSLN's vice-presidential candidate in the 1996 elections. This seemed a clear throwback to the cross-class coalition building that Ortega had promoted in the year or two preceding the overthrow of the Somoza dictatorship.

15. Montenegro interview, 22 May 1996. According to Carlos Fernando Chamorro, "Daniel Ortega became an ally of his traditional adversaries—people who were traditionally more ideological in the front. Daniel was more a pragmatist." Chamorro interview, 16 May 1996.

16. Ryan, *Fall and Rise*, 24; emphasis his. Ryan quotes a 1987 speech by Ortega to illustrate this "orthodox Marxism" even in the National Directorate member most renowned for moderation, and at the very point the market was "triumphing" in Sandinista policy: "The history of Count Dracula is the very history of the exploitation of man by man. Slavery, feudalism, capitalism, imperialism, all prolonging their existence at the cost of the blood of the workers. The vampires had also made themselves owners of Nicaragua, when the adequate weapon to exterminate them had not yet been invented. Not until, that is, Marx and Engels discovered the formula, and Lenin efficiently directed its application, driving the spike into the heart of the monster. Just as Michelangelo penetrated into the depths of human anatomy in order to mould his masterpieces, Marx and Engels penetrated and explored social

phenomena from the beginning of humanity, resulting in the masterpiece which gave to the workers the ideological instrument that their class instinct demanded" (p. 32).

17. Ryan, *Fall and Rise*, 33, 43, 48.

18. It was Humberto Ortega as army chief, according to Chamorro, who was pushing hardest for *Barricada* to be "more officialist and propagandistic." Chamorro interview, 22 July 1998.

19. "Bayardo Arce . . . told Carlos [Fernando Chamorro]: 'Tell Sofía to keep quiet on this subject.' Because I was about to sit down to write something saying that Comandante Ortega didn't know, or was misinformed about, what was happening; that the reality of women in Nicaragua was such-and-such. But from then on, and for a long time after, every time I tried to write something on the issue, Carlos would say, 'It's not convenient for the newspaper. I don't want to provoke a polemic that will affect the newspaper.' The result was, I spent a whole year more without the freedom to write, with Carlos saying, 'Please help me. Just wait for your time.'" All quotes from Montenegro interview, 8 March 1991.

20. Chamorro interview, 18 April 1991.

21. As well, Murillo's polemic came at a time of uncertainty for the *Barricada* cultural supplement she edited, *Ventana* (Window). *Ventana* was struggling in 1990: it ranked lowest in reader surveys, far behind Sofía Montenegro's popular *Gente*. *Ventana* was eventually discontinued in 1991—something Daniel Ortega took personally, in Carlos Fernando Chamorro's estimation. "He was very upset, and he had a personal resentment, about the fact that *Ventana* closed after the [July 1991] congress. He accused me of being responsible for the closure." Chamorro interview, 23 May 1996. In 1998, Chamorro elaborated: "The *Ventana* affair was definitely important [in understanding Ortega's opposition to *Barricada*]. Since its creation as a cultural supplement, *Ventana* had been completely autonomous from *Barricada*. Its payroll and services were covered by the office of the president. When we lost the elections and *Ventana* was transformed into a political pamphlet, it continued being paid for by Ortega's office. By mid-1991, Ortega had accumulated a considerable debt with *Barricada*. And *Ventana* could not resume publishing. So for Ortega, it was humiliating that he could not keep publishing *Ventana* after the 1991 congress, while on the other hand, *Gente*—being part of

Barricada—continued publishing." Chamorro, pers. comm., 25 September 1998.

22. Christian, "Ortega's Leadership Criticized."

23. The quoted passage here interpolates comments from the two 1996 interviews with Chamorro, 16 and 23 May.

24. Quoted in Christian, "Ortega's Leadership Criticized."

25. Carlos F. Chamorro B., "La *Barricada* que necesitamos," *Barricada*, 2 March 1992.

26. Chamorro interview, 23 May 1996.

27. Malespín interview, 17 May 1996. Carlos Fernando Chamorro also recalled that Ortega "accused us of pretending to be journalists and at the same time being politicians." Chamorro interview, 23 May 1996.

28. Chamorro interview, 23 May 1996.

29. Ibid.

30. See the coverage in *Barricada*, 24 January 1994.

31. Noel Irías and Jorge Katín, "Caliente debate FSLN," *Barricada*, 26 January 1994.

32. Ibid.

33. Noel Irías, "Rechazo total a insultos," *Barricada*, 28 January 1994. It was not the first time Guadamúz had spoken out on Ortega's behalf. Indeed, like William Grigsby, Guadamúz seems to have served as a point man for the ortodoxos in campaigns against individuals and institutions identified with the renovationist current. Like Grigsby, too, Guadamúz allied himself with Ortega and the DL current only after years of iconoclastic populist broadsides against Sandinista leadership figures. His actions were similar in the wake of the defenestración: Radio Ya spread rumors that journalists and workers planned to forcibly seize the *Barricada* plant to protest Chamorro's dismissal. Journalists at the paper vehemently denied the charge, claiming it could expose them to violent reprisals. See "Radio Ya inventa 'toma' de *Barricada*," *Barricada*, 25 October 1994.

34. Alegría interview, 10 May 1996.

35. Chamorro interview, 23 May 1996.

36. Montenegro interview, 22 May 1996.

37. Some time after signing the "mayorías" document, Chamorro recalled, he was visited by Julio López, who tried to urge him to leave *Barricada* quietly, in return for future considerations. "We had a long talk

here [at Chamorro's house], appealing to our friendship, et cetera. His final argument was: 'Why don't you quit? Why don't you resign from *Barricada*?' I said, 'Why should I resign if I am running a good newspaper?' He said, 'Well, because you know you are an important figure in the front, and we think about you as a future "political," someone who's going to be in the small group of people in power in the front.' I said, 'I don't have any interest in being part of the leadership of the front. I see myself as a journalist. I am much more convinced now than ever that this is what I should do. And if you don't like it, you make the decision, you know? I'm just waiting. You make the decision to change *Barricada*. I'm not going to resist it, but I'll try until the last day to make a good newspaper.' And that's what I did." All quotes from Chamorro interview, 23 May 1996.

38. See the introduction to the interviews gathered under the title, "What Must be Done to Relaunch Sandinismo?" *Barricada*, 15 May 1994.

39. Montenegro interview, 22 May 1996.

40. Chamorro interviews, 16 May and 23 May 1996; emphasis his. The ortodoxo victory was not total. It had been widely expected that Tomás Borge, the only surviving FSLN founder, would be drafted to fill the newly created post of Sandinista president. Instead, delegates voted against creating the post—an implicit snub to Borge. Likewise, Julio López, whom many had expected to join the National Directorate, was not among those chosen to fill the expanded twelve-person directorate. Both these figures ended up playing leading roles at the postdefenestración version of *Barricada*, roles that may be linked to these setbacks at the congress, as is discussed in greater detail in chapter 4.

41. As the assembly's hesitation attests, the stand of the dominant current of the FSLN was somewhat uncertain. In one of his occasional opinion pieces on topical issues, Carlos Fernando Chamorro described "two contradictory positions" on the issue. One—the position of the bench and other renovationist sectors—viewed constitutional reforms as "a crucial opportunity to deepen democracy and strengthen state institutions [against] excessive presidentialism," a reflection of the renovationists' antivanguardist stand in the internal politics of the front. The other tendency—the ortodoxo/Democratic Left current—"does not reject the foregoing entirely, but in the final instance thinks that reforming the constitution means making a concession: giving something up to the right [wing]." The appraisal seems accurate

to me. Chamorro, "Reforma constituticonal y crisis del sandinismo," *Barricada*, 27 September 1994.

42. Jorge Katín, "Eligen a Téllez, DN: 'Es desacato,'" *Barricada*, 13 September 1994.

43. Jorge Katín, "AS y Bancada FSLN sostendrán encuentro," *Barricada*, 20 September 1994.

44. Carlos F. Chamorro B. and Jorge Katín, "Ortega asumirá curul," *Barricada*, 10 September 1994.

45. Internal document, privately supplied.

46. All quotes from Chamorro interview, 16 May 1996; emphasis his. In a conversation with *El Semanario* after the defenestración, Chamorro described the drafting process as follows: "We put together a series of proposals [after the Special Congress] to preserve the present project of *Barricada,* and all the proposals brought us to a single conclusion: the necessity to affirm even more strongly the autonomy of the newspaper from the Sandinista Front. . . . This was what we outlined to the National Directorate. . . . Obviously, the response we got tended in an absolutely opposite direction." Solórzano, "Carlos Fernando."

47. Chamorro interview, 23 May 1996. Alegría declined comment when asked whether he was indeed Chamorro's source for the information.

48. Alfonso Malespín Jirón, "Renuncian a C. Editorial," *Barricada*, 25 October 1994.

49. "Borge: *Barricada* será un periódico sólo para sandinistas," *La Tribuna*, 26 October 1994. The article states the initiative was approved by 64 votes out of 120, with 3 abstentions.

50. Montenegro interview, 22 May 1996; emphasis hers.

51. Alegría interview, 10 May 1996; Chamorro interview, 23 May 1996. The final edition of the supplement *Gente* to be edited by Sofía Montenegro referred to Campbell in similar, unusually benign terms: "He came with the thankless task of carrying out a *dry cleaning* of the brains [of *Barricada*]. He was chosen for his affable and educated manner, and because he's nice as a person. . . . He speaks slowly and low, [and] has the mission of bringing about a 'peaceful transition' toward *partidismo* and preparing the conditions for an ortodoxo successor . . . We feel for him." "Gente de la semana," *Gente*, 28 October 1994; emphasis in original.

52. Alegría interview, 10 May 1996.

53. Alvaro Cruz Rojas, "Nombran a Borge nuevo presidente de *Barricada*," *La Tribuna*, 31 October 1994.

54. Chamorro interview, 23 May 1996.

55. "Ortega has to deal with Tomás," said Daniel Alegría, "but he doesn't like him. They have to tolerate each other, but . . . they're two antagonists. The pie isn't big enough for both of them." Alegría interview, 10 May 1996.

56. Cruz Rojas, "Nombran a Borge"; Cruz Rojas, "¿Ortega y Borge dueños de *Barricada?*" *La Tribuna*, 2 November 1994.

57. Montenegro interview, 22 May 1996.

58. Arce's letter of resignation appeared in *Barricada* on 1 November 1994.

59. Chamorro interview, 23 May 1996.

60. In his published resignation statement on 3 November, Daniel Alegría asserted: "In honor and truth, I must say that neither Lumberto Campbell nor Tomás Borge censored a single line. . . . My arguments as to what . . . was news and what was not, prevailed; I do not renounce a single one of the editions on which I have worked during these days." Alegría, "Una renuncia amarga," *Barricada*, 3 November 1994.

61. Quoted in Guillermo Fernández Ampié, "Changes at *Barricada*," *Barricada Internacional*, October/November 1994 (*BI*'s translation).

62. "Autonomía vs. partidismo," *Barricada*, 26 October 1994.

63. Alegría interview, 10 May 1996.

64. Alfonso Malespín Jirón, "Periodistas protestan," *Barricada*, 29 October 1994. Two days later, journalists, again wearing gags and this time bearing a coffin, picketed Daniel Ortega's office. The coffin was meant to symbolize "the interment of repression against freedom of the press and free expression." They called for the "democratic space won in the last few years" to be preserved, and pledged: "We will never again be a tool of the FSLN." "Repercussions of Chamorro's Dismissal as Director of *Barricada*," New York Transfer News Collective, 26 November 1994 (<soc.culture.latinamerica>), from *El Diario/La Prensa* (New York City), trans. Toby Mailman.

65. "Respaldan decisión de Asamblea Nacional," *Barricada*, 29 October 1994.

66. Berenice Maranhao, "Miente, miente, algo quedará," *Barricada*, 2 November 1994.

67. *Barricada*, 28 October 1994.

68. Mónica Baltodano, "Carta abierta a cuatro miembros de la DN-FSLN," *Barricada*, 30 October 1994.

69. Maranhao, "Miente, miente."

70. Montenegro interview, 22 May 1996.

71. Alegría interview, 10 May 1996; emphasis his.

72. See Huerta, "Los retos immediatos."

73. Alegría, "Renuncia amarga." Alegría told *La Tribuna* at the time that he resigned "for very personal reasons; I served as editor because I believed in the project that they are destroying. I have open eyes and sufficient knowledge of the facts to know that this daily is going to be converted into a partisan object and [an object] of political clientelism." Alvaro Cruz Rojas, "Espionaje y censura en *Barricada*," *La Tribuna*, 3 November 1994.

74. Cruz Rojas, "Espionaje y censura"; Cruz Rojas, "Despiden a tres periodistas en *Barricada*," *La Tribuna*, 5 November 1994.

75. Montenegro interview, 22 May 1996.

76. Quoted in Huerta, "Los retos inmediatos."

77. See "Ortodoxos confirman control de medios," a Reuters dispatch published in *El Nuevo Diario* on 9 November 1994. The article quotes Tomás Borge as pledging that *Barricada* would seek a "fraternal" relationship with other Sandinista media "now, tomorrow, and forever." "Borge [also] predicted that *Barricada*'s circulation would increase and that, together with the party's radio stations and TV channel, [*Barricada*] would lead the Sandinista Front to victory in the 1996 elections by bolstering its base of support among the poor."

78. Quoted in Guillermo Fernández Ampié, "Political and Labor Conflicts in Full Color," *Barricada Internacional*, December 1994.

79. "16 periodistas proponen salida negociada," *Barricada*, 1 November 1994.

80. Antonio Cruz Rojas, "Quince periodistas se van de *Barricada*," *La Tribuna*, 2 November 1994.

81. Alegría interview, 10 May 1996.

82. Quoted in Fernández Ampié, "Political and Labor Conflicts." According to Fernández, "Many of the other workers at the newspaper—particularly the press operators and those at the bottom of the pay scale—were unsympathetic or indifferent to the journalists' situation. Some even expressed a certain righteous satisfaction, saying that they got no more than

they deserved. . . . In the last four years, more than 100 workers have been laid off, causing general discontent among the paper's staff. The journalists, however, were rarely affected."

83. "Trabajadores de El Amanecer piden auditoria," *Barricada,* 26 October 1994.

84. Borge quoted in Huerta, "Los retos inmediatos."

85. Alvaro Cruz Rojas, "¿Vienen más despidos en *Barricada?*" *La Tribuna,* 30 October 1994.

86. Quoted in Fabián Medina, "Hasta ahora, solo las ganas de cambiar *Barricada,*" *El Semanario,* 27 October–3 November 1994.

87. See "Nombrados subdirector y editor de *Barricada,*" *Barricada,* 4 November 1994; and Alvaro Cruz Rojas, "FSLN no es dueño de *Barricada,*" *La Tribuna,* 4 November 1994.

88. Ironically, they also presage the positions adopted by renovationists in the 1990s, including those at *Barricada* whom Grigsby and the "new guard" displaced.

89. Grigsby interview, 28 February 1991. Apart from the interview, this account of Grigsby's checkered relationship with the front draws from Massing, "Nicaragua's Free-Fire Journalism"; and from my own monograph *Nicaragua, 1991: After the Earthquake,* CDAS Discussion Paper no. 68 (Montreal: Centre for Developing-Area Studies, McGill University, 1992). The latter work is also available at <http://adamjones.freeservers.com/nica2.htm>.

90. On the bombing of *La Primerísma,* see Anne Baldwin, "Solidarity among the Ashes," *Barricada Internacional,* 20 October 1990.

91. For a typically outraged response from an FSLN militant—precisely the sector Grigsby would ally himself with a couple of years later—see William Calero, "Siete preguntas para William Grigsby," *Barricada,* 28 February 1991: "Do you not believe that the [Popular Sandinista Army] is the only bastion that can sustain the revolution? What are your pretensions in seeking to discredit it? Does this position differ from that of the bourgeoisie and imperialism?" and so on.

92. On Grigsby's office wall in 1991, there hung a cartoon drawn for him by a Primerísima listener. It showed Murillo and Grigsby playing chess. Grigsby had just one piece left: but it was Justice, the blindfolded woman holding a set of scales. A frustrated Murillo was complaining, "If it weren't for this lady, you'd have been checkmated long ago."

93. Murillo explained the charge as follows: "I didn't mean to suggest Grigsby received a salary from the CIA. But I did mean to say that you can act as an agent for hostile forces without even knowing it, as a result of your arrogance, your self-righteousness—or, in Grigsby's case, your political ambition, the desire to be acknowledged as a 'voice' and a 'brain.' . . . I don't like to say this, but I was the only person who responded to [Grigsby's] campaign of defamation. I didn't do it because I live with Daniel Ortega. I did it because I think the same criticisms could be made in a much more constructive, helpful, loving, *responsible* way." Murillo interview, 24 April 1991; emphasis hers.

94. Borge interview, 29 May 1996.

95. Grigsby interview, 15 May 1996.

96. A prominent Sandinista elder; father of Joaquín Cuadra Lacayo, who replaced Humberto Ortega as army chief in February 1995.

97. Cruz Rojas, "FSLN no es dueño." According to Carlos Fernando Chamorro, "*Barricada* was owned by a holding company based in Panama. Formally as vice president and member of the board, I had been assigned a small percentage of the shares for legal purposes, just like the other [board] members. But it didn't belong to me, or to Bayardo Arce, or to Joaquín Cuadra. In theory, it all belonged to the party. The formal shareholders simply lent their names. Obviously, this situation changed when Tomás Borge came in. He put up money of his own to cover the [newspaper's] deficits and capitalized that money with real shares of his property." Chamorro, pers. comm., 25 September 1998. Borge's efforts to keep *Barricada* afloat with his personal resources are described further in chapter 4.

98. Cortés, "El funeral" (*Siglo Veintiuno* column). Sofía Montenegro recalled the use to which this line of argument was put during the daily battles of the interregnum period: "We told them, 'This is a political intervention. You are violating the rules and the structures of the newspaper. You are not entitled [to do so]. The only one who can "defenestrate" Carlos Fernando is the Junta Directiva. And since we don't have the Junta Directiva [with Arce out of the country], the only authority here is the editors.'" Montenegro interview, 22 May 1996.

99. "Periodistas de *Barricada* exponen en Asamblea," *La Tribuna*, 8 November 1994. Most of the quoted passages here are drawn from "Nica: *Barricada* Shake-Up," *El Diario/La Prensa*, 8 November 1994;

text provided by the New York Transfer News Collective
<soc.culture.latin-america>, trans. and ed. Toby Mailman.

100. Fernández Ampié, "Political and Labor Conflicts."

101. Montenegro interview, 22 May 1996. Carlos Fernando Chamorro pointed out that his own situation needed to be viewed separately from that of the other departed *Barricada* staffers. "My case was completely different. When I was fired, I never had a quarrel with El Amanecer over money. Nor was I part of the legal claim that was filed later. I was offered an indemnification in October 1994. I accepted, but didn't subsequently claim it—basically for moral reasons. I decided to wait until they behaved justly toward the rest of the staff. These were all private dealings; I never told El Amanecer anything. I simply waited in solidarity with the others. In 1997, I formalized my situation. They accepted the debt and are finally paying me in an indirect manner." Chamorro, pers. comm., 25 September 1998.

102. Montenegro interview, 22 May 1996.

103. Alegría interview, 10 May 1996.

104. For example, Chamorro wrote in *El Nuevo Diario* at the end of November 1994 that *Barricada* had "suffered a total reversal" since the defenestración, "in order to dedicate itself to promoting personal vanities and partisan sectarianism." He minced few words in describing "the extreme manicheanism" of Daniel Ortega, criticizing "his vision of the world in black and white [which] has reached the point of bankruptcy within and outside Nicaragua. . . . He doesn't want to admit that the main intention of this long-planned action was to pave the way for the aligning of the newspaper with his own person, and with the group of 'ideologues' that join him in controlling the FSLN, as also occurred with other Sandinista communications media." Chamorro B., "Religión de una secta."

105. See <http://www.confidencial.com.ni>.

106. Chamorro interview, 23 May 1996.

Chapter 4

1. Grigsby interview, 15 May 1996.

2. Roberto Fonseca, "El periodismo partidista agoniza," *Confidencial,* 8–14 December 1996. In an interview on 27 July 1998, Carlos Fernando

Chamorro stated that the average daily circulation of *Barricada* in 1994 (when promotional print runs were factored in) was actually about twenty-three thousand copies.

3. One of the "closest collaborators" of Tomás Borge told *Confidencial* in September 1997 that "the circulation continues to stagnate between 5,000 and 5,500 copies." "Conato de huelga en *Barricada*," *Confidencial*, 21–27 September 1997.

4. *El Nuevo Diario*, 7 November 1994.

5. Borge, "Saldremos victoriosos." Former *Barricada* personnel made frequent references, in interviews, to ortodoxo statements that the circulation of the new project either would be bolstered by an influx of new readers, or was irrelevant. Daniel Alegría: "Tomás said, given all the economic problems the paper had, that if every militant in the FSLN bought a copy of *Barricada*, the economic problem would be solved. The truth is, . . . nobody buys *Barricada*." Alegría interview, 10 May 1996. Carlos Fernando Chamorro: "What they say is that Julio [López's] conception is much more orthodox than anyone's. He says it doesn't matter for him if they sell two thousand copies, as long as these two thousand copies are really influential on opinion leaders of the front and other sectors of society. He is willing to sacrifice anything for politics, and for this kind of coherent line. But it's not coherent at all. There's no line in *Barricada*. And if there is, it's not influential enough." Chamorro interview, 23 May 1996. Lastly, Sofía Montenegro: "Do you know the account given by Daniel Ortega? That they have three hundred fifty thousand people who are registered as militants of the front . . . And if they all bought the newspaper, what was the problem? They made the decision that if the militants militantly would buy *Barricada*, there would be no economic problems for *Barricada*. It just so happens that the militants militantly *don't* buy it." Montenegro interview, 22 May 1996; emphasis hers.

6. Tomás Borge also stated in 1997 that *Barricada* was "at death's door" and "in a really tragic condition" when the new directorate took charge in October 1994. "In the administrative area," meanwhile, "there was a great deal of disorder, anarchy, and even corruption." Borge, "Sí, hay salida para superar la situación," interview with Roberto Fonseca, *Barricada*, 11 November 1997.

7. All quotes from Grigsby interview, 15 May 1996.

8. The quote in the heading for this section is from a column by Tomás

Borge: "The new management took on the difficult mission of converting the newspaper, not into a party bulletin—as the prognosticators had it—nor into yellow trash [*mamarracho amarillo*] that appeals to deviant desires—but into a broad accessible medium . . . [with] a relative objectivity such as decency demands." Borge, "Saldremos victoriosos."

9. In another apparent pledge of continuity, the slogan was incorporated into the headline of the first interview with Borge published after the defenestración: see "*Barricada:* Fiel a los intereses nacionales," *Barricada*, 2 November 1994.

10. Ibid. In another early postdefenestración interview, this time with *Barricada Internacional,* Borge similarly sought to downplay anticipated transformations at *Barricada.* He stressed only the "contradiction" between the positions adopted by the director of the front's newspaper, and policy positions arrived at through party channels. "We do not agree with the present editorial line of *Barricada,*" he said; but the defenestración had "resolved the political problem" between the paper and the majority Sandinista sentiment. Borge quoted in Guillermo Fernández Ampié, "Changes at *Barricada*" and "Political and Labor Conflicts."

11. Huerta interview, 22 May 1996.

12. Grigsby interview, 15 May 1996; emphasis his.

13. Chamorro interview, 23 May 1996.

14. Grigsby interview, 15 May 1996.

15. Decisive, certainly, in the sense that it was Borge who took the decision to close the enterprise in January 1998.

16. It was Daniel Alegría who used the term: "From the very beginning, [Borge] saw the newspaper very much as his toy." Alegría interview, 10 May 1996.

17. Chamorro, for his part, found Borge's hands-off approach mystifying. "I don't know what Tomás Borge does for *Barricada.* I don't see his hand in the newspaper. You see some silly things . . . when he writes something, some showing off, some self-promotion. But not even too much of that." Chamorro interview, 23 May 1996. Alfonso Malespín, who departed the paper in December 1996, recalled that Borge "was not doing his job. . . . He was there but he wasn't there. He wasn't really running the newspaper. He wasn't there like Carlos Chamorro, who was keeping his eye on the editorial page, the front page, seeing that everything was running smoothly. And he

[Borge] also lacked knowledge of how to run a newspaper." Malespín interview, 17 July 1998. Francisco "Paco" Gómez, brought on as an advisor in the final months of the paper's life (see below), similarly described Borge as "not really a director. He was in his office talking about his stories of the revolution." Gómez interview, 24 July 1998.

18. Grigsby interview, 15 May 1996.

19. Huerta interview, 22 May 1996.

20. Malespín interview, 17 May 1996. The three "political staff" referred to are Pablo Emilio Barreto, whose beat was the various Sandinista organizations; Juan Ramón Huerta, covering political parties and Sandinista policies; and Carlos García in the National Assembly. According to Malespín, these journalists received closer attention than most.

21. "Ramírez consuma plan separatista," Barricada, 10 January 1995; Santiago Paredes Sacasa, "El travestismo político de Sergio Ramírez," Barricada, 13 January 1995.

22. Juan Carlos Sarmiento, "Borge: Cerrado capítulo Ramírez," Barricada, 31 January 1995.

23. "Sergio Ramírez: Cuechero y mentiroso," Barricada, 28 August 1995.

24. Domingo Elizabeth Tercero, "Ramiristas se lavan las manos," Barricada, 19 December 1995; emphasis in original. The paper's treatment of Ramírez was not entirely without its lighter side. A front-page photograph published on the Nicaraguan equivalent of April Fool's Day (28 December 1995) depicted Ramírez and Daniel Ortega shaking hands. The caption read, "Gentleman's Agreement—Sergio Goes with Daniel." An accompanying article quoted Ramírez as calling Ortega "the only candidate for the presidency of Nicaragua" and "the best president in the history of Nicaragua." Only at the end of the article did the reader learn that the article and photograph had originally been published in Barricada on 24 February 1990, the day before the elections in which the Sandinista ticket (Ortega and Ramírez) was de-feated by the UNO coalition.

25. Grigsby interview, 15 May 1996.

26. Another ordinary news story referred to La Prensa as "the official somocista daily." "La Prensa miente, según Zelaya," 31 October 1996.

27. Huerta interview, 22 May 1996.

28. Barricada, 22 November 1995.

29. "La rabia y el odio de La Prensa," Barricada, 2 July 1995. The refer-

ence is to a front-page article, "Ortodoxos planeaban secuestrar a diputados," also published in *La Prensa* on 2 July. The article repeated bizarre allegations originally aired in *El Nuevo Diario* on 27 June concerning an FSLN plot to kidnap wayward National Assembly deputies (including the Sandinista renovationist Dora María Téllez and UNO deputy Luís Sánchez) as a way of forcing their way into negotiations over constitutional change.

30. Ricardo J. Cuadra García, "El pueblo celebró cumpleaños a Daniel," *Barricada*, 12 November 1996.

31. "¡Todos con los oídos abiertos al llamado del FSLN!" editorial, *Barricada*, 10 May 1995.

32. Chamorro interview, 23 May 1996.

33. "Debatir no es insultar," *Barricada*, 16 August 1995.

34. A survey conducted in late 1996 by the Costa Rican firm Demoscopía gave *El Nuevo Diario* 45 percent of the Nicaraguan press market, compared to *La Prensa*'s 37 percent, *Barricada*'s 12 percent, and *La Tribuna*'s 6 percent. Cited in Carlos Fernando Chamorro B., "¿Un cartel publicitario?" *Confidencial*, 9–15 February 1997.

35. Grigsby interview, 15 May 1996; emphasis his.

36. Huerta interview, 22 May 1996; emphasis his.

37. The totals break down as follows:

Barricada, March–August 1994: *Sexually suggestive imagery:* March—15, 19, 20, 24, 26, 28, 30 (heavy concentration around the Semana Santa holiday); April—4; May—2, 30 (Miss Nicaragua, not suggestively dressed or posed) (An 8 May story on breast cancer was illustrated with a photo of a naked breast and a hypodermic syringe; it was not counted as a sexually suggestive image); June—3; July—12 (Miss Latin America, not suggestively dressed), 23, 29; August—2, 15, 25.

Barricada, March–August 1994: *Violent imagery:* March—25 (Mexico—Colosio assassination), 27; April—5, 7, 27 (two instances, one an aircrash in Japan); May—26; June—12 (Rwanda), 30; July—none; August—21.

Total for March–August 1994: 17 sexually suggestive images, 10 violent images.

Barricada, March–August 1995: *Sexually suggestive imagery:* March—9, 14, 18, 20, 22, 24 March; April—2, 7, 10, 12 (two instances), 17, 30; May—none; June—9 (drawing of satanist sex) (A possible example from 24 June—a dramatized photo of a rape victim, topless—was tallied instead under violent imagery, below); July—6; August—5, 6 (suggestive photo of a street prostitute).

Barricada, March–August 1995: *Violent imagery:* March—1, 5, 6 (two instances), 11 (three instances), 13, 21 (two instances), 30; April—11, 17, 20 (Oklahoma bombing), 22 (Oklahoma bombing), 26, 28 (two instances, Rwanda); May—6, 11, 16 (two instances), 17 (two instances), 18, 19, 31; June—5, 19, 24; July—2, 5, 8 (dramatized—story on dying), 12; August—11, 12 (three instances, all from an air crash), 28, 31 (three instances).

Total for March–August 1995: 17 sexually suggestive images, 42 violent images.

38. The interview was conducted on 26 May 1996 and was subsequently translated from tape by Enrique Salgado and Elizabeth García.

39. See, for example, Daniel Ortega's comments to the Spanish publication *El País,* quoted in chapter 3.

40. Borge seemed to allude to his reputation in an opinion piece published a couple of months before *Barricada*'s death: "I am a heterosexual. No one—I am sure—could doubt this assertion." Borge, "Homosexualismo y delito," *Barricada,* 14 November 1997.

41. This and subsequent quotes from Huerta interview, 22 May 1996.

42. Grigsby interview, 15 May 1996.

43. Montenegro interview, 22 May 1996.

44. "What happened is that when the front started questioning political reporters like Jorge Katín, we tried to diminish the pressure by sharing some assignments with Malespín." Carlos Fernando Chamorro, pers. comm., 25 September 1998.

45. This and subsequent quotes from Malespín interview, 17 May 1996; emphasis his.

46. Malespín expressly cited the pages he edited as an antidote to *Barricada*'s political coverage, which was generally perceived to be excessive: "They are clear that they have difficulties among the public when they present political news. But they believe that through *De todo un poco, Gente,* and sports, they can gain this audience."

47. Huerta interview, 28 July 1998.

48. Huerta's phrase.

49. Huerta interview, 28 July 1998.

50. Fonseca, "Periodismo partidista agoniza."

51. Malespín interview, 17 July 1998.

52. According to Juan Ramón Huerta, the dispute arose over a "very strong caricature" directed against Rosa María Zelaya, and published at the behest of editor William Grigsby. Huerta interview, 28 July 1998.

53. "Nada detiene fervor sandinista del pueblo," *Barricada,* 10 October 1998.

54. *Barricada,* 14 October 1996.

55. See, for example, the reference to Alemán as "el candidato somocista." "Borge y Asociadios admite derrumbe de Alemán," *Barricada,* 13 September 1996, and the 8 September 1996 headline, "Candidato arnoldista invade cooperativo en Masatepe."

56. Huerta interview, 28 July 1998.

57. William Roiz Murillo, "Historia de los fraudes somocistas," 23 October 1996. See also the headline of 19 December 1996: "Alemán peor que Somoza" (Alemán worse than Somoza).

58. "¡Que Dios los perdone! Resultados ilegitimos—Seguiremos luchando," *Barricada,* 9 November 1996.

59. "Consuman fraude—¡pobre Nicaragua!," *Barricada,* 23 November 1996.

60. "Por vergüenza, CSE debería renunciar," *Barricada,* 25 November 1996.

61. *Barricada,* 7 December 1996.

62. Fonseca, "Periodismo partidista agoniza." *El Nuevo Diario* claimed that Grigsby had also been opposed to the decision to fire the ninety-two staffers the previous month. See "Cisma en *Barricada,*" 7 December 1996. Grigsby, for his part, refused comment at the time, except to state that he and López had resigned and not been fired. He did not return phone calls in July 1998.

63. The estimate was made by Carlos Chamorro B., "¿Cartel publicitario?" Chamorro cited the total amount of state-sector advertising as "some 60 to 80 million córdobas of the 270 million [in advertising revenue] billed annually."

64. Ibid.

65. "1998: El año de *Barricada,*" *Barricada,* 30 December 1997.

66. Borge, "Sí, hay salida para superar la situación." In an opinion piece published in October 1997, Borge wrote: "*Barricada,* in order to

obtain advertisements, would be obliged to keep silent about the abuses, vices, and errors of those who govern . . . [their] corruption, stupidity, betrayal, and demagoguery. This is impossible. But it means nothing more or less than the absence of advertisements. . . . As a result of the government reprisals—to which a section of private industry has [also] submitted, with notable exceptions—*Barricada* is in an extremely difficult situation." The paper, however, would not "sell out or surrender. We will die with our boots on." Borge, "En Nicaragua no hay libertad de expresión," *Barricada,* 22 October 1997.

67. Borge quoted in "*Barricada* lanza dramático SOS," *Confidencial,* 6–12 July 1997.

68. "1998: El año de *Barricada.*"

69. "*¡Al ladrón, al ladrón!* contra *Barricada,*" *Barricada,* 23 December 1997. These "other communications media" included *La Prensa,* which in December 1996 had switched from afternoon to morning publication; Roberto Fonseca linked this to the material "crisis" at both *La Tribuna* and *Barricada.* Fonseca, "Periodismo partidista agoniza."

70. The lower figure was given by Roberto Fonseca in "El periodismo partidista agoniza," an article that dates from December 1996. Francisco Gómez claimed Borge had told him, upon Gómez's arrival at *Barricada* in autumn 1997, that he had invested a million dollars of his own money in the daily (Gómez interview, 24 July 1998). In his 1997 interview with Roberto Fonseca, Borge claimed to have paid off "an important part" of the debt to Social Security (INSS), "in part with my own personal resources." Borge, "Sí, hay salida."

71. "Banco no aceptó hipoteca a Tomás Borge," *Confidencial,* 21 December 1997–11 January 1998.

72. This according to the financial statement prepared by *Barricada* general manager Soraya Montoya on 13 November 1997, privately supplied. The document cited the total debt to the INSS alone as C$11,088,792—a little over $1 million.

73. "*Barricada* lanza dramático SOS."

74. In the interview with Fonseca, Borge claimed to have spoken with businesses in the Dominican Republic regarding investment in El Amanecer, the publishing enterprise that "subsidizes the newspaper in large measure, although not totally." He also stated, in response to Fonseca's

question, that Humberto Ortega had not indicated interest in investing in *Barricada* on "the few occasions I have spoken with him on this theme"— although "I believe he could be a great investor if that's what he decided to do." Borge, "Sí, hay salida."

75. This and subsequent quotes from Gómez interview, 24 July 1998.

76. It must be stressed that the astonishing twist in the *Barricada* story that Gómez described is impossible to verify independently. "I've never talked about this until now," said Gómez. "But I think now is the time to say what happened." Gómez interview, 24 July 1998.

77. Gómez elaborated that Huerta could not fill the gap left by Borge's absence, partly "because Tomás didn't want him to," and partly because the very notion "panicked" him. Gómez interview, 24 July 1998.

78. This and subsequent quotes from "Notas para un perfil," internal document, privately supplied, [November or December 1997].

Chapter 5

1. "Conato de huelga en *Barricada.*"

2. The letter was signed by fifteen *Barricada* staff and most senior editors on 23 October 1997. Privately supplied.

3. "Daniel Ortega se niega a intervenir en favor de periodistas de *Barricada,*" *Confidencial,* 16–22 November 1997. Ortega reportedly met with Borge at the *Barricada* offices in mid-December, but refused to provide support for the paper. He also seemed openly derisive of Borge's own attempts to keep the paper going: "If Tomás believes he can solve the problem of the newspaper by mortgaging his house, he's wrong." Quoted in "Banco no aceptó hipoteca."

4. Núñez, a lawyer, ran against Daniel Ortega in the February 1996 presidential primary, losing by 84 percent to 16. She was the wife of the late Carlos Núñez, the National Directorate's representative to *Barricada* in the early and mid-1980s.

5. *Barricada,* 23 December 1997. See also Manual Torres Cerda and Vivian Torres, "Crece crisis en *Barricada,*" *El Nuevo Diario,* 23 December 1997: "Workers at the daily insisted that the strike and protests they were

undertaking were strictly labor related," dismissing suggestions that the conflict was a replay of the defenestración of 1994.

6. "1998: El año de *Barricada.*"

7. The cafeteria provided subsidized (i.e., free) meals to *Barricada* personnel and the occasional itinerant Canadian scholar.

8. Carlos García and Freddy García to Comandante Daniel Ortega, 26 January 1998, privately supplied.

9. Mario Mairena Martínez, "Cierra diario *Barricada,*" *El Nuevo Diario,* 31 January 1998.

10. Manual Torres Cerda, "Hoy embargan a *Barricada,*" *El Nuevo Diario,* 2 February 1998.

11. In an ironic echo of the defenestración, the revolt was confined to the editorial side of the operation—though this time the actions of editorial staff were aimed squarely at the directorate of *Barricada* and Editorial El Amanecer, rather than being mobilized in the directorate's defense. Staffer María Antonia López claimed that employees in printing and production had been paid when editorial workers had not, in order to "ensure they didn't join the protest." A majority of staffers—150 out of a total of 230 or 250, depending which report one believes—still had administrative or blue-collar jobs with El Amanecer. López, quoted in Mayela Rodríguez, "Trabajadores embargarán el lunes el diario *Barricada,*" *La Tribuna,* 1 February 1998; staff figures cited in Torres Cerda, "Hoy embargan a *Barricada.*"

12. Torres Cerda, "Hoy embargan a *Barricada.*"

13. "Trabajadores embargarán el lunes el diario *Barricada,*" *La Tribuna,* 1 February 1998. According to Minister Navarro, quoted in the same source, "When an enterprise requests a temporary closure, this does not extinguish contractual arrangements; the employer pays to the worker a small indemnity, equivalent to one week's salary; but if the closure is complete, then the owner must pay *preaviso,* vacation pay, and other benefits. In *Barricada*'s case, there are workers who have worked [at the enterprise] for more than fifteen years, for which they must receive one month's salary for every year worked." Rejecting charges that the ministry's actions against *Barricada* were politically motivated, Navarro claimed, "We have treated this case with a great deal of tact, in order to avoid having the Sandinistas make charges of political pressure. But now we are going to be energetic in ensuring that the 283 workers at *Barricada* receive their back salaries."

14. Huerta interview, 28 July 1998.

15. Mayela Rodríguez, "Hoy demandan a Editorial El Amanecer," *La Tribuna,* 2 February 1998.

16. Moises Castillo Zeas, "INSS embarga a *Barricada,*" *El Nuevo Diario,* 4 February 1998.

17. Montenegro interview, 20 July 1998; emphasis hers. Daniel Alegría also described receiving a similar offer from Núñez, which he rejected out of hand. Alegría interview, 21 July 1998.

18. All figures from Huerta interview, 28 July 1998.

19. "Representantes del Comite Provisional de *Barricada,*" internal document, privately supplied [February 1998].

20. "Propusieron treinta y dos nombres para sustituir el de *Barricada,*" *Confidencial,* 22–28 February 1998. The "beer hall" comment appeared in this same article.

21. "Empañan terrenos de *Barricada,*" *Confidencial,* 8–14 February 1998.

22. See the series of reports in *Confidencial,* 15–21 February 1998, 2–3.

23. "*Nueva Barricada,* una publicación para el siglo veintiuno," internal document, privately supplied.

24. This and all subsequent quotes in this section from Huerta interview, 28 July 1998; emphasis his.

25. This was true of all my major interlocutors in the summer of 1998, although I do not believe in trial by consensus, and the charges against Ortega are unproven at the time of writing.

26. Huerta edited a short compilation of statements and articles on Zoilamérica's allegations: see *El silencio del patriarca* (Managua: El Renacimiento, 1998). Note that the name chosen for the "publisher" (the project was "financed by the friends of Zoilamérica") is close to Renacer, the company name planned for the new *Barricada* enterprise.

27. "Today the moral and political credibility of the Sandinista leadership is in question—in the case of Tomás Borge, on account of *Barricada,* and in the case of Daniel Ortega, on account of his stepdaughter['s allegations]." Huerta interview, 28 July 1998.

28. See Jones, *Press in Transition.*

29. In rural areas of northern Nicaragua, according to a foreign-aid worker with whom I spoke in 1991, newspapers were usually purchased in

bulk (at a steep discount) days or weeks after they were published. They were bought not mainly for informational purposes, but for use as toilet paper—though the aid worker assured me that literate peasants read them first.

30. Cortés interview, 9 April 1991.
31. Blandón interview, 15 April 1991.
32. Chamorro interview, 27 July 1998.
33. Rothschuh interview, 16 April 1991.
34. Huerta interview, 28 July 1998.
35. Chamorro interview, 27 July 1998; emphasis his. For more excerpts from this interview, see Adam Jones, "*Barricada* and Beyond: Journalism in Nicaragua," *Harvard International Journal of Press/Politics* 4, 4 (Fall 1999): 127–31.
36. Juanita Darling, "Sandinista Paper Returns, but Ex-Staffers Aren't Impressed," *Los Angeles Times*, 22 July 2000.

Sources

Printed and Manuscript Sources

"1998: El año de *Barricada.*" *Barricada,* 30 December 1997.

Alegría, Daniel. "Una renuncia amarga." *Barricada,* 3 November 1994.

Alisky, Marvin. *Latin American Media: Guidance and Censorship.* Ames: Iowa State University Press, 1981.

Annunziata, Lucia. "Democracy and the Sandinistas." *Nation,* 2 April 1988.

———. "Why the Sandinistas Lost: Eleven Years of Nicaraguan Revolution." *Dissent,* Summer 1990, 307–14.

Arce Castaño, Bayardo. "The New *Barricada.*" *Barricada,* 30 January 1991.

———. "Para un debate sobre los medios sandinistas." *Barricada,* 5 March 1992.

Baca, Vicente. "La formación de periodista." *Pensamiento Propio,* no. 34 (July 1986).

"Banco no aceptó hipoteca a Tomás Borge," *Confidencial,* 21 December 1997–11 January 1998.

Barricada. "Ajustes en la estrategia editorial de *Barricada* (octubre 1994)." Internal document.

———. "Nuevo perfil editorial de *Barricada:* Aprobado por el Consejo Editorial del periódico." Internal document, December 1990.

———. "Principios y normas éticas de *Barricada.*" Internal document, April 1991.

———. "Reglamento del consejo editorial de *Barricada.*" Internal document, [1991?].

Barricada. Editorial Council. "Evaluación cualitativa del diario *Barricada.*" Internal document, April 1992.

Barrios de Chamorro, Violeta. "The Death of *La Prensa.*" *Foreign Affairs* 65 (Winter 1986/87): 383–86.

Black, George. *Triumph of the People: The Sandinista Revolution in Nicaragua.* London: Zed Press, 1981.

Booth, John A. *The End and the Beginning: The Nicaraguan Revolution.* 2d ed. Boulder: Westview Press, 1985.

Borge, Tomás. "Saldremos victoriosos." *Barricada,* 25 July 1995.

———. "Sí, hay salida para superar la situación." Interview with Roberto Fonseca. *Barricada,* 11 November 1997.

Boudreaux, Richard. "The Great Conciliator." *Los Angeles Times Magazine,* 6 January 1991, 8–14.

Castillo, J. R., y Asociados. *La Tribuna: Encuesta de opiniones, Mayo 1994.* Report. Managua: J. R. Castillo, May 1994.

Centro de Investigdaciones de la Comunicación (CINCO). *A New Newspaper for Nicaragua.* Project report. Managua: CINCO, February 1995.

Chamorro B., Carlos Fernando. "*Barricada:* Crónica para el entierro (oficial)." *Confidencial,* no. 80 (8–14 February 1998).

———. "*Barricada:* En el punto de no retorno." *Barricada,* 25 July 1992.

———. "La *Barricada* que necesitamos." *Barricada,* 2 March 1992.

———. "¿Un cartel publicitario?" *Confidencial,* 9–15 February 1997.

———. "El debate sobre *Barricada.*" *Barricada,* 27 May 1994.

———. "Front Page Battlefront." *Barricada Internacional,* 8 July 1989, 36.

———. "La religión de una secta." *El Nuevo Diario,* 30 November 1994.

———. "Renovation or Political Death in 1996." *Barricada Internacional,* May 1994.

———. "El sistema político y el rol de la prensa en la futura situación de la region." In *Periodismo, derechos humanos, y control del poder político en Centroamerica,* ed. Jaime Ordóñez, 119–21. San José: Instituto Interamericano de Derechos Humanos, 1994.

Chamorro, Jaime. "How *La Prensa* Was Silenced." Trans. Steven Blakemore. *Commentary* 83 (January 1987): 39–44.

———. "*La Prensa:* Role of the Opposition Press in Nicaragua." In *Media, Freedom, and Development: Comparing Experiences,* ed. Andrew W.

MacFarlane and Robert Henderson, 64–68. London: University of Western Ontario Graduate School of Journalism, 1989.

Christian, Shirley. *Nicaragua: Revolution in the Family.* New York: Random House, 1985.

———. "Ortega's Leadership Criticized by Sandinistas." *New York Times,* 24 March 1992.

Close, David. *Nicaragua: Politics, Economics, and Society.* London: Pinter Publishers, 1988.

———. *Nicaragua: The Chamorro Years.* Boulder: Lynne Rienner, 1998.

Colburn, Forrest D. *Post-Revolutionary Nicaragua: State, Class, and the Dilemmas of Agrarian Policy.* Berkeley: University of California Press, 1986.

"Conato de huelga en *Barricada*." *Confidencial,* 21–27 September 1997.

Corresponsales de guerra: Testimonio de cien días de sangre, fuego, y victoria. Managua: Editorial El Amanecer, 1984.

Cortés Domínguez, Guillermo, and Juan Ramón Huerta Chavarría. "Critical Journalism in the Daily Barricada." Monograph prepared for the Degree in Journalism, School of Journalism, University of Central America (UCA), Managua, submitted 30 June 1988.

Cruz, Arturo J., and Mark Falcoff. "Who Won Nicaragua?" *Commentary,* May 1990, 31–38.

Cruz Rojas, Alvaro. "FSLN no es dueño de *Barricada*." *La Tribuna,* 4 November 1994.

———. "Nombran a Borge nuevo presidente de *Barricada*." *La Tribuna,* 31 October 1994.

Dassin, Joan R. "The Brazilian Press and the Politics of Abertura." *Journal of Interamerican Studies and World Affairs* 26 (August 1984): 385–414.

"The Debate Spreads Out." *Barricada Internacional,* 22 September 1990.

Diederich, Bernard. *Somoza and the Legacy of U.S. Involvement in Central America.* New York: Dutton, 1981.

Dirección de Información y Prensa de la Presidencia. *Acuerdos de la concertación económica y social y la política exterior del gobierno de*

Nicaragua. Managua: Dirección de Información y Prensa de la Presidencia, 1990.

Dunkerley, James. "Reflections on the Nicaraguan Election." *New Left Review* 182 (July–August 1990): 33–50.

Dye, David R., and William Gasperini. "Sandinistas: From Revolution to Evolution." *In These Times,* 14–20 March 1991.

Edmisten, Patricia Taylor. *Nicaragua Divided:* La Prensa *and the Chamorro Legacy.* Pensacola: University of West Florida Press, 1990.

Estrada, Eduardo. "El recelo nos autocensura." *Pensamiento Propio,* no. 34 (July 1986).

Everingham, Mark. *Revolution and the Multiclass Coalition in Nicaragua.* Pittsburgh: University of Pittsburgh Press, 1996.

Fernández Ampié, Guillermo. "Changes at *Barricada.*" *Barricada Internacional,* October–November 1994.

———. "The FSLN's Most Serious Crisis." *Barricada Internacional,* September 1994.

———. "Journalists in Nicaragua: Behind the Headlines." *Barricada Internacional,* August 1995.

———. "A Modest Publications Boom." *Barricada Internacional,* 22 September 1990, 28–29.

———. "Political and Labor Conflicts in Full Color." *Barricada Internacional,* December 1994.

Flórez-Estrada, María. "Tres voces, dos proyectos." *Pensamiento Propio,* no. 34 (July 1986).

———. "La verdad es dialéctica." *Pensamiento Propio,* no. 34 (July 1986).

Fonseca, Roberto. "El periodismo partidista agoniza." *Confidencial,* 8–14 December 1996.

Fox, Elizabeth, ed. *Media and Politics in Latin America: The Struggle for Democracy.* London: Sage, 1988.

Frente Sandinista de Liberación Nacional. "Una alternativa para Nicaragua: Propuesta a la nación." Electoral platform 1997. Managua: FSLN, March 1996.

———. "Anteproyecto: Principios y programa del FSLN." Managua: FSLN, March 1991.

———. "Posición del FSLN ante la problemática nacional. *El Nuevo Diario*, 7 March 1991.

———. "Proyecto de estatutos del FSLN." Managua, 1991.

Frente Sandinista de Liberación Nacional. Departamento de Agitación y Propaganda. "Anteproyecto del programo radial 'De Cara al Pueblo.'" Internal document, Managua, [1986?]

———. "Perfiles de los medios de comunicación." Internal document, Managua, 1985.

———. "Rol de los medios de comunicación en la propaganda sandinista." Internal document, Managua, 1985.

Fried, Mark. "Sandinismo for the Nineties." *NACLA Report on the Americas,* April 1990.

Gilbert, Dennis. *Sandinistas: The Party and the Revolution.* Cambridge, Mass.: Basil Blackwell, 1988.

Goldman, Francisco. "Sad Tales of *La Libertad de Prensa:* Reading the Newspapers of Central America." *Harper's,* August 1988, 56–61.

Hodges, Donald C. *Intellectual Foundations of the Nicaraguan Revolution.* Austin: University of Texas Press, 1986.

Hoyt, Katherine. *The Many Faces of Sandinista Democracy.* Athens: Ohio University Center for International Studies, 1997.

Huerta, Juan Ramón. "Los retos inmediatos de *Barricada.*" *Barricada*, 2 November 1994.

———. *El silencio del patriarca.* Managua: El Renacimiento, 1998.

Instituto de Estudio del Sandinismo. *El sandinismo: Documentos básicos.* Managua: Editorial Nueva Nicaragua, 1985.

Invernizzi, Gabriele, Francis Pisani, and Jesús Ceberio. *Sandinistas: Entrevistas a Humberto Ortega Saavedra, Jaime Wheelock Román, y Bayardo Arce Castaño.* Managua: Editorial Vanguardia, 1986.

Jones, Adam. "*Barricada* and Beyond: Journalism in Nicaragua." *Harvard International Journal of Press/Politics* 4, 4 (Fall 1999): 127–31.

———. "Beyond the Barricades: The Sandinista Press and Political Transition in Nicaragua, 1979–1991." *New Political Science,* no. 23 (Fall 1992): 63–90.

———. "Beyond the Barricades: The Sandinista Press in Transition, 1979–1991." Master's thesis, McGill University, 1992.

———. "The Death of *Barricada*: Politics and Professionalism in the Post-Sandinista Press." *Journalism Studies 2, no. 2* (May 2001):*243–59*.

———. *Nicaragua, 1991: After the Earthquake.* CDAS Discussion Paper no. 68. Montreal: Centre for Developing-Area Studies, McGill University, January 1992.

———. *The Press in Transition: A Comparative Study of Nicaragua, South Africa, Jordan, and Russia.* Hamburg: Deutsches Übersee-Institut, 2001.

———. "Revolutionary Journalism in Nicaragua: Predicament and Potential." *Socialist Alternatives 2*, 1 (Winter 1993): 166–87.

Kattenburg, David. "News from the *Frente*." *This Magazine,* June–July 1993, 36–39.

Kinzer, Stephen. *Blood of Brothers: Life and War in Nicaragua.* New York: Putnam, 1991.

"Ley creadora del Colegio de Periodistas de Nicaragua." *Periodistas,* September 1995.

Luciak, Ilja A. *The Sandinista Legacy: Lessons from a Political Economy in Transition.* Gainesville: University Press of Florida, 1995.

M and R Consultants. *Estudio: Lectores medios escritos en Nicaragua: El caso* Barricada. Report. Managua: M and R Consultants, August 1994.

Maranhao, Berenice. "Miente, miente, algo quedará." *Barricada,* 2 November 1994.

Massing, Michael. "Nicaragua's Free-Fire Journalism." *Columbia Journalism Review* 27 (July-August 1988): 29–35.

Mattelart, Armand, ed. *Communicating in Popular Nicaragua.* New York: International General, 1986.

McClintock, Cynthia. "The Media and Redemocratization in Peru." *Studies in Latin American Popular Culture* 6 (1987): 115–34.

McCoy, Jennifer L., and Shelley A. McConnell. "Nicaragua: Beyond the Revolution." *Current History,* February 1997, 75–80.

Montenegro, Sofía. "¿Es revolucionario el FSLN?" *Nuevo amanecer cultural* (supplement to *El Nuevo Diario*), 14 May 1994.

————. *La revolución simbólica pendiente.* Managua: Centro de Investigaciones de la Comunicación, 1997.

Media in Latin America and the Caribbean: Domestic and International Perspectives. Windsor, Ont.: University of Windsor, 1985.

"A New Format for a New Era." Editorial, *Barricada Internacional,* 28 July 1990, 3.

"Nicaragua's New Media Law: Freedom and Social Responsibility." *Envío,* special edition: "Institutionalizing Democracy in Nicaragua's Revolution," October 1989.

Nichols, John Spicer. *Cuban Mass Media: Organization, Control, and Functions.* Columbia, S.C.: Association for Education in Journalism and Mass Communication, 1982.

————. "The News Media in the Nicaraguan Revolution." In *Nicaragua in Revolution,* ed. Thomas Walker, 181–99. New York: Praeger, 1982.

————. "*La Prensa:* The CIA Connection." *Columbia Journalism Review* 27 (July–August 1988): 34–35.

Norsworthy, Kent W. "The Mass Media." In *Nicaragua without Illusions: Regime Transition and Structural Adjustment in the 1990s,* ed. Thomas Walker, 281–95. Wilmington, Del.: Scholarly Resources, 1997.

Núñez, Carlos. "El debate entre la verdad y la infamia." In *Hacia una política cultural de la revolución popular sandinista.* Managua: Ministerio de Cultura, 1982.

————. "La reacción y sus ejes de enfrentamiento ideológico." In *Hacia una política cultural de la revolución popular sandinista.* Managua: Ministerio de Cultura, 1982.

Núñez, Orlando. "The New Sandinista Utopia." *envío,* July 1994, 38–42.

Orme, William A., Jr., ed. *A Culture of Collusion: An Inside Look at the Mexican Press.* Coral Gables, Fla.: North-South Center Press, University of Miami; distributed by Lynne Rienner, Boulder, 1997.

Pedelty, Mark. *War Stories: The Culture of Foreign Correspondents.* New York: Routledge, 1995.

Pierce, Robert N. *Keeping the Flame: Media and Government in Latin America.* New York: Hastings House, 1979.

"Proyecto de Código de Etica Profesional de los Periodistas de Nicaragua." *Periodistas,* September 1995.

"A Rather Extraordinary Congress." *envío,* July 1994, 10–13.

"The Revolution and the Electoral Defeat: Resolutions Taken at the FSLN Assembly." *Barricada Internacional,* July 14 1990.

Rosset, Peter, and John Vandermeer. *Nicaragua, Unfinished Revolution: The New Nicaragua Reader.* New York: Grove Press, 1986.

Rothschuh Villanueva, Guillermo. *Comunicación: La cuerda floja.* Managua: Editorial Tierra Arada, 1986.

———. *Vuelta de siglo.* Managua: Universidad Centroamericana, 1997.

Rothschuh Villanueva, Guillermo, and Carlos Fernando Chamorro B. *Los medios y la política en Nicaragua.* Managua: Centro de Investigaciones de la Comunicación/Friedrich Ebert Stiftung, 1995.

Ruchwarger, Gary. *People in Power: Forging a Grassroots Democracy in Nicaragua.* South Hadley, Mass.: Bergin and Garvey, 1987.

Ryan, Phil. *The Fall and Rise of the Market in Sandinista Nicaragua.* Montréal: McGill-Queen's University Press, 1996.

Salwen, Michael B., and Bruce Garrison. *Latin American Journalism.* Hillsdale, N.J.: Lawrence Erlbaum Associates, 1991.

Sarmiento, Juan Carlos. "Continuar el profesionalismo perdido." *Barricada,* 2 November 1994.

Selser, Gabriela. "The Battle for Public Opinion." *Barricada Internacional,* 2 June 1990.

Solórzano, Edgard. "Carlos Fernando: 'Regresión Total.'" *El Semanario,* 27 October–3 November 1994.

Straubhaar, Joseph D. "Television and Video in the Transition from Military to Civilian Rule in Brazil." *Latin American Research Review* 24, 1 (1989): 140–54.

Tirado, Víctor. "Sandinism's Renewal." *Barricada Internacional,* August 1991, 17.

"Tomás asume *Barricada.*" *Barricada,* 31 November 1994.

Torres, Rosa María, and José Luis Coraggio. *Transición y crisis en Nicaragua.* San José, Costa Rica: Editorial DEI, 1987.

Torres Cerda, Manual. "Hoy embargan a *Barricada.*" *El Nuevo Diario,* 2 February 1998.

Vickers, George R. "A Spider's Web." *NACLA Report on the Americas* 24, 1 (June 1990): 19–27.

Vilas, Carlos M. "The Contribution of Economic Policy and International Negotiation to the Fall of the Sandinista Government." Trans. Lena M. Gilman. *New Political Science* 18–19 (Fall/Winter 1990): 81–102.

———. "Family Affairs: Class, Lineage, and Politics in Contemporary Nicaragua." *Journal of Latin American Studies,* May 1992, 309–41.

———. *The Sandinista Revolution: National Liberation and Social Transformation in Central America.* New York: Monthly Review Press, 1986.

———. "What Went Wrong." *NACLA Report on the Americas* 24, 1 (June 1990), pp. 10–18.

Walker, Thomas W., ed. *Nicaragua without Illusions: Regime Transition and Structural Adjustment in the 1990s.* Wilmington, Del.: Scholarly Resources, 1997.

Williams, Philip J. "Dual Transitions from Authoritarian Rule: Popular and Electoral Democracy in Nicaragua." *Comparative Politics,* January 1994, 169–85.

Interviews

1991

Alegría, Daniel. Editor in chief, *Barricada Internacional.* Managua, 25 February 1991. (In English.)

Blandón, Nelba. Chief censor, Office of Communications Media, Ministry of the Interior, 1982–86, under direct supervision of Comandante Tomás Borge. Managua, 15 April 1991. (In Spanish, trans. Jane Curschmann.)

Castro, Sergio De. Member of *Barricada* editorial council; former editor of *Barricada Internacional.* Managua, 22 April 1991. (In English.)

Cerna, Pablo. Staff writer, *Barricada* supplement *Gente;* author of thesis on Nicaraguan caricaturist and former *La Semana Cómica* director Róger Sánchez. Managua, 4 April 1991. (In Spanish, trans. Jane Curschmann.)

Chamorro, Carlos Fernando. Director and editor in chief, *Barricada;* head of FSLN's Department of Agitation and Propaganda, 1984–87; son of former *La Prensa* director Pedro Joaquín Chamorro and Nicaraguan president (1990–96) Violeta Chamorro. Managua, 28 February, 19 March, 3 April, 12 April, 17 April, 18 April, 28 April 1991. (In English.)

Cortés, Guillermo. *Barricada* senior writer and columnist; former war correspondent; former journalist with *El Pueblo* (1979–80); coauthor of dissertation on objectivity and professionalism at *Barricada.* Managua, 9 April, 15 April, 9 May 1991. (In Spanish, trans. Jane Curschmann.)

Cuadra, Pablo Antonio. Director, *La Prensa.* Managua, 26 April 1991. (In English.)

Curschmann, Jane. Staff writer and translator, *Barricada Internacional.* Managua, multiple informal interviews. (In English.)

Flores, Aleyda. *Barricada* photographer. Managua, 9 May 1991. (In Spanish, trans. Jane Curschmann.)

Fonseca, Roberto. Editor of *Barricada* supplement *De todo un poco.* Managua, 9 May 1991. (In Spanish, trans. Jane Curschmann.)

Grigsby, William. Managing Director of radio station La Primerísima; former reporter at *El Nuevo Diario;* functionary at FSLN's Department of Agitation and Propaganda in mid-1980s. Managua, 28 February 1991. (In English.)

Guevara, Onofre. *Barricada* senior writer; former journalist with pre-1979 Socialist Party press. Managua, 2 April 1991. (In Spanish, trans. Jane Curschmann.)

Henríquez, Juan Alberto. Coeditor, *El Pueblo.* Managua, 8 April 1991. (In Spanish, trans. Jane Curschmann.)

Irías, Noel. Editor of *La Semana Cómica* at time of interview; *Barricada* journalist in the 1980s and again in the 1990s. Died in 1996. Managua, 22 March 1991. (In Spanish, trans. Jane Curschmann.)

Kreimann, Max. *Barricada* business manager. Managua, 4 April 1991. (In Spanish, trans. Jane Curschmann.)

INTERVIEWS

Martínez, René. Production manager, *La Semana Cómica*. Managua, 22 March 1991. (In Spanish, trans. Jane Curschmann.)

Montenegro, Sofía. Director and editor in chief of *Barricada* supplement *Gente; Barricada* international editor, 1980-84; *Barricada* editorial page editor, 1985-88. Managua, 8 March, 10 March, 15 March, 2 April, 3 April, 11 April, 1 May, 6 May 1991. (In English.)

Murillo, Rosario. Director of former *Barricada* cultural supplement *Ventana* (ceased publication 1991); poet; former director of Sandinista cultural union (ASTC); companion of ex-president Daniel Ortega. Managua, 24 April 1991. (In English.)

Reyes, Xavier. *Barricada* subdirector and member of editorial council; managing editor, 1984-87; former *Barricada* war correspondent. Managua, 13 April 1991. (In Spanish, trans. Jane Curschmann.)

Rothschuh, Guillermo. Communications theorist, Department of Sociology, University of Central America (Managua); advisor to *Barricada* editorial council; former advisor to FSLN's Department of Agitation and Propaganda. Managua, 16 April 1991. (In English.)

Selser, Gabriela. Staff writer, *Barricada Internacional;* former *Barricada* war correspondent. Managua, 9 May 1991. (In Spanish, trans. Jane Curschmann.)

1996

Alegría, Daniel. (See also 1991.) *Barricada* editor, 1992-94; editor in chief, October-November 1994 (resigned November 1994). Managua, 10 May 1996. (In English.)

Borge, Comandante Tomás. Founding member of Sandinista Front (1961); member of the FSLN National Directorate, 1979-96; minister of the interior, 1980-90; FSLN assistant general secretary, 1994-; director of *Barricada,* 1994-98. Managua, 29 May 1996. (In Spanish, trans. Enrique Salgado and Elizabeth García.)

Chamorro, Carlos Fernando. (See also 1991.) Director of *Barricada,* 1992-94 (dismissed October 1994); director, Centro de Investigdaciones de la Comunicación (CINCO); chief of FSLN's Department of

Agitation and Propaganda, mid-1980s. Managua, 16 May, 23 May 1996. (In English.)

Chomsky, Diane. Editor and translator, *Barricada Internacional.* Managua: informal conversations, May 1996. (In English.)

Fernández Ampié, Guillermo. Journalist and political writer, *Barricada Internacional.* Managua: informal conversations, May 1996. (In Spanish, trans. Diane Chomsky.)

Grigsby, William. (See also 1991.) Editor in chief of *Barricada,* 1994–96. Managua, 15 May 1996. (In Spanish, my translation.)

Huerta, Juan Ramón. *Barricada* journalist, 1982–94; *Barricada* editor, 1994–97; editor in chief, 1997–98. Managua, 22 May 1996. (In Spanish, transcribed by Carmén Miranda Barrios, my translation.)

Largaespada, Mildred. Editor, *Gente* supplement, 1991(?)–94. Managua, 10 May 1996. (In English.)

López, Julio. *Barricada* subdirector, 1994–96. Managua, 8 May 1996. (In Spanish, my translation.)

Malespín, Alfonso. *Barricada* journalist and political writer, 1990–94; editor of *De todo un poco* supplement, 1994–96; editor of *Gente* supplement, 1995–96. Managua, 17 May 1996. (In English.)

Montenegro, Sofía. (See also 1991.) Director of *Barricada* supplement *Gente,* 1992–94; member of *Barricada* editorial council, 1992–94 (dismissed November 1994). Executive director, Centro de Investigaciones de la Comunicación (CINCO). Managua, 22 May 1996. (In English.)

1998

Alegría, Daniel. (See also 1991,1996.) Former *Barricada* editor. Managua, 21 July 1998. (In English.)

Chamorro, Carlos Fernando. (See also 1991, 1996.) Former *Barricada* director, now director of *Confidencial.* Managua, 22 July, 27 July 1998. (In English.)

Gómez, Francisco ("Paco"). Former advisor to *Barricada.* Managua, 24 July 1998. (In English.)

Huerta, Juan Ramón. (See also 1996) Former editor, *Barricada.* Managua, 28 July 1998. (In Spanish, my translation.)

Malespín, Alfonso. (See also 1996.) Former *Barricada* staffer. Managua, 17 July 1998. (In English.)

Index

advertising
  at *Barricada*, 77–79, 196, 213–14
  state-sector, 25, 213–14
Ajustes declaration. *See Barricada: Ajustes* decla-
  ration of; Chamorro, Carlos
  Fernando: *Ajustes* declaration and
Alegría, Daniel, 175
  as caretaker editor of *Barricada*, 147–50,
  157, 159–60
  relationship with Tomás Borge, 148, 153,
  159–60
Alemán, Arnoldo, 212–13
  Barricada advertising and, 213–14
Arce, Bayardo, xxv, 56, 154–55, 183–84
Association of Nicaraguan Women (AMN-
  LAE), 71–72

Baltodano, Mónica, 108, 121, 135, 161–62, 185
Barricada (newspaper). *See also Gente*
  advertising at, 77–79, 196, 213–14
  Ajustes declaration of, 142–44
  autonomy experiment, 1991–94, xx–xxiii,
  54–74, 103–18
  blue-collar staff at, 75–76, 165–66, 290n
  Buzón de Santa Rosa and, xxi, 97–98
  ceasefire with contras and, 46–47, 255n
  challenges after defenestración, 177–79
  circulation of, 25, 75, 196, 210–11,
  250–51n, 282n
  in comparative perspective, 231–37, 269n
  conceptions of journalistic objectivity,
  9–10
  concertación and, 47, 53–65

corruption scandal at, 80–83, 262n
De todo un poco, xx, 68
editorial council of, 55–58
editorial profile of (1985), 43
editorial profile of (1994–98), 190
editorials of, 189–90
Excélsior model and, 50, 255n
founding, 1–6
Gramscian conceptions and, 244–45n
horoscope of, 68
human-interest coverage, 44–45, 69
human rights and, 96–98
internal crisis of 1987, 35–36
interregnum following dismissal of
  Carlos Fernando Chamorro, 145–63
liberal influences on, 58–62
material crisis (1991–94), 74–83
material crisis (1994–98), 196, 210–15,
  221–22
mobilizing imperative at, xviii, 6–11,
  28–38, 84, 180–81, 247–48n
"negotiated exit" at, 164–67, 172–74
New Editorial Profile of, 43, 56–58,
  63–64, 201–02, 219
1991 relaunching, 62–66
1996 election coverage, 211–12
as opinion leader, 65–66
ownership of, 280n
"piñata" scandal and, 93–94, 264–65n
political commissariat at, 28–29
post-defenestración (1994–98),
  xxiv–xxvi
pricing strategies, 80

305

Grigsby, William
    as *Barricada* editor, 168–72, 194, 182–84
    conflict with Rosario Murillo, 170,
        279–80n
    resignation of, 212–13
    Group of 29, 101, 121–22. *See also* ortodoxos

Huerta, Juan Ramón, 150–51, 160–61, 166,
        180–81, 227–30
    Daniel Ortega sexual abuse scandal and,
        227–29
    on closure of *Barricada*, 224–25
    on New Editorial Profile, 201–2
    on post-1994 *Barricada*, 199–205, 210
    study of critical function at *Barricada*
        and, 43–44
    as war correspondent, 200
Kreimann, Max
    corruption scandal at *Barricada* and, 77,
        80–82
    on *Barricada* finances, 76–78, 261–62n

Lenin, V. I., and "vanguard" concept, 8,
        246n
López, Julio, xxvi, 108, 121, 168, 184–85
    resignation of, 212–13

Malespín, Alfonso, 167
    on autonomy experiment, 110, 206–7
    on post-defenestración *Barricada*, 185,
        208–9
    on relations with UNO government,
        86–87
Marx, Karl, and Marxist conceptions of the
        press, 6
Montenegro, Sofía
    after defenestración, 174–75
    conflicts with Sandinista Front, 34–35,
        130–31
    founding of *Barricada* and, 1–3
    Gente and, 70–74, 158–59, 260–61n
    Nueva Barricada and, 225–26
    on conflict with Daniel Ortega, 130–31
    on internal crisis at *Barricada* (1987),
        35–36
    on 1991 elections, 256–57n
    on relations with East Bloc countries,
        33–35
    on violence, 99–100
"Moral economy of journalism," 39–40,
        44

Murillo, Rosario
    Barricada and, 104–05
    conflict with William Grigsby, 170,
        279–80n
    on 1991 elections, 256n
    on "piñata" scandal, 264n
    open letter on *Barricada,* 267n
    Ventana and, 105, 273–74n

New Editorial Profile. *See Barricada:* New
        Editorial Profile of
Nicaragua
    media culture of, 20–21, 271–72n
    1990 elections, 51–52
    1996 elections, 211–13
    UNO government of, 64, 77–78, 83–90,
        188–89, 195–96
Norsworthy, Kent, 269n
Nueva Barricada (newspaper project), 226–27
El Nuevo Diario (newspaper), 244n, 258n
    relations with *Barricada,* 23, 66–67
    "yellow journalism" in, 66–68

Ortega, Daniel, 120, 140–41
    alliance with ortodoxos, 122–23
    relations with *Barricada,* xxii–xxiii,
        112–13, 126–35, 188–89
    relationship with Tomás Borge, 153
    sexual abuse scandal of, 227–29
Ortega, Humberto, as army chief, 94–95
ortodoxos, xvi, xxii–xxiii, 101, 121–27, 135–41,
        242n. *See also* Sandinista National
        Liberation Front: internal politics of
    relations with *Barricada,* 84–86, 100–01,
        103–06, 125–27, 135–36, 268–69n

Periodismo amarillo. See yellow journalism
La Prensa, 244n
    relations with *Barricada,* 20–23, 66
    relations with Sandinista government,
        20–23
professional imperative, xviii–xix, 11–13,
        39–45
El Pueblo (newspaper), 249n
Punitive Forces of the Left (FPI), 102–3
Qualitative Evaluation. *See Barricada:*
        Qualitative Evaluation of

Ramírez, Sergio, 107, 140–41, 186–87, 284n
Renovationists, xxiii–xxi, 103–11, 123–24,
        186–87, 242n. *See also* Ramírez, Sergio

relationship with *Barricada*, xxiii–xxi,
103–11
Revolutionary Worker-Peasant Front
(FROC), 102
Reyes, Xavier
internal crisis at *Barricada* and, 35–36,
253–54n
on political commissariats at *Barricada*,
28–29
report on *Barricada*, 216–20, 227
Ryan, Phil, 24, 47–48, 128–29, 248n

Sánchez, Róger, 36–38
Sandinista National Liberation Front
(FSLN). *See also Barricada:* relations
with FSLN National Directorate;
relations with Sandinista National
Liberation Front
internal politics of, 91–93, 119–21, 128–29,
135–42, 270–71n, 275n
macro-pluralism of, 13–21
Marxism of, 128–29, 272–73n
material relationship with *Barricada*,
23–28
media policies of, 249n
1991 congress of, 124–26, 271n
"piñata" scandal of, 51, 93–94, 257n

political relationship with *Barricada*,
28–38, 90–103
Special Congress of, 119, 123–26, 139–40
Tercerista faction of, 128–29
"turn to the market," 47–48
"vanguard" concept and, 8–9
violence and, 98–103, 266n
Scott, James C., 39
Selser, Gabriela, 40–41

Terceristas. *See* Sandinista National
Liberation Front: Tercerista faction of
Tirado, Victor, 112

United States
influence on Nicaraguan media, 16
role of Central Intelligence Agency, 14

Vargas, Marcio, 31–32
and internal crisis at *Barricada*, 35–36,
253–54n

Wheelock, Jaime, 32

"yellow journalism." *See also Barricada:* yellow
journalism and
and *El Nuevo Diario*, 66–68

.